The Segregated Origins of Social Security

The Segregated Origins of Social Security

African Americans and the Welfare State

Mary Poole

The University of North Carolina Press

Chapel Hill

Set in Charter by Tseng Information Systems, Inc.

The paper in this book meets the guidelines
for permanence and durability of the Committee
on Production Guidelines for Book Longevity of
the Council on Library Resources.

This book was published with the assistance
of the Thornton H. Brooks Fund of the
University of North Carolina Press.

Library of Congress Cataloging-in-Publication Data
Poole, Mary, 1960–
The segregated origins of social security : African Americans
and the welfare state / Mary Poole.
p. cm.
Includes bibliographical references and index.
ISBN 978-0-8078-3024-6 (cloth : alk. paper)
ISBN 978-0-8078-5688-8 (pbk. : alk. paper)
ISBN 978-0-8078-7722-7 (ebook)
1. African Americans—Economic conditions—20th century. 2. African
Americans—Government policy—History—20th century. 3. African
Americans—Segregation—History—20th century. 4. Social security—
United States—History—20th century. 5. Welfare state—United States
—History—20th century. 6. Racism—Political aspects—United States—
History—20th century. 7. United States—Social policy. 8. United
States—Politics and government—1933–1945. 9. Depressions—1929—
United States. 10. New Deal, 1933–1939. I. Title.
E185.8.P66 2006
368.4′00973—dc22   2005034985

For my father,

with love and gratitude

Contents

A section of illustrations follows p. 116.

Acknowledgments

I am struck by wonder as I sit down to contemplate all of the people who have been a part of the creation of this book. I hope to acknowledge as many as I can. My first academic community at The Evergreen State College initiated my focused study of systems of inequality. Thank you especially to Don Finkel, David Marr, Nancy Koppelman, and James Martin. The big questions that are the backdrop of this book first appeared through my work as an analyst for the Washington State Senate Ways and Means Committee, and I am grateful to my community there for all that I learned, especially to Stan Pynch, Steve Jones, Susan Nakagawa, Sue Breen, and my co-teacher at TESC, Randy Hodgins. The book itself was conceived in graduate seminars at the Rutgers University History Department, and I am indebted to the excellent faculty of Rutgers, all of whom are supportive, engaging, and inspiring, especially T. Jackson Lears, Ginny Yans, and Deborah White. Rutgers University provided generous funding, freeing up my time and energy for this project.

I owe so much to Alice Kessler-Harris, who nurtured the project with extraordinary attention, care, and kind support; she taught me to be rigorous with research, to stand by my interpretations, and to seek and find community to sustain the work. Alice shared her pathbreaking research on gender and Social Security with me through the writing stages, and this book has benefited greatly from her generosity. Hasia Diner helped especially with the interpretation in chapter 4, on the work of black organizations. David Levering Lewis has been very supportive and offered an invaluable critique of chapter 2, on southern Democrats. The theoretical questions that drive this book, about the nature of meaning and identity, were developed through close work with Joan Scott, and her influence is present on every page. I thank her for many things, for pushing me to see beyond conventional limits, and for exemplifying a spirit of open, shared intellectual inquiry.

Amy Forbes, Becca Gershenson, Karen Balcom, Liz Smith, Annie Nicolosi, and Jennifer Nelson read and responded to early versions of this work, and I am grateful for their willingness to slog through the mud and help me find what was worth keeping. Thank you especially to Nancy Carnevale for her unwavering friendship and support of this project over many years and to Rebecca Hartman for many cups of coffee drunk late into the night as we dissected and reconstructed the New Deal. Friends and family gave me places to stay and other kinds of support that made this work possible. Thank you especially to Tina, Marianna, and Juli Nannarone and Sonia Thurmond.

Others read and responded to the entire manuscript through later stages of development. Thank you to Eileen Boris, Edward Berkowitz, Robert Lieberman, and Nancy MacLean. Beryl Satter has been a close friend and collaborator throughout many drafts and shared with me her important work on housing activism in Chicago. Many others read parts of the manuscript, including Skip Berger, Juli Nannarone, Rob Halpern, and Jeremy Morrison. Beatrix Hoffman shared her research, insights, and friendship. Dan Katz has been a great friend through this process, and he inspires me with his work. Pat Jerido has contributed to the book in many ways as a valued member of my intellectual community. Carol Poole read parts of the manuscript and edited others and has been a tremendous source of support, fresh ideas, and intellectual challenge over the years.

Two current sources of inspiration have fed me and influenced this book in inestimable ways. The first are my colleagues at Prescott College, who create and sustain a rich, interdisciplinary intellectual community and remind me daily of the interrelatedness of all things. Thank you to all of the faculty, especially Doug Hulmes, Dan Garvey, Ellen Abell, and Gret Antilla, and my colleagues in cultural and regional studies. The book is also fed by my work in East Africa, which gives me hope that human beings can move beyond even the most entrenched systems of inequality and shows the powerful role that education can play. Thank you Gerry Garvey, the Maasai Environmental Resource Coalition, Kaitlin Noss, Ann Radeloff, the nine students who pioneered the first course in Kenya, and my friends in the Prescott Rotary. I am also grateful to John Poole, whose love and insight made it all possible, and to Meitamei Olol Dapash, my brother and co-conspirator, for his vision.

Dozens of librarians provided invaluable assistance to this project. Thank you to the staffs of the Rutgers University Libraries in New Brunswick and Newark; New York Public Library; Schomberg Center for Research in Black Culture; Franklin D. Roosevelt Presidential Library; National Archives in College Park, Maryland, and Washington, D.C.; University of Chicago Library; State Historical Society of Wisconsin; Columbia University Rare Books and Manuscripts; and Library of Congress. Thank you especially to the Prescott College library staff for so much support. The University of North Carolina Press has been wonderful to work with; thanks especially to Chuck Grench and Stevie Champion.

The book would not have been possible without the enthusiastic interest of family and friends and the community they provide. Jean Poole, my mother, tops this list; her pride and joy have been wind to my wings. Jonathan Best has been intimately involved with this project from its first breath. He has read every draft with an intelligent eye, helped me keep it simple and direct, made me coffee and gave me space, and loved me through the process. Thank you to students of the Rutgers honors history class on race in U.S. history and to all of my students at Prescott College who challenge me daily to "find the hope." This book is dedicated to my father, Mark E. Poole, for introducing me at a young age to the pain and cost of the racial divide in America and teaching me through example to never give up on the work of its dismantling.

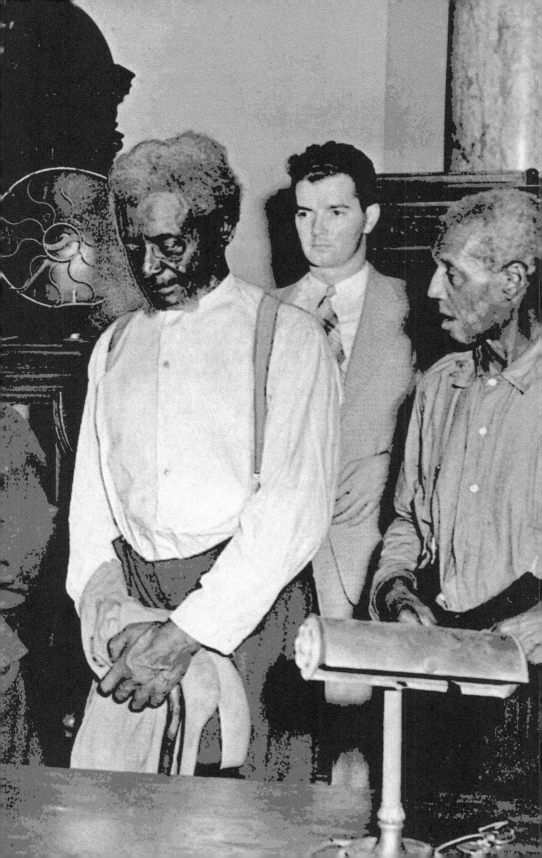

The Segregated Origins of Social Security

Introduction

The greatest challenge of my work as a teacher of the history of race in America is addressing my students' beliefs that racial equality is a hopeless cause. These beliefs are only rarely articulated. But once, in the honors history class that I taught at the Rutgers University campus in inner-city Newark, in the middle of a polite discussion about the racialization of poverty in the 1960s, a student asked, "Hasn't the government already done everything it can to help African Americans?" All eyes turned to me, indicating that a taboo had been broken, or perhaps the secret agreement of some others in the claim. At once the class jumped into gear and began to fight about affirmative action, with white and black students assuming leadership of opposing camps. The energy of the class had shifted dramatically, with students clamoring to be heard, stabbing the air with their index fingers as they leaped out of their seats to defend their "pro" or "con" position. The students were now *engaged* in a relevant topic; ostensibly I was doing my job. Yet I found myself deflated, struggling to stay present. I suspected that my students were not learning anything from the discussion, stuck as their arguments were in tired, circular grooves. But more than that, a pervasive hopelessness framed the comments of both the "pro" and "con" speakers, to which I found myself unable to respond. I noticed that the group was eager to defend or critique the *fairness* of affirmative action in theory, whether it was deserved and by whom, but was unwilling to consider even briefly whether it has been, or could actually be, effective. Becoming more alert, I began to see that my students had no vision of what racial equality would look like—they did not imagine it. Every speaker tacitly confirmed, by what they did not say, that racial inequality is an eternal part of the natural landscape and all efforts to change it have failed. Many Americans ensconced in white neighborhoods, schools, and workplaces may believe that the rise in the number of black politicians and movie stars means that racial inequality is gradually losing ground. But for my students in Newark, racial segregation was a fact of daily life; they did not enjoy the luxury of abstraction. Their arguments revealed, whatever their position, a belief that racial inequality is too deeply entrenched to challenge, too complex to change, and that the proof of this lies in the failure of government policy.

Having structured my classes around a normative narrative of race relations in America—a story of the inevitable cycles of opportunities seized and hopes dashed—I had unintentionally reinforced this hopelessness. I had taught that the promise of the Reconstruction era was answered by the backlash of Jim Crow segregation; the victory of the brave boycotters in Montgomery in the passage of the Civil Rights Act was lost in the shadowy tangle of contemporary racial inequality. Raised in the post–civil rights era, my students come to class believing that legal rights gained through that movement guarantee, if not equality, at least equal opportunity. They therefore tend to believe that the continuing problem of racial inequality is one of individual weakness, of "white" inability to overcome deep-seated prejudice, and, especially, of "black" inability to keep from being pulled under by centuries of oppression.

These two contradictory beliefs, that equal opportunity has been achieved and that racial equality is ultimately a hopeless cause, are embedded in our ways of seeing the U.S. welfare state. Americans, at least as represented in the media, do not generally think of welfare as an investment in the common good, like public schools, as a necessity in an economy that has more workers than jobs and that has no other means to provide for people who are unable to fit into the job market. From the beginning, welfare has carried a stigma: those who receive it have failed as individuals and are a burden on society. And that stigma has a color. The welfare state is literally colored by the "black, welfare-dependent underclass," which serves as a pillar of the American cultural imagination. That term does not actually describe the diverse majority of people who have been enrolled in welfare programs at any given time, most of whom are "white." It expresses, instead, assumptions about the meaning of both "welfare" and "black." Both have been degraded through association with the other in a society that assigns economic and social value to all things considered "white" and self-made. The specter of the "black, welfare-dependent underclass" has greatly affected society's relationship to all African Americans and to all welfare recipients.

Through this study, I have gone back to the origins of the U.S. welfare state to add a piece to the puzzle of the relationship between race and welfare. Americans know that race and welfare are somehow connected, though they may disagree on the nature of that connection. But it is less commonly known that the founding legislation that created the American welfare state discriminated on the basis of race. The Social Security Act of 1935, which created all of the nonmedical programs of our basic welfare system, structurally channeled most African Americans away from the programs designed for workers and, at least in theory, into public assistance. Some aspects of this discrimination were not addressed until the 1950s and 1960s, years after the Act's passage, during which time the families and communities belonging to this group lost out on the baseline of economic security that the Act afforded to covered workers; other aspects continue to discriminate today. Sweeping welfare reforms in the 1960s initiated an expansion of poverty programs, which came to absorb greater percentages of all American families, but it did not revisit the basic structure of the welfare state that related to some citizens as workers and others only on the basis of their proven poverty.

Although the knowledge that the U.S. welfare state was established on a discriminatory basis may be distressing, I believe that it also offers the seeds of a challenge to the hopelessness expressed by my students. The history of the Act reveals that there was a beginning to the relationship between race and welfare, which suggests that there can also be an end. It shows that the government has not done "everything that it can" to undermine inequality, that, indeed, it has contributed to the ghettoization of African Americans through public policy; it points to ways that government might play a different role. Most important, the history reveals that public policy has contributed most to inequality through the belief of policymakers that race is real, that human beings really are "black" or "white."

In telling this story, I am humbled by the shoulders on which I am privileged to stand. Many scholars have written about the history of the American welfare state and the Social Security Act from a variety of perspectives. Initially, Social Security was addressed by historians through the questions and themes that drove studies of the New Deal generally, some of which have exerted a strong influence over interpretive threads that have developed since then. Specifically, a liberal interpretation, which celebrated the New Deal for implementing a progressive and humane social policy, was challenged by historians on the left, such as Barton Bernstein, who argued that these policies were employed to salvage capitalism more than to humanize its effects. While the earlier historians grappled with such an immense and important history as the New Deal, the Social Security Act itself received scant attention.[1]

Over the past three decades, Social Security has been addressed through a different set of questions posed by scholars of poverty and social welfare, who have looked to the Act for insight into the origins of the American welfare state. At first, these questions of origins led to the formation of two opposing schools: developmental theories suggested that welfare states in the United States and Europe evolved out of industrialization, whereas social democratic theories argued that they resulted from demands made by organized labor. Read through these lenses, the Social Security Act was an inevitable outcome of capitalism, a progressive advance in labor's fight against capitalism, or a capitalistic society's means to the social control of workers.[2] An alternative view, referred to as the institutional-political process perspective, has suggested that the timing and features of welfare systems are determined less by the tendencies of capitalism and more by the particular institutional context within which a welfare system is born: the capacity of a state institution to administer policies that are already in place and the political landscape. This approach has exerted a strong influence on welfare history.[3]

A separate though overlapping approach has been taken by historians of women, who have sought to understand the ways that ideas about gender and women have influenced welfare state formation. This work has been theoretically dominated by what is known as the "maternalist" interpretation, which emphasizes the roles of elite white women in the development of federal social programs for women and children.[4] Maternalism is philosophically consistent with the other main theoretical approach to come out of women's history: the "two-channel" welfare state model originally articulated by Barbara Nelson. Nelson has suggested that the American welfare state developed around two separate channels, one growing out of unemployment compensation programs and designed to serve "earned," "legitimate" benefits to mostly white, male industrial workers, and another that evolved from widows' pensions and served mostly poor, white widows in keeping with poor law tradition. These interpretive frameworks converge in an analysis of the Social Security Act and have been used to construct much of women's welfare history since then, including the most detailed history of the development of the act by a women's historian, Linda Gordon, in her *Pitied but Not Entitled: Single*

Mothers and the History of Welfare. Other scholars, especially Gwendolyn Mink, have applied the maternalist interpretation to explore the imposition of Anglo-American norms on nonwhite welfare recipients.[5]

The Social Security Act represents a critical moment in large and important narratives of twentieth-century U.S. history. It is not surprising that, as a consequence, it has been approached through theoretical interpretations of those larger histories: of the New Deal, of U.S. social policy and state formation, and of the relationship between U.S. women and the state. All of this work has provided significant insight into the various contexts into which the Act was born; the task that has not yet been fully accomplished is to reconstruct the details of the development of the Act from within.

This is especially the case regarding the question that inspired this book: How and why did the Social Security Act come to discriminate on the basis of race? The current consensus on this question has been built primarily on two very important works about larger histories: Harvard Sitkoff's *A New Deal for Blacks*, and Jill Quadagno's *The Transformation of Old Age Security*. Sitkoff's book provides a ground-breaking, thorough account of the many discriminations experienced by African Americans through New Deal programs. He saw this discrimination as ultimately incidental to the greater, progressive story of the New Deal, in which, he concluded, the "seeds" of the later civil rights movement were planted. Though it has heavily influenced subsequent assumptions about the Social Security Act, Sitkoff's work is not actually about the Act and only devotes a paragraph to it. Quadagno's book is the most widely cited on the cause of discrimination in the Act; historians have widely accepted her argument that black workers were excluded from the Act at the behest of southern congressional leadership. However, her conclusion was drawn largely through an analysis of interest groups and the positions that they would be expected to assume on the Act. This analysis adds immensely to our understanding of the larger context through which the Act was constructed and what we might expect to have been the cause of discrimination, but it does not answer the question of what actually happened on the ground.

Concurrent with these studies, some historians have also begun to dig more deeply into the history of the Social Security Act's development. Edward Berkowitz has suggested that historians turn away from "esoteric debates" about the origins of welfare states and build the history of social welfare programs, which he says "remains a relatively unexplored topic." Berkowitz directs our attention to the Wisconsin reformers who re-searched and drafted the Act and who are featured in the chapters that fol-low.[6] Gareth Davies and Martha Derthick, after undergoing a close reading of reports of the Committee on Economic Security (CES), found that this same group from Wisconsin played a larger role in the exclusion of black workers from the Act than has been acknowledged, though they argue that this was necessary for administrative reasons. Linda Gordon recon-structed the collaboration of interest groups and policymakers in the de-velopment of Aid to Dependent Children (ADC). And Alice Kessler-Harris has provided a detailed look at the process through which gender was in-corporated into Old Age Insurance (OAI, now Social Security) and Unem-ployment Insurance (UI), showing a direct relationship between cultural ideas about gender and the people who made the policy.[7]

For this book, I dug into congressional records, committee meeting minutes, staff reports, private correspondence, and personal papers to re-construct the step-by-step development of the Social Security Act, paying particular attention to the different ways through which the Act discrimi-nated against African American people. What I found is surprising and does not easily mesh with either the historical narrative about the Act or common assumptions about how public policy is made discriminatory. As this study will illustrate, the Act was not made discriminatory through a fight between liberal northerners and racist southerners, a view charac-terized by Robert Lieberman as "Sweden vs. South Africa,"[8] but because policymakers shared an interest in protecting the political and economic value of whiteness. I found that African Americans were not denied the benefits of Social Security because of the machinations of southern con-gressional leadership, as is assumed. The Act was made discriminatory through a shifting web of alliances of white policymakers that crossed re-gions and political parties. The members of the group that wielded the greatest influence on these developments were not southerners in Con-gress, but President Franklin D. Roosevelt's own people. They were the liberal reformers who researched and drafted the Social Security Act, who genuinely sought to build a fairer and better world, and devoted their waking hours to that challenge, but whose vision was steeped in racial privilege.

What I have found and reported here may help to advance our under-standing of this important history in several ways. First, this study suggests that the New Deal administration played a much more complex role in the history of race in the twentieth-century United States than has been described elsewhere and calls for another look at that larger history. Second, it challenges the "Solid South" interpretation of New Deal history that credits southerners in Congress with the discriminatory aspects of New Deal legislation and in that way suggests that racial politics in the New Deal era cannot be understood solely as the diametric opposition of two regionally centered parties. Third, this history sheds light on the structural basis of inequality in the U.S. welfare system and how that policy might have been designed, and thus might be formulated in the future, to further equality. Fourth, because this structure incorporated the inequalities of the existing economy into federal policy, rather than attempt to mitigate those inequalities, this study can provide insight into current debates about privatization of federal programs like Social Security. Finally, I found that networks of women New Dealers had a different impact on the development of the Social Security Act than has been reported elsewhere, and that assumptions about the influence of the *maternalist* perspective on our welfare state, as well as on the racialization of welfare, need to be revisited.

THE SOCIAL SECURITY ACT was developed through the fall of 1934 and passed by the Seventy-fourth Congress in the summer of 1935. The Act, part of Roosevelt's second New Deal, took on a broader set of challenges than those faced by the first round of New Deal legislation passed in 1933. These earlier initiatives, including the Agricultural Adjustment Act (AAA), the National Recovery Act (NRA), and the Federal Emergency Relief Act (FERA), were designed to mitigate the impact of the immediate economic crisis. The Social Security Act, by contrast, was intended to initiate long-range economic reform and to implement a social welfare safety net that would restructure the future relationship between U.S. citizens and their government. The Act was not widely popular beyond the network of liberal reformers affiliated with FDR's administration. It was fought by business interests and supporters of more radical initiatives, as well as by millions of advocates across the country for a more generous old-age pension system than the Act promised to provide.

In June 1934 FDR announced the appointment of a cabinet-level CES to develop a plan for the "cradle to grave" welfare system that would be introduced during the next congressional session. He named Frances Perkins, secretary of the U.S. Department of Labor, to chair the CES; other members included Henry Morganthau, secretary of the U.S. Department of Treasury; Harry L. Hopkins, director of FERA; and Henry Wallace, secretary of the U.S. Department of Agriculture. Perkins quickly assembled a staff, and a preliminary report of the CES was produced by September. The CES approved the final staff report in December, Roosevelt gave his stamp of approval, and the Social Security Act was introduced in the House of Representatives (as HR 4120) and the Senate (S 1130) in January 1935 as the Economic Security Act. The bill was reconstructed in the House, at which time it was renamed the Social Security Act and passed by both houses of Congress by June 1935. To minimize confusion, the word "Act" refers to the Social Security Act throughout this text.

The final Act included ten titles and created ten separate programs: two insurance programs (UI and OAI) and eight public assistance programs for specific groups of economically disadvantaged people. The insurance programs and Old Age Assistance (OAA) were financed through a combination of contributions by employers and employees of particular types of businesses. The most prominent of the public assistance programs was OAA, which was passed to appease demands by millions of Americans for a pension for people over age sixty-five. It has since been surpassed in prominence by the second program, ADC (which later became Aid to Families with Dependent Children—AFDC), which distributed monthly grants for the maintenance of poor children. The Act created four other programs that targeted poor or disabled children: Maternal and Child Welfare, Services for Crippled Children, Child Welfare Services, and Vocational Rehabilitation. It also established a program to provide "aid to the Blind" and provided additional funds for public health work.

This book focuses on the four programs created by the Act that were the largest and most controversial and that have most impacted the future development of the U.S. welfare state: UI, OAI, ADC, and OAA. It offers an analysis of the ways that racial discrimination was structured into these programs.

Of the many minority groups in the United States in the 1930s, this book addresses the group identified as *Negro*, a group considered in this time and place to comprise a separate, biologically determined *race*. American "Negroes" were diverse. Many were the product of both Western European and West African ancestry; some had Native American ancestry, and some, especially in cities on the East Coast, were immigrants from the West Indies or other former Spanish and French colonies. Some descended from families that had been free for generations, though most descended from slaves held in bondage in southern states until 1865.

In spite of this mixed heritage, "Negroes" were defined according to a "one drop rule," whereby all people with any African ancestry were of a single race. Skin color was of secondary importance in determining identity. Very dark skin would ensure identification as "Negro," but the opposite was not true for either marginally dark skin or very light skin; there were many "white" people with "dusky" skin and many "Negroes" with very fair skin, blond hair, and blue eyes, such as Walter White, the executive director of the National Association for the Advancement of Colored People. Although there were no consistently reliable physical markers, the borders that separated "Negroes" from the rest of society were clear to all and virtually impenetrable. Those borders were drawn by culture, class, and language. In the dominant culture, if a person was classified as "Negro," he or she could not be a doctor or an author, minister or child, but only a "Negro doctor" or a "Negro child." "Negro" was the preferred term; though "colored" was still used to describe people with African heritage through the 1960s and 1970s, "Negro" with a capital *N* was the term used by African American leadership in the 1930s. "Black" was coming into use, especially in leftist political circles, but even there "Negro" was usually preferred.

As is still true in the United States, the language of race made real—natural—what had been invented; "white" and "Negro" were understood to refer to two essentially different types of humans, and as those words were spoken, they created the reality to which they referred. The language of race is problematic, always, because it embodies and therefore reproduces inequality. In the 1930s "white" was used universally to describe the majority of U.S. citizens. "White" was not strictly a racial category like "Anglo-Saxon" or "Caucasian"; it specifically identified Americans of European descent who claimed to have no African heritage. The one-drop rule did not apply to other races. A white person could have a Cherokee or Mexican great-grandmother without losing whiteness, but even the most remote ancestral ties to the African continent would disqualify an individual from being classified as "white." Even more than "Negro," "white" was used, as it had been for centuries, to create a false homogeneity out of a diversity of origins and cultures for no other purpose than to artificially enhance the value of certain people and property. In America, people of African descent have continuously struggled to define themselves with a word, because words, like "colored" and "Negro," come to absorb the racist stereotypes of a time and place and must be replaced with others. But "white" has never needed to be replaced because the word continues to confer privilege on those it defines.

The language of race creates problems for writing history. First, one could argue that it is not accurate to refer to "Negroes" in 1930 as anything else; that was the term that a clearly identified segment of Americans chose for themselves. Yet the meaning of the word has changed in the last seventy years, and it evokes stereotypes that the words "black" and "African American" were adopted to challenge. Second, it would be accurate to use the term "white" to define the majority of Americans in the 1930s, because that is how they were defined at the time. However, this use also misleads; the singular use of "white" through the centuries gives the concept the appearance of being eternal and essentially real, as if "white" defines the unchanging, true essence of a group of people rather than the sociopolitics of a society. Third, in 1930 neither "Negro" nor "white" defined the same groups that we refer to as "black" and "white" today. The borders that have defined these categories have shown themselves to be fluid through the ages. "White" had a different meaning in the 1840s, for example, when native-born Americans challenged the whiteness of Irish immigrants, and in the 1890s "white" had to be defined through the courts by including and excluding Serbian and Japanese petitioners for U.S. citizenship, which was limited at the time, for immigrants, to "white men."[9]

In this book, I tend to adopt the language of the time to help us remember that racial categories are socially constructed. The exception to this approach is my use of the term "African American" or "black" rather than "Negro" when not quoting or describing the perspective of others who would not have used that term. "African American" describes origins rather than racial assignment and thus is, it can be argued, a more accurate way to describe the group that was defined by their "drop" of African heritage.

Other minority groups were similarly defined racially and isolated from white society, and were similarly affected by the Social Security Act, especially Mexicans, some of whom lived in the West when that land was Mexico; immigrants from Asia working as farm labor and living primarily in the Southwest and on the West Coast; and Native Americans. This book does not focus on these groups because all minorities other than African Americans were invisible to policymakers in the context of the Act and therefore have not left a mark on their records. I have included every reference to these groups that I found.

This text explains the process through which the Social Security Act was made discriminatory, the different groups of policymakers who were involved, and how their perspectives on race were reflected, directly and otherwise, in the policies they made. After the first chapter, which describes the backdrop of the 1930s, Chapters 2–5 relate the involvement of particular groups of participants and explores their understandings of the meaning and significance of race. All of these chapters and the Conclusion respond to the question, "How did the racialized worldviews of these groups factor into the policy that they participated in creating?" What I found was not evidence of a single, dominant cultural understanding of the meaning of race, but many diverging and overlapping explanations, explanations that ultimately were embedded in the social policy created through the Social Security Act.

From one perspective, the Social Security Act was the crowning glory of Franklin Roosevelt's liberal New Deal, and those who created it have much to be proud of: they persevered in the face of vociferous opposition, put together a monumentally complex piece of legislation in a very short period of time, and saw its passage through a skeptical Congress. They built into American public policy the idea that the federal government has a responsibility to provide a safety net for its citizens. But that perspective cannot stand as the truth of the meaning of the Act because it was not shared by everyone; for those who were excluded, the Act embedded a different idea into the federal welfare system, the idea that not all citizens are equal, nor are they entitled to equal rights and protections.

one

So Now Mr. President, We Are Looking for Something

African Americans, the Social Security Act, and the Great Depression

To the Senate, governed by a body of well educated men that are elected to make law for both races to live under: Now, I see a bill posed now in Congress about old age pension[s] and it [is] all for one race. Now, you are a body of men to look for the Ethiopian as well as the caucasian races. . . . [T]he Ethiopian race is the foot stool, and when he get[s to] the age of 65 years, he or she need[s] help to live on in this country.[1]

We the *colored* citizens of Plainfield Union County played our part in the overthrow of the Republican Party. . . . This club put life in the Democratic party of Plainfield. . . . So, don't forget us, who have been in this country since 1619, and helped Geo Washington, ran Cornwallis to England. We helped you in all wars. So now Mr. President[,] we are looking for something.[2]

For most of the country's 12 million African Americans, the Great Depression of the 1930s brought with it unemployment, extreme poverty, and a loss of even the meager economic opportunity secured through the 1920s. But this destruction and despair also gave birth to a moment of possibility and a glimmer of hope for a wholly different place in the United States. The crash of the economy profoundly shook the country's class structure, and differing groups of Americans began to ponder the economic platform on which life in this country was built. Even more important, significant numbers of working people began to openly question their place in the economic hierarchy that kept the racial divide in place. Cries to "share the wealth" rang across the land, and as many as 20 to 25 million people—out of a national population of 123 million—petitioned Congress to enact the Townsend plan to redistribute the wealth of the land to all of the people, they said, who had earned it. The ranks of leftist political organizations promoting the rights of workers swelled, and the interracial Congress of Industrial Organizations (CIO) was founded. Perhaps astonishingly, none of the mass movements of mostly white people in this period officially subscribed to a doctrine of white supremacy, and some even encouraged interracial collaboration.[3]

Possibilities also existed in the arena of federal policy. Franklin Roosevelt's New Deal had already shown promising signs that, for the first time since the Reconstruction era, racial justice might fit into some small corner of the federal agenda. Early New Deal programs had not been promising on the whole: they did not alter the discriminatory treatment established by institutional segregation. On the other hand, the directors of the Federal Emergency Relief Administration (FERA) made efforts to combat discrimination, and a diverse spectrum of families was kept alive by government assistance. Roosevelt had named Mary McLeod Bethune, a dark-skinned African American woman, to his cabinet, and more leaders of "Negro" churches and other organizations were pledging their allegiance to the Democratic Party, creating a voting bloc that could not forever be ignored. The expansive reach of the New Deal was reordering society, and some of the more radical leaders of African American communities recognized that they had the potential to cause a dramatic reconfiguration of the social order. But that same reach could also, in the words of Ralph Bunche, "cement the Negro in a permanent position of segregated inferiority in the society."[4]

The Social Security Act was instrumental in determining whether and how this moment of opportunity would be seized. FDR had committed his administration to establishing a permanent safety net. If that safety net had been modeled after the temporary program and built in barriers to discrimination, it would have inevitably eroded, rather than strengthened, the economic disparity between communities on the basis of race, and therefore perhaps the seeming permanence of the racial divide. Three proposals were introduced in Congress to create foundational programs for this permanent system, and each expressed different perspectives about the purpose of social welfare and the obligations of governments to citizens; each had a different plan for the coverage of African Americans. The passage of the Social Security Act concluded this moment of opportunity and laid the seedbed for what has followed.

Racial Inequality and the Great Depression

> Dear sir[:] I am writing you for some information. I am out of work
> and have a wife and four small children. I have registered at the Un-
> employment office and also at the W.P.A. office and they have not
> give[n] me any thing to do and I have not got any thing to go up
> on for my little children. I have no food and no money at all and no
> work and cant find nothing at all to do. I have beg[ged] them for
> work at the W.P.A. office at Port Allen and the office people do not
> give me any straight talk at all. If I was call[ed] to go to war they
> would give me straight talk at once if they kneeded me. Now dear
> sir I am much in need so I am begging you please help me . . . if I
> could find any work at all I would not ask the government for any
> help at all.[5]

As the words of this "colored" man from Walls, Louisiana, convey, in
the mid-thirties the vast majority of African American families were under
siege. In the ghettos of northern cities and southern plantations alike,
most of these families lived precariously. Initially, they turned to extended
families and churches, but these communal resources were quickly exhausted. In northern areas after 1933, they relied on FERA for survival,
supplemented by help from the local Urban League or "Negro charities."
However, they typically lived without access to health care, and relief
grants did not provide enough to meet all of a family's needs. In 1935 most
families in rural African American communities still lived without elec-
tricity and indoor plumbing. They received less assistance in all forms than
their northern and urban counterparts and struggled even more for the
basics of physical survival.

Like this Louisianan, "colored" men and women throughout the country expressed a willingness to do any kind of paid work in order to survive, but they were often unable to find even the most demeaning, underpaid jobs. Centuries of racial discrimination had worked to keep them in
job categories where their labor could be most easily exploited and they
themselves could be kept most financially insecure. When the depression
hit, race lines hardened, and all African Americans were vulnerable to
being fired from even this work to make room for white workers. After
Franklin Roosevelt's election in 1932, they began to turn to the federal government in unprecedented numbers, asking for help in obtaining work so
they could care for their families.

The depression caused a crisis because of the history that preceded it. The wealth produced by the labor of African Americans continued to be stolen after the slaves were freed, and generations of black families struggled to build their lives with no economic base, no family and community resources for down payments on houses, business starts, or college educations. The struggle continued even through the flush decades of the 1910s and 1920s, because opportunities for earning were so limited by discrimination and segregation. Young African American men who migrated north found some openings in manufacturing, the mechanical industries, transportation, and trade; in 1930 roughly a quarter of all "Negro" workers were employed in such jobs, primarily in northern states. But even these apparent gains did not signify a major shift in economic opportunity. African American men were let into industry, but only into its bottom rungs. They were hired by ironworks and meatpacking plants, not to weld or butcher, which were skilled jobs, but to spend long days cleaning furnaces in scorching heat, or mopping blood off of a cutting room floor, for very low wages.[6] As E. Franklin Frazier summed it up during the boom year of 1927, "There are two types of business in New York in terms of Negro hiring policy: those that employ Negroes in menial positions and those that employ no Negroes."[7]

Even these jobs were lost to white workers during the depression, when unemployment rates spiked. Since the end of the Civil War, northern African American families had relied heavily on women's work as domestic servants for survival, and they continued to do so in these years. Domestic service was the largest category of employment for all women, though the field was particularly dominated by the descendants of slaves. In 1935 one-fifth of all "Negro" workers were domestics. Older women typically worked in slightly better-paid institutional settings, and younger women were subject to the greater insecurity, and sometimes sexual harassment, that went with work in private homes.[8] Wages fell with the economy. In southern states, women earned between $2 and $4 dollars for a week of 12- to 14-hour days scrubbing floors, cooking over hot stoves, cleaning toilets, ironing, and changing diapers. In northern states, even fledgling domestic workers' unions considered $10 per week "good" pay. Estimated yearly earnings in 1934 were $579 for women cooks, $788 for male cooks, and $559 for housekeepers. These figures are miniscule compared to the average salaries of upper-middle-class professionals and others, including most upper-level New Deal administrators, who earned $5,000–$10,000 per year, an income considered to be merely "comfortable." They are extremely low when compared to the 3.7 million families living in "moderate" comfort, earning $3,000–$5,000 per year, or even those 9.9 million families at a "minimum comfort" level earning $1,500–$3,000, including social workers employed by private agencies. The bulk of African American urban working women—especially those who were sole earners—was among the poorest of the 11.7 million families living on "subsistence and poverty" wages, with incomes of less than $1,500 per year.[9]

Though African Americans in northern cities typically experienced less overt forms of social discrimination than those in the rural South, their economic opportunities were still strictly controlled. Social segregation in the North did "not cover the whole gamut of interpersonal relations" but was "spotty."[10] Intermarriage was restricted, but not forbidden; dancing and swimming were generally segregated activities, but not eating and drinking. White society could exert tremendous social pressure to maintain de facto segregation in these areas, but generally its efforts were not supported by law and could be subverted in various ways.

This was not the case when it came to housing and education, issues that more directly determined the ability of African American communities to establish an economic base. In northern cities, all people identified as "Negro" were concentrated in the slums. They were prevented from moving by the artificial creation of housing shortages in these areas and by discriminatory codes that kept rents unjustly high. Segregation in housing served to maintain a system of economic exploitation. It was imposed informally through the unacknowledged agreement of the housing industry that the presence of a single African American family in a neighborhood lowered property values. Residential segregation enabled institutional segregation—through schools and hospitals, for example—which in turn facilitated the continued ghettoization of African American professionals and the substandard education of African American children.[11]

In many ways, the North appeared to African Americans to be less discriminatory than the South, as they were free to ride integrated subways with diverse commuters in New York City, speak directly to white merchants, and drink at the same water fountains. Yet the economics of race in the North had much of the same outcome as the economics of race in the South: the maintenance of an underpaid, vulnerable group of laborers.[12]

African Americans living in the South fared no better, even before the depression. More than 9 million of the country's almost 12 million African Americans still lived in southern states, two-thirds of these in poor rural areas. Most were agricultural laborers who were kept indebted to the owners of the land that they worked. In 1934 the average income for all African American families in two Georgia black belt counties was less than two hundred dollars per year. "Negro" tenants and sharecroppers were structurally prevented from getting ahead; plantation owners would not allow them to sell their own crops and often paid them in scrip rather than cash, which could be redeemed only at typically overpriced plantation stores.[13]

The plight of rural African American southerners was made much worse by changes in the agricultural landscape. Through the 1920s industrial farms had begun to gobble up family farms, turning farmers into industrial-style laborers. In 1934 only a tiny fraction of the 6.3 million farms in America were large-scale, yet they employed more than a tenth of all farmworkers. Farm foreclosures created a surplus of labor and led to a drop in agricultural wages—from $47 per month in 1920 to $15 in 1933. After the depression hit, workers flooded the farm market, exacerbating the low wages. As opportunities for farmwork decreased, unpaid family laborers tripled.[14]

Southern agriculture had only begun to move in the direction of the more large-scale industrialized farming that dominated agriculture in the West. The larger western farmers were creating associations to monopolize the canning and processing of foods like vegetable oils. These associations took advantage of the depression to accelerate the process of driving smaller farms out of business. In response, the more industrialized farmworkers in the West engaged in a series of strikes in the mid-1930s. These strikes, which in 1933 "swept California agricultural districts," were "the most extensive strikes of their kind" in the United States, involving 65 percent of the state's entire crop value for that year. Most of the strikes were led by the Cannery Agricultural Industrial Workers Union, but others were directed by independent, mostly Mexican and Chicano unions.[15]

In 1935 African American agricultural workers were almost completely contained within some of the lowest paid and most vulnerable sectors of farming, trends that only worsened their situation. They were barely represented either among the country's three million farm owners, who were mostly white, or among the hired laborers on western industrial farms, also exploited labor, who were mostly immigrants from Mexico, Japan, and the Philippines. In the South, African Americans dominated tenant farming and sharecropping, a peasant farm system where workers used plantation land and then split their harvest with landowners. Share-cropping occupied 44 percent of "Negro" agricultural workers, but only 16.4 percent of white agricultural workers; in 1935, 70 percent of the country's two million tenant farmers were African American.[16] Life for ten-ant farmers and sharecroppers could be brutal. Families lived in shacks and subsisted on cornmeal and pork fat; even small children typically did strenuous labor, often from dawn to dusk. It was especially hard for African American tenant farmers, who were the first to lose their farms when competition increased, and sharecroppers, who even in the good times received much lower wages than their white counterparts for the same work.[17]

The generally poor economic position of African Americans was exacer-bated by the depression, which began with the stock market crash in the fall of 1929. Yet widespread unemployment had been a fact of life among them for at least three years before then: it had already affected those "last to be hired and first to be fired" by the end of 1926. The widespread com-petition for jobs created by the depression made life even harder. In 1930, 40 percent of all African American workers were unemployed compared to roughly 25 percent of the country's total workforce.[18] The jobs of these workers were not just evaporating; they were being replaced in droves by unemployed white workers. As one "Negro newspaper" reported, "Nearly every job that has been classified as a Negro job is being contested for by other workers."[19] White workers were even taking over city garbage col-lection and scavenger wagons, as well as moving into socially demeaning jobs such as those of hotel porters and domestic servants.[20]

More devastating, perhaps, was the destruction of African American–owned businesses throughout the country and with it the loss of an in-cipient economic base. In the early thirties New York City's Harlem ex-perienced the massive failure of locally owned businesses; afterward the mostly Jewish immigrant–owned businesses that bought them out refused to hire Harlem residents.[21]

African American workers were barely organized at the time of the drafting of the Social Security Act, a result of their economic vulnera-bility and discriminatory union practices. Throughout the twenties and thirties they were unable to overcome one of the chief obstacles to union representation: their exclusion from the American Federation of Labor (AFL) affiliate unions. Some individual "Negro unions," most notably the

Brotherhood of Sleeping Car Porters, won concessions from employers through organized efforts in the early 1930s; the interracial Southern Tenant Farmers Union was founded in the summer of 1934 to give voice to farmworkers who were being squeezed out by planters. The International Ladies Garment Workers Union (ILGWU) organized African American women garment workers after 1933, and local unions affiliated with the Communist Party went to great lengths, in some cases, to reach out to African American workers. But generally, even after the founding of the CIO in November 1935, African American workers had no place from which to negotiate with employers. For example, domestic workers in Cleveland attempted to organize in early 1934 as the Household Workers Welfare Association, and two hundred women initially joined. However, they were derailed when the AFL refused their application for a charter.[22] A report claimed that only seven unions for domestic workers were active in 1939, and that none of them offered unemployment or disability assistance.[23]

One of the cruelest consequences of employment discrimination was that it limited the options and strategies available to African Americans as they struggled to provide for their children. Forty percent of African Americans were eighteen or younger in the mid-1930s.[24] In many northern cities, black children with widowed mothers could get help through Mothers' Pension programs or other private programs, though in the poorer South, programs were either nonexistent or channeled limited funds to white widows and their children. In the Deep South, children in rural areas routinely worked alongside their parents in the fields or factories, and school was a luxury.

In 1937 many African Americans expressed their urgent need for jobs through a census taken by the U.S. government of the nation's unemployed. The census, financed by FERA, was designed to gather information on the "numbers, classes, geographical distribution, and occupations of unemployed persons" to use in the development of programs for re-employment, relief, and social security. But many of those canvassed believed that the purpose of the census was to place them in a work program or otherwise help them find a job. The respondents, who were well represented by African Americans, overwhelmingly voiced a desperation for work. One man wrote: "Sire I am a colard man and is cripple in Both of my feets and not able to do Standard work so I am asking for help in the name of jesus. . . . I will Be more than glad for you to get me A disability license in order that I can Earn a living for my family[.] I have tried to get a disability license and they see my condishon But they fail to give them to me."[25] Letters requesting "assistance" generally defined that term as help getting paid work. As one respondent said: "Kindly see if you cannot find some kind of Employment for Me. I am physicaly able and cap-able to fill the Position's asked for. . . . This is my third time to appeal for financial assistance of the Government hoping [I] may be more successful this time."[26] Even mothers with overwhelming domestic burdens asked for work. One woman had been "trying to get some work for over 6 year & they wont pay any attencion to me I am a widow woman & have no help whatever & they cut me off of the relief April, 1937. . . . I can work & wants work. . . . [I] have got my name down in every employment office in town."[27] A mother with an "education up to the first year in high school" needed a job to feed her eight hungry children: "[I]f you do not give me or my husbin some work I could not live[.] I go days and two days without a thing to eat[.] Children crying[,] I am hungry[,] what shall I do[?] . . . I coud not get no job to do a thing for you all white people."[28]

The first round of New Deal programs sought to provide jobs and job protection, but African Americans rarely benefited from them. The cotton acreage reduction program of the Agricultural Adjustment Agency (AAA) hurt sharecroppers, tenant farmers, and other agricultural laborers, though it benefited southern plantation owners and northern industrial corporations that owned plantations in the South. Sharecroppers and tenant farmers received only a tiny share of government compensation for decreasing farm production, and many were evicted as a result. Generally, the larger the farm, the greater the benefit that farm owners realized through AAA.[29] African American workers were also structurally discriminated against through National Recovery Administration (NRA) codes. The codes allowed employers to pay different wages to workers for the same work and excluded occupations dominated by "Negroes," including domestic service. The NRA also exacerbated the displacement of African American workers in job categories that required higher wages for all workers. A minister in Alabama reported that employers frankly acknowledged that "if they must pay higher wages they will pay it to white folk."[30] Following the implementation of a particular discriminatory NRA code, Adrienne Baxter, of Danville, Illinois, pleaded for help from President Roosevelt in August 1933: "It is painful to think that the labor by which the negro earns his daily bread, often becomes a long suicide . . . out of so many of the rich and powerful, no one thinks of the mortality which decimates his brothers, thus forced to eat homicidal bread. . . . I beg of you on bended knees and plead with you to give your attention to this dreadful situation that [is] happening in Danville, Illinois."[31]

The most vulnerable workers, especially agricultural and domestic workers, were funneled by the federal government into FERA. One government report claimed that agricultural workers were more represented on Emergency Relief than any other group in 1934; according to another report, close to half of the workers on relief in many American cities were domestic servants.[32] Emergency Relief was a godsend to African American families during these years, as they had been excluded from other forms of assistance. In northern states they generally received relief in amounts appropriate to their poverty and greater than their representation in the population.[33] However, these workers obtained relief in lieu of the jobs that they sought through government work programs like the Works Progress Administration (WPA) and the Civilian Conservation Corps (CCC) or assistance through NRA to help them keep working.

But an opportunity was on the horizon in the form of public pressure to encourage government to take a firmer stand in the provision of social welfare. A second demand was growing not just for work, but for the benefit that accompanied work: old-age pensions. And many of the voices that called for social welfare also demanded that it be distributed equitably among all citizens.

Three Plans for Social Welfare

The Social Security Act was only one of three bills presented to Congress during the seventy-fourth session seeking to create a permanent welfare system. The other two, the Lundeen Bill and the Townsend Bill, represented mass movements of people who organized and sent petitions demanding that Congress enact their respective plans. All three bills sought to influence the larger economy through the social welfare systems they created. Because they were based on very different understandings of the political economy and human nature, the welfare systems that they designed would have far-reaching and very different impacts on American society.

Both the Lundeen and Townsend measures intended not only to provide security to workers, but also to redistribute the country's wealth. Yet the Worker's Unemployment and Social Insurance Bill, or Lundeen

Bill, was the only one of the three to create a system that unambiguously protected against racial discrimination. Introduced by Ernest Lundeen, a Farmer-Labor Party representative from Minnesota, the bill sought to create an unemployment insurance program that would be funded by significantly taxing the incomes and estates of wealthy citizens, basically redistributing wealth between rich Americans and members of the working classes. It was only two pages and five hundred words long, therefore vague regarding the design of the program it would create.

But the Lundeen Bill was not at all vague regarding its intent to provide for African Americans. It stated that unemployment benefits "shall be extended to all workers, whether they be industrial, agricultural, domestic, office, or professional workers, and to farmers, without discrimination because of age, sex, race, color, religious or political opinion or affiliation."[34] The measure was endorsed by five international AFL unions, six state AFLS, and three thousand AFL locals, as well as by "substantially all" independent radical unions and unions for the unemployed. Fraternal and veterans societies were also major supporters, as well as a lengthy list of Communist-affiliated organizations. Petitions containing over a million signatures in favor of the Lundeen Bill were presented to Congress on three separate occasions. A *New York Post* poll of its readers concluded that 83 percent preferred the Lundeen Bill over either the Social Security Act or the Townsend Bill.[35]

Some government administrators were very concerned about the equal treatment that different categories of workers received in the Lundeen Bill. Alex Nordholm, a staff member of the Committee on Economic Security (CES), which drafted the Social Security Act, worried that, "[w]ith one stroke of the pen skilled toolmakers, lawyers, doctors and ditchdiggers are to be treated alike in the matter of benefits?" The bill, he argued, regarded "workers" and "farmers" as "synonymous" and extended unemployment coverage to sharecroppers and even unpaid farm family members. Nordholm, who headed up the CES research on the Lundeen bill, estimated that the federal government would have to confiscate all individual and corporate incomes over $5,000 and 100 percent of the estates of decedents to pay for it. Nevertheless, he acknowledged that even at present levels of unemployment, all Americans could probably be provided for in this way.[36]

Like the Lundeen Bill, the Townsend Bill may have been more of a statement of philosophy than a polished plan of action. The heart of the

Townsend plan was a 2 percent tax to be levied on all financial transactions that would be paid into a fund from which every U.S. citizen aged sixty-five and older would receive a pension of $200 per month. For recipients, the only stipulation was that they spend the pensions within thirty days to keep the money circulating in the economy. It was understood that this plan would enhance employment by encouraging older people to retire; it would also give them a vital financial role in their families and communities. The measure's larger goal was to redistribute wealth through the transaction tax, gradually emptying "eastern banks" (which, Townsendites argued, had caused the country's economic problems by hoarding wealth) and returning that wealth to the people who had earned it. There were various national and local societies created during this period to advocate for old-age pensions, but the Townsend movement was by far the biggest. The movement loomed large in Washington, and, Edwin Witte confided to a friend, "[a]ll members of Congress are afraid of the Townsend people."[37] Supporters of the plan had secured enough votes to substitute the Townsend Bill for the Social Security Act on the House floor; they were only prevented from doing so by the passage of a gag rule that prohibited the addition of amendments to the Social Security Act. At the movement's peak period, Congress received 1,500 letters a day from individual supporters and Townsend clubs, and an estimated 20–25 million people signed petitions.[38]

In spite of its size, the Townsend movement has received little attention from historians and deserves more than it will get here. The movement has been framed by Alan Brinkley's work on two other popular protest movements in the 1930s, one led by Huey Long and the other by Father Charles E. Coughlin, and seen primarily through the eyes of its contemporary detractors as "an impossibly expensive and unworkable delusion" promoted by a starry-eyed physician and a professional huckster.[39] Yet to be written is a history of the movement on its own terms. The ideology behind the Townsend movement, as represented by the publications it left behind, appears to have been undergirded by a critique of the country's economic structure drawn from Christian ethics, democratic patriotism, and socialism. Its leadership may have been questionable, but the issues raised by its membership are revealing.

The Townsend movement's main assault was on resource hoarding by the wealthy. Over and over, Townsendites asked their representatives, "Why should a small percent of the people of this great America possess over 90% of all of the wealth, which the two past generations have produced?" They insisted that they had a right to the wealth produced by the country, not on the basis of their individual contribution, but collectively as workers and as Americans. They asked the CES:

> Has it ever occurred to your economic committee that the two preceding generations have builded [*sic*] these United States from a veritable wilderness into the greatest technologically developed country on earth? Has your committee ever stopped to consider that had it not been for the labor, the intelligence, the human sacrifices, the endurance of all the hardships that are connected with frontier life that the United States of America would still be a wilderness and that all of the millions and billions of wealth created during these two generations would never have existed?[40]

Rank-and-file unions often supported the Townsend plan, weaving their own analyses of class-based oppression with the plight of the aged. They argued that the "unemployable" class was created through the disposal of middle-aged and older people, which led to pauperism.[41]

The diverse makeup of the movement has not yet been fully researched, though we do know that some "Negro" and racially mixed Townsend clubs existed.[42] Generally, old-age pension movements across the country appear to have leaned toward class solidarity as opposed to racial solidarity. Members of the Old Age Pension Society of Biloxi, Mississippi, critiqued the exclusion of agricultural and domestic workers from the Social Security Act, saying: "No white man will be paid a decent wage while there is cheap colored labor. . . . This is the only 'colored problem' that we have: and state malipulation [*sic*] of unemployment insurance and pensions could easily perpetuate southern poverty."[43] The National Old Age Pension Association, another old-age pension movement usually referred to as the "Pope Plan," claimed in its official publication that if "any state, county or district, in its administration of the Old Age Pension, seek to mistreat or leave out any deserving old man or woman, white or black, then the National Old Age Pension Association and the NATIONAL FORUM will start a fight which will be too rough even for a den of lions or a hell full of devils. The aged black man or negro 'mammy' can suffer as much from hunger and privation as can a white person."[44]

Townsendites drew on a contemporary discourse, associated with the Technocratic movement, asserting that ample wealth existed for everyone, and poverty was caused through inefficiency and unequal distribution. According to one historian, this assumption was "widely accepted" among economic and political thinkers in the 1930s. These included Stuart Chase, who contended that increased efficiency would enable all Americans to live comfortably on $5,000 a year, the salary level for middle- and upper-middle-class professionals, and John Maynard Keynes, who described the depression as a crisis of abundance, not of scarcity. The Technocratic movement claimed that efficiency and redistribution would lead to reduced workweeks and an increased standard of living for all Americans. Townsend followers drew on the Technocratic argument that the "machine age" was dangerous to employment and production because it led to an undue accumulation of wealth in the hands of a few. Using the metaphor of the human circulatory system, they argued that money had been "frozen in financial channels" that cut off circulation to the whole body and prevented fair distribution throughout.[45]

Unlike the Townsend Bill, the Social Security Act was not born from a movement of average Americans; unlike the Lundeen Bill, it did not have the endorsement of a particular sector of society. The Social Security Act was drafted by government experts in the fields of economics and social welfare. It was complex and not generally understood by the public before its passage. Of the three bills, the Social Security Act was the only one that discriminated against African American workers.

The CES staff analyzed and produced reports on the Townsend and Lundeen proposals, and their critiques were very influential on Capitol Hill. The Townsend Bill, because of its widespread popularity, came under particular attack, and a team of CES staffers was designated to undermine it. The Lundeen Bill was also scrutinized. Edwin Witte declared that it was "a cruel travesty on the unemployed of the country, who are led by this propaganda to expect full wages while idle but actually would get nothing at all were the bill to be enacted into law." He sought to derail its supporters by noting that the bill was endorsed by leftist organizations; indeed, Witte claimed that it was "excellent propaganda for the 'front line trenches' in the battle for communism."[46]

Neither the Lundeen proposal nor the Townsend plan were ever brought to a vote in either house. Because of concern over the support for these bills, House Democrats passed a measure increasing the number of signatures necessary to bring a bill to the floor from 145 to 218. This measure was opposed by all Republicans, Farmer-Laborites, and Progressives, as well as by the 70 Democrats who broke ranks with their party. A gag rule was then imposed to prevent either bill from being substituted for the Social Security Act through a floor amendment during consideration of the Act. The Social Security Act passed both houses of Congress in June 1935, and a negotiated final bill was signed into law by President Roosevelt.

The Social Security Act did create a national pension program, Old Age Insurance (OAI), later renamed Social Security, but that program was not available to most Americans. OAI was created for industrial workers and their families, and it did not cover workers whose jobs were seasonal, part time, or paid too little to allow for insurance contributions; some groups of workers were explicitly excluded in the Act, as discussed in the chapters that follow. The program created in the Act to respond to the demands of the Townsendites was Old Age Assistance (OAA), which would provide small grants—up to $30 per month—to indigent older adults if they could document that they were poor. OAA was not a pension program that recognized the contribution of older citizens, but a welfare program that provided for society's dependents.

Resistance continued after the Act was passed. One of the biggest challenges of the Social Security Board between 1935 and 1939 was trying to convince states that they had to impose means tests—requiring proof of poverty—on people applying for OAA. Many Townsend-influenced states wanted to use OAA to establish a genuine pension program that recognized the contribution made by, not the poverty of, older Americans. The fights waged by states for what they called "flat pensions" culminated in the 1939 amendment debates. Texas succeeded temporarily in running its OAA program like a pension system based on age, not poverty, but when it ran out of funds six months later, the federal government insisted that only "needy" people be served.[47]

History has paid little attention to the Lundeen and Townsend Bills, the losers in the struggle to design the foundation of the U.S. welfare state, though the popularity of these plans suggests that they may have more closely represented Americans than did the Social Security Act. Both were constructed by people inexperienced in policy-making. Their economic formulas were simplistic, as were their plans to administer the programs that they created, for their framers did not have the resources of the federal government at their disposal. But each of these plans expressed an understanding of the meaning of work and citizenship that deserves our scrutiny. Both plans advocated equal recognition for all Americans—

bankers, meat packers, and housewives—whose labor, paid or unpaid, had "built the wealth of the country." They sought to construct a social welfare system on the basis of citizenship, not according to one's positioning in the labor market. In so doing, these plans would have challenged the country's racial hierarchy by forging a direct relationship between the people and their government that was not negotiated through a discriminatory economic structure.

Today we regard the Social Security Act as the embodiment of liberal social policy, the program that has gone further than any other to provide real economic security for Americans. But in 1935, for the millions of the country's most vulnerable workers, the Act's passage signaled the defeat of more radical possibilities and the opportunities they presented to challenge racial divisions among working people. The cries for old-age pensions, for wealth redistribution, and for an end to hoarding were silenced by acceptance of the Social Security Act and the creation of Old Age Assistance. At the same time, the possibility for equalizing opportunity through the welfare state was also missed, and the gap in economic security widened between citizens assigned to different categories by race.

If a discriminatory old-age pension program did not represent the expressed will of the people, how did it come to be created? One logical place to look for an answer is with the southern Democrats who controlled both houses of Congress in the mid-1930s, lawmakers who had a vested interest in the scope of the Act and in the spectrum of people it would cover. We turn our attention first to them.

two

The Not-So-Solid South

Southern Democrats in Congress

On April 26, 1935, Senator Josiah Bailey of North Carolina rose from his seat on the Democratic side of the floor to speak about the controversial Costigan-Wagner Anti-Lynching Bill (S 24), drafted with the aid of the National Association for the Advancement of Colored People (NAACP). If passed, the bill would give the federal government authority to intervene in state and local judicial processes in order to punish local officials who neglected to bring lynch mobs to justice. Bailey and all other southerners on Capitol Hill vehemently opposed the measure, which obviously targeted southern states. Although Congress had considered similar antilynching bills through the twenties, none had ever come close to passing.

But by 1935, the bill's supporters had swelled, and southerners were compelled to take action. Bailey now addressed the issue, not to convince his colleagues of the rightness of his position, but to filibuster—to talk continuously, refusing to yield the floor to other business—to prevent the measure from being brought to a vote. Filibusters are rare because they require participants to be unified and willing to stand firm under a great deal of pressure. For eight long days southern members took turns, one after the other, reading from prepared speeches, quoting from long passages in the Bible, at times to a nearly empty room as other senators entered and left the chamber. Each speaker in turn, after expressing outrage about the bill, defending southern institutions, and charging their northern colleagues with political agendas and hypocrisy, eventually made their way back to the historical context of the bill, especially the period of Reconstruction and the Fourteenth Amendment. They echoed over and over Bailey's insistence that "I will say with my last breath" that the Civil War was not fought over slavery but over states' rights, that slavery was "merely the match which set off the explosion of war." The filibuster was successful. After eight long days, the sponsors of the anti-lynching bill let it die without a vote.[1]

The unity shown by southern members of Congress against federal anti-lynching legislation was known to be solid and unbreakable; it is this unity that has led to a characterization of southern lawmakers in the 1930s as the "solid South." On other issues, southern members voted like all other members, representing diverse southern constituencies and shifting alliances with various voting blocs. Only on federal antilynching legislation did southerners march in lockstep; indeed, members from no other region of the country expressed such unity over a specific issue. Because lynching was widely recognized to be a crime directed primarily by white mobs against African Americans and used to maintain white hegemony in the South, historians have logically assumed that the solidarity of southern members was not just about preventing antilynching legislation but represented a greater unity on protecting the southern racial order and white supremacy.

This understanding of the "solid South" has been used to frame historians' approach to the Social Security Act. Scholars have assumed that southerners in Congress acted in unison to deny the benefits of the Act to the African American workforce in the South. This assumption appears to make sense for three reasons. First, the most blatantly discriminatory aspect of the Act originated in Congress, where agricultural and domestic workers were explicitly excluded from the programs created by the Act for workers—Unemployment Insurance (UI) and Old Age Insurance (OAI). Since the vast majority of the southern African American workforce fell into these two categories, it has been assumed that they were being specifically targeted by those exclusions. Second, during this period southerners dominated the House and Senate leadership, and as a group they wielded enormous power to determine what legislation passed and in what form. And third, segregation was legally sanctioned in the South, and the region had a long history of using the law to undermine the economic power of African Americans.

But a closer look at these southern lawmakers and their involvement in the Social Security Act reveals a much more complex picture. The southern congressional leadership of the mid-1930s did share a belief in white supremacy, if that term is defined as the desire to protect the value and property of whiteness. But white supremacy, so defined, may not have been the real issue that unified southern Democrats in opposition to other members of Congress. In the 1930s the meaning of race, and of white supremacy, was not just constructed region by region, but was also a part of the broader U.S. culture and society; racial politics revolved not just around the opposition of *black* and *white*, but also around the opposition of *North* and *South*. So to understand southern unity in this period, we must ultimately look beyond the parameters of the South to the relationship of the South to the nation.

Southerners in Congress

What is most striking about southern members of Congress in 1935 is their diversity on matters related to race; these southern lawmakers exhibited a wide spectrum of perspectives about relations between the races and the use of public policy to affect those relations. The umbrella of white supremacy could cover many diverse racial ideologies. This is not surprising when one considers that southern race systems varied across states and between rural and urban areas. As an observer in the thirties, Ralph Bunche noted that while the "Negro presence" is a "dominating influence" in southern politics because it ensures the continuation of the one-party system, in fact "[t]he southern political system is highly decentralized and almost anarchistic . . . not fascistic." After conducting an extensive analysis of southern racial politics, V. O. Key argued that, despite outsiders' "misconceptions" to the contrary, southern whites were not "equally concerned about the race problem." Different factors, such as the relative proportions of African American and white people, local economies, and political machines, determined local race relations and therefore the demands placed on U.S. lawmakers.[2]

Legislators from southern states not only represented diverse constituencies, but they also negotiated their stand on white supremacy with other aspects of their political identities and agendas. In the white South of the 1930s, a person's views on "Negro rights" did not determine his or her mainstream political identity as liberal or conservative, for example. In Bunche's view, there were two main types of liberals in the South: interracialists, who sought tolerance between the races through education and Christian ethics, and economic reformers. Bunche argued that these liberal identities did not necessarily overlap, that economic liberals exhibited an array of attitudes about race that were not seen as inconsistent with their liberal views on economics, views that today might even be considered radical. Bunche's insight helps to explain the politics of a senator like Theodore Bilbo, of Mississippi, who came to be recognized nationally as one of the most racist demagogues in the South; yet he was also one of the most loyal New Dealers in the Senate and was known at home as a strong supporter of social welfare and other progressive agendas.[3] In 1935 southerners did not view these positions as contradictory.

White supremacists did not all agree on whether southern "Negroes" should be granted any of the same rights as white southerners and, if so, which of the spectrum of rights they should be granted. For instance, Senator Pat Harrison of Mississippi strongly opposed political rights or economic autonomy for African Americans and worked to keep them in the rural South, where their labor could be easily exploited. Harrison said: "The negra is one of the largest and most important factors in our [southern] labor supply. By training and tradition, the negra is better adapted to the Southern type of agriculture. . . . With respect to his working ability, his goodness, and his trustworthiness, the negra can't be beat."[4] At the same time, however, Harrison promoted federally administered aid to education for African American children; he even sponsored an education bill that would safeguard equal funding for "Negro schools" and had the endorsement of the NAACP. He also admired and supported Harry L. Hopkins, director of the Federal Emergency Relief Administration (FERA), who campaigned against racial discrimination in his program.[5] For Harrison, education and government assistance for southern African Americans and their political and economic rights were different issues.

Harrison's views on southern race relations contrast with those of Theodore Bilbo. Bilbo, concerned mainly with competition between African American and white workers, led the repatriation movement to "return" African Americans to Africa. He loudly trumpeted his belief that "Negroes" were biologically inferior and incapable of change.[6] Josiah Bailey, a devout southern Baptist and staunch critic of the New Deal, argued that white supremacy was not inconsistent with recognizing the shared humanity of "Negroes." He claimed: "I have no prejudices against the colored people. . . . They are human beings, made in the image of God, entitled to human sympathy and to human help."[7] Virginia's Harry F. Byrd, another New Deal foe, sought "political stability and economic progress" by supporting both Jim Crow segregation and state antilynching legislation and through his long-standing membership in the Committee for Interracial Cooperation.[8] Hugo Black of Alabama courageously spoke on behalf of economic rights for African American workers in southern states, but not the right to vote, in which he claimed they were not interested; he also called intermarriage "deplorable" and supported laws that prohibited it.[9] While all southern members opposed federal intervention to punish lynching, among themselves they disagreed, some expressing embarrassment and even disgust at this blot on the reputation of the South. Opponents considered lynching to be the province of the lower classes, a problem that southern states would rectify in time. Other members vaguely defended their right to control African Americans outside of the law.[10] There was no consensus among southern members of Congress on whether there was a "Negro problem" in the South and, if so, how to solve it.

Northerners had difficulty making sense of the southern New Dealers in Congress. Contemporaries in the administration downplayed southerners' support of New Deal legislation, suggesting that those who voted for the recovery program did not genuinely support it but were either expressing party loyalty or had been "charmed" by President Roosevelt.[11] However, this would not necessarily make them any different than politicians throughout history who have been motivated by political expediency and patronage as well as conscience.

Some southern lawmakers fought the New Deal agenda, particularly social welfare policies, throughout FDR's tenure. But others fiercely defended the creation of a social welfare state, claiming that it was a traditional product of the Democratic Party. Senator Tom Connally, of Texas, an ardent states' rights advocate, refused to use the term "New Deal," arguing that the recovery legislation "was just a part of the Democratic tradition."[12] Representative Thomas Lindsay Blanton of Texas castigated Republicans for neglecting old-age pensions during their long control of the White House following the Civil War. He likened Republicans' begrudging acceptance of social welfare legislation to a "hightoned" forger thrown into an Arizona jail: the forger initially turned up his nose at the sow's belly he was given to eat but in time came to the table.[13]

Words such as these can, of course, always be discounted as political rhetoric. But some southern members were also engaged in passing social welfare legislation without directives from the White House. It was the southern-controlled Seventy-third Congress that forced Roosevelt's hand on old-age assistance by nearly passing the Dill-Connery Bill without an official position by the president or other administration support. The Dill-Connery measure provided federal funds to pay one-third of the cost of state old-age pension systems. The same was true of the Wagner Labor Relations Act passed in 1935, again with congressional support but without the White House's backing. The Wagner Act, which has been called the single most important U.S. labor legislation in the twentieth century, prohibited employers from interfering with worker organization and from discriminating against union members. According to one historian: "No one, then or later, fully understood why Congress passed so radical a law with so little opposition and by such overwhelming margins."[14]

Some southern members of Congress expressed support for distributing social welfare to African Americans without, apparently, alienating their colleagues. When Representative Arthur W. Mitchell, of Illinois, the only African American representative in Congress, lauded FDR on the floor of the Senate for helping "Negroes in the South" through New Deal programs like relief, John M. Robsion, a Republican from Kentucky, noted that a number of southern Democrats applauded the speech. Further, southern lawmakers pointed the finger at one another for participating in discriminatory practices. Louisiana Democrat Huey Long, in calling for fully federally funded Old Age Assistance (OAA) pensions, asked: "Who most needs a pension in Louisiana? The colored people are among the poorest people we have in some instances. About one-third to 40 percent of our people are colored people. They do not vote in many of the southern States. How many of them will ever get on the pension roles? . . . That may seem like cheap demagoguery, but I'm not afraid to say it."[15]

It is widely accepted that no Social Security legislation would have passed the Seventy-fourth Congress without the commitment of several well-placed southerners. Edwin Witte, executive director of the Committee on Economic Security (CES), credited passage in the Senate to Pat Harrison, chair of the Senate Finance Committee. He said that "with a less adroit" chairman, the Act would not have fared as well or at all.[16] Harrison's biographer claims that Harrison genuinely believed in the Act's vision; at one point he even tried to insert a catastrophic illness provision, though doing so was politically suicidal in the face of opposition from the American Medical Association. At the time Harrison himself said: "I know of no legislation since I have been in Congress, in whose passage I have taken a part, of which I am prouder of my part than this social security legislation."[17] Harrison supported the measure despite the fact that virtually all of the letters received on Capitol Hill relating to the Act were, according to Witte, "critical or hostile."[18]

The southern members most involved in the development of the Social Security Act sat on the House Ways and Means Committee or the Senate Finance Committee, where the bill was sent for consideration; these committees tended to include the most powerful members of each house. Veteran Robert Doughton, of North Carolina, who sponsored the House version of the Act, chaired the Ways and Means Committee. In 1935 Doughton was seventy-two, and though he had been born during the Civil War, he embodied elements of both the Old and New South. North Carolina was more urban and business-oriented than Deep South states, and its constituents were some of the most liberal on race issues. Doughton himself spoke a language of progressive reform that would have been easily recognized in other urban areas of the country.[19] To get the Social Security Act through the House, he relied most heavily on two younger members of his committee: Fred Vinson of Kentucky and Jere Cooper of Tennessee. Vinson and Cooper were perhaps the House's most strident supporters of the Act. They worked long hours to redraft the bill and knew it inside and out.[20] A fourth southerner on the House committee, David J. Lewis of Maryland, was the son of a Welsh miner who had begun working in coal mines at age nine. Lewis was a strong advocate of workers and cosponsor of the Social Security Act.[21]

Of the two fiscal bodies, the Senate Finance Committee was generally regarded as less cooperative with administration policy. Chairman Pat Harrison, the senior senator from Mississippi, whose ancestors included two U.S. presidents—William Henry Harrison and grandson Benjamin Harrison—had lost his father at age seven to wounds received in the Civil War. A preeminent politician, Pat Harrison had lived in Washington for twenty-five years and was one of the best golfers on Capitol Hill. He was a personal friend of FDR, writing him "Dear Frank" letters since the 1920s, and was one of the president's most consulted advisers in Congress.[22] Another defender of the bill on the Finance Committee was Tom Connally, also the son of a Confederate soldier, who had been recently elected to the Senate after seven terms in the House. Connally was known equally for his "almost reverential faith in the Democratic party and its traditional beliefs" and his "responsive[ness] to large oil and financial interests."[23] Hugo Black, later a U.S. Supreme Court justice and one of the brightest minds in Congress in the 1930s, was an economic liberal and a consistent supporter of the rights of labor. In addition to his support of African American workers, Black advocated more radical approaches to social welfare that involved income redistribution and medical insurance.[24]

Senator Harry Byrd, a consistent enemy of New Deal legislation, led the opposition to the Social Security Act. Byrd, the youngest son of Virginia's most powerful family, had earlier enjoyed a familial friendship with FDR (his brother Admiral Richard E. Byrd remained a "warm" friend) but broke with him early in his presidency. Virginia politics in the thirties revolved around the fight of Byrd and Senator Carter Glass against the challenge posed by New Deal supporters; Byrd was a "defender of the faith" of southern rights.[25] Thomas Gore of Oklahoma also detested the New Deal and all it stood for. He so opposed massive government expenditures for relief that he voted against the Federal Emergency Relief Act in 1933. When discussing race relations in the South, Gore "spoke the language of Social Darwinism."[26]

The diversity of interests and alliances of southern members of Congress can be seen in an extensive analysis published by V. O. Key in 1950, which shows voting records of southerners in the House and Senate between 1933 and 1949. Of the 598 roll call votes taken during those years, southern Democrats voted as a bloc against Democrats from other regions only nine times, five of them opposing federal antilynching legislation.[27] Still, those nine ballots reveal something, and the question remains: Did southern members of Congress vote as a bloc to uphold an agreed-upon position on white supremacy? Also, was excluding the African American workforce from the benefits of Social Security one of the priorities that unified this diverse group of southerners?

The Exclusion of Domestic and Agricultural Labor

Agricultural and domestic workers, along with casual workers, were explicitly excluded from the Social Security Act for the first time when the bill underwent redrafting in the House Ways and Means Committee. Public hearings started in both the Senate and House committees on January 21, 1935. During the next three weeks, Ways and Means met both morning and afternoon, and in the beginning most of the committee's twenty-five members were in attendance. For the same period of time, hearings were held in the Senate Finance Committee. Both committees heard much of the same testimony offered by dozens of representatives of interested groups.

The bill was initially explained to the committees by CES executive director Edwin Witte. Some committee members expressed resentment toward the CES staffers who were brought in to help them with the finer points of the legislation. The many titles of the bill were so complex, especially the taxation features, that members had a hard time understanding them. At one point Senator Harrison complained that "either we're dumb or they can't express themselves." But both committees took their task seriously — Ways and Means held more than twenty executive sessions — and literally examined every word of the bill as it was introduced.[28]

On April 5, 1935, the Ways and Means Committee passed out a revamped version of the bill (retitling it the "Social Security Act"), which included two important changes. First, the substitute bill excluded all agricultural, domestic, and casual workers from the two social insurance programs created by the act: UI and OAI. This change was retained when the bill passed from the House to the Senate on April 19; it also remained as the bill passed out of the Senate Finance Committee on May 20 and out of the full Senate on June 19.[29] Second, the Ways and Means version eliminated language in the original bill that required state old-age assistance systems to provide a "reasonable subsistence compatible with decency and health" through OAA grants. These two revisions have been interpreted as evidence that southern Democrats on the committee sought to deny the benefits of the Act to African Americans.

The explicit exclusion of agricultural and domestic workers is thought to be the aspect of the bill that most fostered discrimination, and this issue was discussed in hearings and debated on the House and Senate floors. Of the two excluded groups, Congress paid the least attention to domestic workers, or "servants," who seem to have been all but invisible to the lawmakers. We can assume that this was a function of gender and race, as 90 percent of domestics in private homes were women and 45 percent of these were African American, and the fact that they were unorganized. Though lumped together with agricultural workers in "standard" exclusions from regulatory and welfare legislation, domestic workers were perceived as a separate group, evidenced by legislators' lack of concern about offending or neglecting them.[30] The few scattered comments made about them expressed the interests of employers or taxpayers, not the workers themselves. On the House floor, Representative James W. Wadsworth Jr. of New York expressed concern that domestic workers would not be taxed under OAI and therefore would not carry their share of the "burden," instead imposing themselves on the tax-funded public assistance provided through OAA. Fred Vinson said that they did not earn enough in a lifetime to build up a pension under OAA, but Wadsworth disagreed.[31]

The disagreement between Wadsworth and Vinson was left unresolved and forgotten; in general, members did not demand or receive much information about domestic workers. Earlier, in a hearing of the House Ways and Means Committee, CES staffers acknowledged that, although they had generated mounds of actuarial data on the proposed insurance programs and on groups of workers, they had not even estimated basic costs associated with domestic workers. The committee did not pore over the details on this issue as they had most other aspects of the bill, reflecting both a lack of interest and the fact that they had less information to work with.[32]

Beneath the seeming indifference, the majority of lawmakers would have had a personal investment in preventing the coverage of domestic workers for the simple reason that they employed them in their homes. Household servants worked in up to three million homes throughout the country, but were particularly concentrated in the urban homes of middle- and upper-class families, and in the Southeast, where even lower-income white families often hired a cook or laundress.[33] As competition increased with the dawn of the depression, the wages of domestic workers plummeted, and more middle-class and upper-working-class households outside of the South were able to afford domestic help. Most employers hired a single domestic worker and half of all domestics lived in.[34] The few times lawmakers referred to domestic workers, they tended to do so in personal terms. Senator Harrison asked administration staffers: "Suppose my wife had trouble with the cook and had to fire her, and had to hire one every 2 weeks, and in the aggregate of 13 weeks there were four persons employed to cook, would I come under the provisions of the act?"[35]

Though committee members may have had a personal economic interest in looking the other way in regard to pensions and UI for domestic servants, some of them at least would have had personal relationships with the domestics who worked and lived in their homes, with whom they shared a kitchen and the physical care of their children. In southern states especially, the disregard shown to domestic workers seems strange in light of the idealization of servants in American culture of the thirties, specifically southern domestics who were presented as "mammy," that southern icon of the "Negro" maternal presence who willingly gave her life for the family she served. This period saw a revival of stories of mammies "as the protectors of 'white' children . . . a white child's best friend, a secure refuge against the world."[36] Some southerners saw in the resurrection of mammy a hope for rekindling southern pride to face the onslaught of the depression. Yet animosity was frequently expressed toward the real 1930s incarnation of the southern household servant, who worked for money, not love of the white family, and therefore did not meet the standards of the myth. A letter to the editor of the *Jackson Daily News* speculated that OAA would lead to idleness among domestic servants. " 'No more work in white folks' homes for Mandy!' shouted a fat and perspiring mammy who couldn't possibly be more than 55, yet she claims to be 70 [to qualify for a pension.]"[37]

Some members of Congress might have seen the testimony of Rosa Rayside of the New York Domestic Workers Union before the Senate Committee on Labor. Rayside and her union endorsed the Lundeen Bill because "[i]t is the only unemployment insurance bill which does not exclude domestic workers." No doubt she was African American, as she emphasized the devastating effects of exclusion on "Negro" women, and the committee chair asked her to assess the bill on behalf of "colored" people. Her articulate, well-researched testimony clearly illustrated the misery of domestic workers during the depression.[38]

The exclusion of agricultural workers was considered to be dicier than that of domestic servants, because farmers—employers and employees alike—were recognized constituents. Moreover, there was good reason to assume that southerners would have had a regional stake in the issue, since a disproportionate number of southern farms would fall under the Social Security Act. Under the original Act, only employers with four or more employees would be required to contribute to the programs to pay for OAI and UI benefits for their workers.[39] In 1935 most of the country's 6.8 million farms (84 percent) hired no outside labor.[40] Of the farms that did, almost 70 percent employed less than three workers. Ten states deviated from this norm: in most of the Deep South states, as well as in California and Arizona, an agricultural worker was far more likely to be employed by a bigger farming operation and therefore might have been covered by UI without a specific exemption.[41]

In all ten states, these workers were likely to be categorized as something other than "white." There were three types of larger-scale agricultural employment. A quasi-industrial agricultural system had made a strong foothold in California, Arizona, Florida, and Texas, employing almost 300,000 workers annually who mainly picked fruits and vegetables. Moderate-size farms, those that employed more than eight workers, were concentrated in these and a few other southern states, especially Louisiana and Arkansas. The third type of labor—cotton sharecropping— was all but nonexistent outside of the South. Whereas tobacco plantations had an average of two or three sharecroppers, cotton plantations had an average of eight. It is unclear whether sharecroppers would have been included under the Social Security Act had they not been specifically excluded. They were considered "employees" under the laws of some southern states, but an argument could also have been made that they were self-employed. Without specific exemption, however, cotton sharecroppers on plantations with four or more workers might have been covered by the Act. Nationally, only 20 percent of agricultural workers were classified as "Negro" and less than 7 percent as "other races." These workers were concentrated in the areas with the largest farms. African Americans comprised between 40 percent and 77 percent of waged farmworkers in southern states and 51.5 percent of sharecroppers. Mexicans, Chicanos, recent Filipino immigrants, and Japanese American laborers made up 40 percent of California's farmworkers.[42]

The exemption of all agricultural labor from the Social Security Act would obviously have had an impact on African American workers, and assumably at least some representatives of states with plantation economies would have supported the exclusion of agricultural workers from the Act. In a less direct way, all of the southern lawmakers who helped to shape the Act obviously benefited politically and economically from the racial hierarchy in southern states. That hierarchy had made African American agricultural laborers one of the most vulnerable classes of workers in America and politically impotent to demand coverage in the Act.

Yet, surprisingly, the record shows that southerners in Congress did not join forces to exclude agricultural workers. Even though the original bill that had been drafted by the president's Committee on Economic Security did not specifically exclude agricultural workers, Witte's CES staff was the driving force behind adding the exclusion to the House bill. The exclusions were promoted by southern Democrats in the House, but primarily by those who had allied with the New Deal; southern Democrats as a group were divided on the issue.

Southern Democrats were not solidly unified to exclude farmworkers because the exclusions were not in their best interests. For one thing,

members of Congress did not get explicit direction from either farm lobbies or farmers in their districts. In the mid-1930s the lawmakers were
beholden to a national farm lobby, which, in the words of a 1932 veteran Washington reporter, was "the most powerful single-industry lobby
in Washington."[43] The farm lobby was centered in the West, though by the
late twenties it had won access to lawmakers from the Midwest and, by the
early thirties, the South. The lobby was composed of four primary organizations: the radical Farmers National Council, the more conventional
National Board of Farm Organizations (called the "AFL of agriculture"),
the National Grange of Patrons of Husbandry (the largest organization),
and the conservative American Farm Bureau. These recently consolidated
groups (prior to which legislators had had to choose from a "bewildering
8,600 organizations" of farmers) had seen ten years of lobbying culmi-
nate in the Agricultural Adjustment Act. This measure was popular in farm
organizations nationwide, including the South, where 94 percent of cotton growers participated in 1935. "For southern New Dealers, the Farm
Bureau's relief program was electoral bedrock."[44]

Initially, Southern members of Congress, only newly incorporated into
the farm lobby fold, were unsure whether excluding agricultural workers
from UI and OAI was in the lobby's interests. When Pat Harrison first raised
the issue of excluding agricultural workers in Senate Finance Committee
hearings, he was far more interested in finding out what representatives
of agriculture, especially Secretary of Agriculture Henry Wallace (a member of the CES), had to say than anything else. Harrison badgered Edwin
Witte into revealing which members of the CES agreed with the inclusion
of agricultural workers and who on the CES Advisory Council was pro or
con. His questions expressed a genuine interest in what agricultural representatives and Roosevelt's administration wanted.[45]

The legislators do not appear to have received much insight from the
farm lobby. The lobby did not send representatives to testify on the bill before the Senate and House committees. By the 1940s, the leading farmers'
organizations supported extending OAI to farm labor, and at least one faction claimed that it had always supported such inclusion.[46] The CES Advisory Council, composed of representatives of business, labor, and social
services, included a representative of the farm lobby, Louis J. Taber of the
National Grange, though he apparently did not attend meetings regularly.
The council voted to advocate compulsory coverage of agricultural and
domestic workers, and no controversy over the issue was reported, leading

to the assumption that Taber might have been sympathetic to inclusion, assuming that he was present during the vote.[47]

There is also little evidence that southern farmers strongly opposed including agricultural workers under OAI and UI. The written record suggests that southern legislators received only a handful of complaints from constituents about that possibility. Representative Willis Robertson, of Virginia, wrote Representative Robert Doughton that the Social Security Act would impose a burden on agricultural districts like his and Doughton's, and his main concern was for small farmers.[48] The few letters received stand in contrast to the literally millions of southerners who petitioned Congress for old-age assistance through the Townsend Plan and to the scores of letters received by southern members in 1935 requesting help in securing cotton reimbursements stemming from property lost during the Civil War.[49]

Southern editors also expressed diverse views of the Social Security Act, yet the most noticeable feature of editorials is the sparsity of commentary. Fred Sullens, editor of the *Jackson Daily News* and a personal friend of Senator Harrison, argued that after Social Security, "able-bodied men [would] sit around in idleness on front galleries, supporting all their kinfolks on pensions, while cotton and corn crops are crying for workers to get them out of the grass."[50] But other southern editors supported government assistance; their greatest complaint was that more aid would go to the North than to the South. This was a dominant theme in the few editorials on the subject appearing in the *Charleston News and Courier*, a consistent critic of New Deal policies and an ardent states' rights advocate. Several commentaries declared that the South would be shortchanged because of the assumption that African American southerners required less relief.[51] The *Atlanta Constitution* supported relief and the Social Security Act but did not comment often.[52]

Even if they were concerned that the inclusion of farmworkers would have given African American southerners more independence, lawmakers would also have been aware of the potential impact of exclusion on the economies of southern states. Plantation owners might have sought to keep sharecroppers from receiving government assistance in any form to prevent them from participating in the larger economy outside of the plantation system. But business communities would have benefited from any infusion of money into southern pockets. In the Deep South, white-owned businesses depended on the buying power of African Americans, as retail stores were not segregated in 1935. Southern members of Congress were also aware that their states' agricultural workforces were on the verge of starvation, and, whether for economic or humanitarian reasons, they had an interest in addressing that fact.[53]

Most southern members of Congress did not see the exclusion of agricultural workers as an opportunity to control and oppress black laborers, but as evidence that the Social Security Act discriminated against the South as a region. Their main concern had to do with the differential impact of the bill on the economies of industrial and agricultural areas of the country. The Act would have the effect of charging rural consumers for the implementation of UI and OAI, because prices on manufactured goods would need to be raised to cover employer and employee contributions to those programs, but prices on agricultural goods would not be similarly raised. Mostly northern industrial workers would benefit from these increased prices.

In Senate Finance Committee hearings, southern Democrats actually led the fight to include farmworkers in UI and OAI. Their first impulse was to question the logic and fairness of any exemptions, and their comments reveal a sobering awareness that the exclusions would intensify inequality, making the poorest people in the country even worse off. When informed by William Green of the American Federation of Labor that only employees of companies that hired four or more workers would be covered under UI and that this condition was imposed "to exempt the farmers and the farm population," Tom Connally asked, "Why exempt them?" When told that the CES felt that it was "unjust" to extend UI over that "class of people," Connally noted that the cost of UI would ultimately be paid by them, in the form of higher prices "for everything they consume, and they will get no benefit from it." Hugo Black agreed that the "lower income-tax brackets" would pay for UI; he said that he might offer an amendment to get "a part of this contribution from those who have higher incomes and who do not buy any more of the consumable products than the employees themselves."[54]

A similar problem existed through the structure of UI, prompting southern lawmakers, though they generally fought for state administration across the board, to argue *against* state administration of that program. Senator Black noted that wealth tended to flow from poorer to wealthier states, and that organizing UI by individual states would exacerbate that tendency, as employers in poorer states would be taxed on profits realized elsewhere. He said that truly uniform taxation systems could not recognize county or even state borders, because poorer communities might not be able to meet a tax burden even though the people worked harder than those in wealthier regions.[55]

Although the original administration bill had not specifically excluded agricultural and domestic workers, it was the testimony of two White House representatives that appears to have settled the issue in favor of exclusion. The exclusion of farmworkers was first raised in the Ways and Means Committee by Representative Daniel Reed, a Republican from New York. In response to Reed's question on whether farmers would be covered by OAI, Edwin Witte said that they would and that the CES bill included everyone because everyone grew old and needed coverage. But, he observed, "You may deem it wise to exclude certain occupations. That certainly is within your right." When Ways and Means did not pick up on the suggestion, treasury secretary Henry Morganthau raised it again much more directly when he strongly recommended that agricultural and domestic labor be exempted because including these groups would pose too great an administrative problem: workers were widely dispersed, making collection difficult to enforce.[56]

According to Witte, the committee adopted Morganthau's recommendation in executive session "practically without dissent," though not primarily because of the administration's directive. Rather, he explained, the members were concerned that farmers would object to being taxed for the OAI program for their employees; moreover, they were "merely follow[ing] established practice" in excluding these groups.[57]

In contrast to the Senate, the leadership of the House fiscal committee argued strongly in favor of excluding agricultural and domestic workers. This was especially true of Representatives Doughton, Vinson, and Cooper, who showed more enthusiasm for the New Deal administration than their counterparts in the Senate. In the Senate Finance Committee, southern Democrats like Tom Connally and Hugo Black had challenged the exclusion of these workers. But on the House floor, it was northern Democrats who questioned the exclusions, while southerners defended them. Representative Albert J. Engel of Michigan argued, as southern senators had done, that exempting farmworkers would worsen the situation of the lowest-paid workers because they would ultimately pay a large percentage of industry's contribution through increased prices. In response, Vinson and Cooper tried to divert his attention by pointing out that farmers, if they were poor, would be eligible for OAA, and the issue was dropped. Doughton, Vinson, and Cooper were working in concert with FDR's people on this issue, not with southerners in the Senate.[58]

In the House, representatives of rural districts leveled the main critique of the exclusions: that they were an assault on farmers in all regions. In particular, rural Republicans goaded southern Democrats by suggesting that they were neglecting the farmers in their districts. Representative Charles L. Gifford of Massachusetts said that farmers would be "paying the bill" for industrial workers' UI and OAI and "the farmers' representatives here must know and apparently approve of it." Gifford concluded that farmers would be, in a sense, going to the aid of industry, and "great is my surprise that it is being endorsed by those usually so watchful of their interests."[59]

But these taunts lost all of their steam when southern Democrats called the Republicans' bluff. On April 17, on the House floor, Fred Vinson announced: "We have been actually criticized because agriculture, casuals, and domestics, and certain other people have been exempted from Title VIII [OAI]. I would like to know, and I am willing to yield my time for reply, what member of this House is willing to stand on this floor and say that agriculture, domestics, and casuals should be taxed for old-age benefits." Ernest Lundeen, of Minnesota, sponsor of the Lundeen Bill, which covered farmers and domestic workers under old-age and unemployment programs, replied that people with incomes over five thousand dollars should be taxed to fund social welfare, as proposed in his own alternate bill. Vinson replied: "Do not dodge it, my friend. . . . Does the gentleman from Minnesota assert that the farmers of his district should pay that tax?" After a pause, Vinson continued: "The gentleman is eloquent as usual, but it is the eloquence of silence. I say to you there were real reasons why those exemptions were made." Lundeen said that he would respond later but never did.[60]

Vinson argued that agricultural and domestic workers could not be included because of the administrative difficulties that had been identified by the CES staff and by Secretary Morganthau. He claimed that these workers had been covered in the president's bill only because the bill's framers (whom he referred to as "we"), "knew that the House and Senate would not keep it in," suggesting that the administration did not genuinely believe that these workers could be covered but sought to shift the blame for their exclusion and politicize the issue. His basic argument was that Congress did not have a political stake in the issue of exclusion. The discussion ended there. Senator Huey Long would later hold up funding for the Social Security Act with a one-man filibuster in part, he said, because the bill excluded farmers. He was the only legislator to take any real action on their behalf.[61]

It would appear that, despite some regionally specific interest in the question of exclusion, southern members of Congress as a group allowed the exclusion of agricultural and domestic workers for the same general reasons as did members from other regions. Regarding agricultural workers, they did not get much direction either from the national farm lobby or, seemingly, from constituents. And what direction they did receive was mixed because of the differing interests of southern states and constituents, including those of plantations and businesses. Regarding domestic workers, most of the lawmakers would have had a personal interest in looking the other way and letting them slip through the cracks, for there would be no reprisals from such a vulnerable, unorganized group. A decisive factor was the administration's insistence that inclusion would be extremely difficult to implement and could jeopardize the whole system. But even more decisive was the lack of sufficient interest in the issue among members of Congress and their constituents, and this was true for all regions of the country.

Southern Democrats in Congress thus did not unite to exclude farm laborers and domestic workers from the Social Security Act. But does that mean that they were not united behind the desire to deny economic security to African Americans? Would the southern bloc that appeared during antilynching debates have surfaced if the interests of workers and state economies had been less entwined? To begin to explore these questions, it is useful to look at the other major program created by the Social Security Act—OAA—and the racialized politics through which that program was reconstructed in Congress.

State Administration of Old Age Assistance

There may not have been a "solid South" behind the exclusion of agricultural workers, but something approaching unity was demonstrated in debates about the program created in the Social Security Act for indigent older people who did not qualify for OAA: Old Age Assistance. One of the main concerns of southern Democrats was that OAA, if federally administered, would impose rules with which states would not want to comply. Southern lawmakers, especially in the Senate, were especially concerned about a requirement in the original bill that states provide recipients of OAA "a reasonable subsistence compatible with decency and health."[62] This language left the door open, they argued, for the federal government to deny funds to states that did not provide for citizens adequately and, it could be inferred, equally. As a result, this requirement was stricken from the House's revised bill—apparently at the request of the southern members of both Senate Finance and House Ways and Means Committees. Some legislators were undoubtedly motivated, at least in part, by the desire to deny equal assistance to southern African Americans.

The issue of whether states would fully control OAA under the Social Security Act was raised very quickly in hearings of the Senate Finance Committee, and though the topic was not initiated by a southern Democrat, it was raised in the context of states rights. Following the introduction of the bill by its sponsor, Senator Robert F. Wagner of New York, Senator William King of Utah asked whether "the purpose [of OAA] is not to have the Federal Government supervise the action of the State, or to deny the State the power which it now exercises in dealing with its own residents." Wagner repeatedly assured King that this was not his intent. King questioned whether OAA would only be used to supplement state efforts and "to stimulate a case where they have not made ample provisions to enact legislation more human in character, calculated to care for the needs of the people." Wagner replied, "Exactly."[63]

But the senators' concerns were not put to rest, and the issue of state control of OAA, now raised by southern Democrats, dominated the second day of hearings. Connally and Byrd forced Witte to admit that federal officials would have the final say about the definition of "reasonable subsistence."[64] Byrd attacked the bill for giving "dictatorial powers" to the federal government: "You can deny the entire payment to the State, even though this money comes from the State originally and goes into the Federal Treasury, you can refuse to have it go back to a State unless the State does the things which your dictator under this bill sets up." He said that the law gave the federal government the right to "set up certain standards of living."[65] Hugo Black came to Byrd's support; they argued that the Senate, not the administration, should decide what constituted a "reasonable subsistence."[66]

Then and later, however, the argument over the "reasonable subsistence" language was primarily *between* southern Democrats. Pat Harrison led his defense of the president's bill by insisting that the Social Security Act as written did grant states control over how OAA funds would be spent. He maintained that OAA would provide an infusion of funds for floundering state governments, and that it would be done with an "absolute minimum of Federal participation." He asserted: "It is right and proper for the States, where old-age pensions laws began, to go on administering these laws in their own way, for their own people."[67]

This drama was not repeated in the House Ways and Means Committee, where the reasonable subsistence clause was not even referred to until the eighth day of hearings. At that time, the issue was raised by George Haynes, executive director of the Department of Race Relations of the Federal Council of Churches of Christ and one of the few African Americans to be heard by the fiscal committee of either house. Far from supporting the reasonable subsistence clause as a protection for African Americans, Haynes took issue with that language for a different set of reasons. He maintained that it could lead to discriminatory treatment; "in many communities there is a prevailing idea that Negro persons can have such a reasonable subsistence on less income than a white person." There was no substantive response to his argument; indeed, few committee members were even present to hear it. His testimony reveals that the political implications of the "reasonable subsistence" language were neither clear nor agreed upon.[68]

The real action on OAA in the House took place during floor debates about the Ways and Means version of the bill, where southern Democrats dominated the discussion. As in the Senate Finance Committee, a small group led by southern Democrats quickly displayed an intense interest in state control over OAA. Immediately after Doughton introduced the bill, Representative Edward E. Cox of Georgia raised the issue of state control, asking whether the reasonable subsistence clause would require grants to be uniform within states. Doughton assured Cox that pensions would not have to be uniform. But Cox kept hammering the point until he received the explicit assurance that he obviously sought—that different amounts could be awarded to different persons within a state. A second group of southern congressmen, consisting of New Deal allies Vinson, Cooper, and Doughton, defended the bill and responded to the concerns of Cox and others throughout the floor debates, assuring them that states would get to determine levels of grants and who would receive them.[69]

The language used in these debates suggests that some members specifically sought to ensure that their states could discriminate by race under the Social Security Act, and these were not limited to southern lawmakers. For example, John Robsion of Kentucky and Thomas A. Jenkins of Ohio joined Senator Cox in considering whether people would have to be treated the same "under like conditions," a clear reference to the "separate but equal" language of contemporary segregationist race politics. Representative Charles F. McLaughlin of Nebraska pushed the issue further, arguing that "individual need" could determine the amount of a person's grant, opening the door for discriminatory treatment based on perceptions of the lesser "needs" of minority groups.[70]

It was widely understood that southern members of Congress led the charge for state control over OAA and did so in part to protect their "right" to establish lower grant levels for African Americans. In a letter to FERA director Harry Hopkins, Edwin Witte said that the federal limit of fifteen dollar per OAA recipient included in the original bill had caused problems with "the South." Witte wrote: "While the present bill does not require southern states to pay pensions of $30.00 per month to their negro population, this is the impression that the bill has created and it seems impossible to get this out of the minds of the public officials of southern states as well as their members of Congress."[71] Shortly afterward he told Raymond Moley, a Roosevelt adviser, that the reasonable subsistence clause had been stricken from the House bill because this was the major objection of the southern members to [the OAA section of] the bill, as they feared that someone in Washington would dictate how much of a pension they should pay to the negroes."[72] Witte reported that FDR had agreed to eliminate the reasonable subsistence clause after being lobbied by southern members of the Ways and Means Committee. He also said that there was no intent by the bill's sponsors or drafters to use this provision to police discrimination in the South. Witte noted that it had never occurred to anyone involved with the original bill that the reasonable subsistence clause would evoke the "Negro question."[73]

It thus appears that southern Democrats in both houses of Congress, along with members from other regions, fought for state control over OAA so they could set up unequal grant structures for "white" and "Negro" constituents. Yet the story does not end there. The unequal distribution of OAA grants to southern African Americans would result, in part, from an unequal distribution of federal OAA money to southern states, which caused great fear among southern members of Congress.

First, OAA was created to be a matching-funds program, and there was widespread concern that southern states would be unable to afford the state match and therefore be ineligible for the federal money. The South was especially hard-hit by the depression. By the early thirties, state governments had already cut the salaries of their employee, and whatever meager relief programs existed before the stock market crash quickly dried up. Many southern states were heavily in debt before the depression struck, having "gotten caught up in the speculative mania of the 1920s." Mississippi stood $14 million in arrears in 1932, and Arkansas had to default on a massive highway construction bond, the refunding plan for which could not see full repayment of even the principle until 1977. Other southern states instituted sales taxes and severely reduced appropriations.[74] There would be very little state funding available for OAA.

This issue broke the unity of southern Democrats. Many southern Democrats in the House, particularly those recently elected on a New Deal ticket, were happy to toss states' rights out the door in favor of obtaining increased federal funding for OAA, even if it meant relinquishing all claims to administration of the program to the federal government. Of the roughly two dozen House members who spoke on behalf of greater or full federal funding of OAA, and therefore federal control of the program with attendant requirements for equal grants to all, fifteen were from southern states. They spoke as "citizens" of the United States in their appeal for federal aid, and they claimed that the Act, as it stood, discriminated against southern states that could not afford OAA matching funds.[75]

The South was also disadvantaged in another way. Only 16.5 percent of the nation's population over age sixty-five lived in twelve southern states; by contrast, New York State alone accounted for 10 percent of this population. By tying the main federal assistance funds to a class of people underrepresented in the South, southern states stood to receive less money. Southern African Americans, who comprised just 7 percent of the South's population over agbe sixty-five, would gain the least of all.[76] In addition, many more northern states than southern states already had old-age pension systems; in May 1934 only three of the thirty existing state pensions programs were in the South, and these were not mandatory statewide as well as extremely underfunded. States with prior existing pension programs would get federal money immediately; they would not have to pass legislation to establish programs first, and they could use existing state pension funds to match federal funds.[77]

Those members of Congress who wanted more federal funding at any cost tended to be newer representatives of southern states who were perhaps more vulnerable to widespread constituent threats to throw out elected officials who did not enact the Townsend Plan. In fact, a great deal of concern was expressed throughout the House floor debates about the amount of mail members were receiving from Townsend supporters. In their focus on seizing as much federal funding as possible, they showed little interest in the debate over language waged by their colleagues, and they posed a potential roadblock to the campaign for state control of OAA. They garnered strength to pass the Russell amendment to the Social Security Act, over the objections of the administration and southern leadership, which would assist states that would initially be unable to come up with matching funds for OAA, giving the federal government greater control over the program.[78]

The Roosevelt administration knew the extent of the poverty of southern states. By early February it was commonly understood that southern states would be unable to match federal allotments for Aid to Dependent Children, and we can assume the same for OAA. Research conducted by Katherine Lenroot of the Federal Children's Bureau concluded that "[t]he southern states would, on the whole, fall very far short of ability to match."[79] These facts help to explain the comments of southerners who said repeatedly that as the bill stood, OAA was, for the South, "a veritable gold-brick," a "hollow mockery."[80] Representative William M. Colmer of Mississippi asserted that southern states would not benefit from OAA without help, and so the bill would draw a line, "similar" to the Mason-Dixon line, "that would divide this great country of ours into two sections," those with old-age pensions and those without.[81]

As shown in the Senate committee debates about the unequal effects of UI on rural and urban regions, southerners feared that the Social Security Act would discriminate against the South, and it was in the context of this fear that southern African Americans would be marginalized even further than other southerners. This dynamic can be seen most dramatically in the solution found to the problem of where to find state matching funds for OAA.

It turns out that there was a pot of money in most southern states that had so far escaped the ax of budget cuts. After the Civil War, the U.S. government established a federal pension system, but only for Union soldiers. The government paid for the pensions by increasing certain tariffs that hindered attempts to rebuild the southern agricultural economy. Over time, southern states created their own pension systems for Confederate soldiers, and these pensions were sacred to white southerners. Southern representatives could not eliminate the programs, but they could redirect the funding.

The first person to hit upon this idea was Representative Wright Patman, of Texas, who had suggested to CES chair Frances Perkins, back in December 1934—before the Social Security Act was introduced in Congress—that OAA be merged with existing Confederate pension programs and that equal grants be awarded for all pensioners. Because, as Patman noted, this would involve lowering the veterans' pensions considerably, it seems to have been suggested only to enable states to match federal funds. Perkins did not understand the significance of the request, and Patman was apparently put off by her and Witte's unwillingness to discuss his proposal.[82] Later, in testimony before the Ways and Means Committee, Patman made it clear that he had little interest in preserving state control over OAA, or in ensuring the right to provide unequal grants, arguing that OAA was a "direct responsibility of the Federal Government." His main concern was that states would be unable to match federal funds.[83]

The proposal did not reappear until May 1935, when a deal was struck between the Senate Finance Committee and the Roosevelt administration in a "Confidential Hearing" that sealed the fate of African Americans in regard to OAA. At this hearing, Senator Hugo Black asked Frances Perkins whether the pensions that all southern states paid to their Civil War veterans could be used to offset a state's matching funds for OAA. This time, Perkins quickly agreed to the scheme, which would secure the support of southern members for the Social Security Act, because it would enable them to make the state match, though at the same time it would ensure that the bulk of federal money for OAA would go to (white) southern veterans and their families. Perkins gave her full support to the unequal distribution of OAA grants. She insisted that payments within states did not have to be uniform and that states could "pay one class of people . . . for a particular reason" and still get federal matching funds.[84] Edwin Witte followed up with a letter to Senator Harrison, saying that federal funding might even be available for veteran pensioners who are "65 years of age" but "not needy"; in an attachment to the letter, Witte admitted that "[t]he pensions paid to Confederate veterans will probably be higher in most of the southern States than the pensions paid to other needy persons under old age pension acts." Witte's letter also indicated that southern states spent between $10 and $12 million annually for these pensions, no small amount, most of which the federal government would meet.[85] This allowance would obviously give southern states license to use OAA for patronage and to discriminate against African Americans.

In fact, this was the means by which African American southerners were most discriminated against through OAA. All OAA grants in southern states were low; fifteen southern states ranked lower than all other states in average OAA grants. Average grants for African American southerners were even lower than those for white southerners. In Mississippi, for example, "Negroes" received an average of $7.00 per month and "whites," $11.00. However, the larger gap was between those who received OAA and those who received veterans' pensions. Alabama gave average payments of $7.68 to OAA recipients and $27.60 to 1,720 Confederate pensioners or their survivors. Southern states gave as much as $50.00 per month to veterans, usually in fixed amounts, and as little as $4.11 to OAA recipients. By 1937 all southern states had veterans' pension programs, but several had not yet established OAA programs.[86]

The inequality of this plan surfaced in 1937, when southern states first applied for federal funding to match the Confederate pensions. Jane Hoey, director of the Federal Bureau of Public Assistance, initially tried to reject southern state plans, and the Social Security Board backed her up, because, she said, "It seems impossible, in the light of southern tradition and southern State law, for the States to administer funds to Confederate pensioners on an identical basis with old-age assistance."[87] However, legal council for the administration established that legislative intent allowed OAA federal funds to be used for this purpose. In an apparent response to Hoey's suggestion that the policy discriminated, the council responded, "Plans for public assistance are, in one sense, discriminatory by definition."[88]

One interesting aspect of the deal reached on OAA and Confederate pensions was that the Senate negotiator was not Pat Harrison or Tom Connally, who held more typically white supremacist views, but Hugo Black, probably the most "liberal" member of the Finance Committee in his support of African American workers and denunciation of economic discrimination. Black's own justification for initiating what would clearly be a discriminatory policy was, ironically, based on the concept of equity. He asked whether it would be "fair" to use federal funds for Confederate veterans pensions as "the Federal Government itself pays a pension to the Union soldiers and their dependents?" Black, a man with a solid grasp of U.S. political history, would have been aware of the role of northern veterans' pensions in winning and maintaining loyalty to the Union following the Civil War.[89]

Black's call for fairness, for more equitable treatment for the South, and his evocation of the period following the Civil War mirrors the interpretation offered most consistently by southern senators and congressmen in their demand for state control of OAA. One after another, speakers on the floor of both houses argued that state administration of OAA was necessary to prevent the federal government from intervening in state affairs and assaulting the power of state governments.

States' Rights, Federal Intervention, and the Meaning of Whiteness

To understand southern involvement in the Social Security Act, one needs to appreciate what southerners meant by "federal intervention." Since the civil rights era, the term has been used to refer to federal action against discriminatory practices in southern states; the government intervenes with troops to restrain the screaming mobs and allow crisply dressed African American children with intelligent, wary faces to enter through the doorways of previously segregated schools. The term evokes a picture of a tolerant and progressive nation intervening to root out southern racism, a victory of federal over states' rights, of North over South. The truth of that moment in Little Rock, Arkansas, may well be described through such a binary view as the triumph of good over evil. But the larger story of race relations between the regions and the role of federal intervention is more complicated. Looking at the southern perspective on federal intervention breaks down these polarities and leaves us with a more complex picture of American race relations in the mid-1930s.

To understand the southern perspective, we must return to the 1870s, the era of Radical Reconstruction and the role that era played in the minds of white southerners. Reconstruction was the period following the Civil War when the assumption of power in Congress of a radical arm of the Republican Party prevented, for a brief moment, the reconquest of the planter class that had dominated the South before the war. During this period, which lasted between two and seven years depending on the state, African Americans moved quickly into public life and began to build an economic base. Several southern legislatures were dominated by African Americans, fourteen of whom were elected to the U.S. House and Senate; surprising numbers of "Negro" families managed to buy property. The era was brought to an end by the realignment of southern planters and northern business leaders and by the withdrawal of federal support for the freed slaves. In the era that followed, which has been labeled "Jim Crow segregation," segregation law dominated the region until civil rights victories in the 1950s and 1960s.

In the 1930s southerners across the political spectrum argued that the South's race problem was caused, not by slavery and the Civil War, but by Reconstruction. This was true for the Ku Klux Klan, which by 1935 counted FDR and the New Deal among its greatest enemies, but also for most southern liberals, including those who developed some of the New Deal's most radical programs.[90] The view was expressed most eloquently by the Nashville Agrarians, a group of twelve southern writers who held a variety of perspectives on race and "Negro rights," but were unified by a disdain for industrialism and progress and by a glorified vision of the leisured lifestyle of the antebellum South. They were outraged over the destruction of that lifestyle through Reconstruction. Contemporary southern race relations, they argued, were a direct result of those years of "horror." Robert Penn Warren, one of the twelve, used this as a justification for rejecting the insistence of northern "radicals" that the South should extend political rights to African Americans; instead, he backed the "realistic" view that "the hope and safety of everyone concerned rested in the education of the negro." This belief, he acknowledged, "might be, in the mind of a person who had witnessed the Reconstruction, an expedient insurance against the repetition of just such a disaster."[91]

This view was initially incorporated into the historical narrative and organized as the Dunning School, which characterized Reconstruction, with apparently unconscious irony, as the "blackest" page in American history and focused on corruption and inexperienced African American leadership. This perspective has since been overturned, first by W. E. B. Du Bois and later by Eric Foner and others who have dug into the historical record and exposed the radical promise of Reconstruction for giving birth to a different racial order in the South. But for white southerners in the thirties, Reconstruction was not a matter of scholarly debate. It was extremely present, still being fought over, and the defining event in many of their lives, even if it had occurred in their childhoods or before they were born.[92]

In this worldview, where all that was good and true was lost through "Yankee aggression" and the freedman's "betrayal," the "Negro" signified defeat and was for many southerners "the symbol of the South's humiliation."[93] The federal government had marched south to invert the racial order, according to these white southerners, liberating the slaves and taking away the authority and autonomy of the former ruling class. Through Reconstruction, northern whites, who set up schools for the children of freed slaves, who helped them negotiate with plantation owners and even buy their own plot of land, had aligned with "Negroes" against southern whites. This alignment threatened the economic and social value—the very meaning—of whiteness in the South. To restore that value, African Americans had to be returned to their former state of dependence. Du Bois understood the significance of the mythology of Reconstruction to white southerners, which is why he devoted himself to rewriting that history from the perspective of the freed people; his book *Black Reconstruction* was published in 1935.

The greatest privilege that whiteness bestowed in the southern race system was independence, and this continued to be true after emancipation. Race and dependence were so deeply connected that southerners' ability to see was literally "colored" by their belief. In a telling example of the social construction of race, Gunnar Myrdal reported that white southerners in this era commonly claimed to have a special ability to identify "Negroes," but what they actually identified was a set of behaviors that denoted dependence rather than physical characteristics reflecting African ancestry, which had to have been very pronounced in order to be seen. According to Myrdal, a white southerner who saw a dark-skinned man "carrying himself with assurance and ease, actually *does not see his color*." He literally "does not believe his eyes." This was especially true for women. A white woman in the company of an African American man was seen to be "Negro." Myrdal concluded that white southerners' "theories of 'white womanhood' obviously blinded them in a literal sense."[94]

Southern African Americans could use behavior that signified dependence as a form of currency. Myrdal observed that "Negro beggars who make their appeal in [a paternalist, deferential] old relationship will often be amply and generously rewarded by white people who are most stingy in paying ordinary wages." He observed that "[t]heir Negro dependents and their own relations to them play a significant role for white peoples' status in society." Myrdal suggested that "Negro dependence" had value to white society, and some African American leaders used it to barter for influence. This behavior had value because every "yes, Sir" uttered by a black man reinforced the opposite status of the white man to whom he bowed his head. When the southern ruling class could no longer derive its identity, its illusion of control and guaranteed independence, from legal ownership of other human beings, it found other ways to continue the dependence of African Americans, to create itself in contrast. Of course, this was true not only in the South.[95]

But without possessing the validation and protection provided by legal slavery, and having lived through Reconstruction and seen how quickly alignments could shift, white southerners in the thirties knew that the privilege bestowed by whiteness—in fact, their designation as "white"— was not necessarily guaranteed. Reconstruction promised to reconfigure the racial order, and though the redemption may have unified whites beyond regions, it did so in a fragile fashion that left southern whites unsure of their status. Racial categories were fluid; this is clear when we see how the same stereotypes landed on, and constructed the identities of, different groups of black and white southerners.

Upper-class and educated southern whites characterized "poor whites" and "Negroes" with the same stereotypes, constructing both groups as the uncivilized opposite of the upper-crust white South. Nashville Agrarian Robert Penn Warren wrote that "to the Southerner, the 'poor white' in the strictest sense is a being beyond the pale of even the most democratic recognition; in the negro's term, 'po' white trash,' or so much social debris."[96] In the words of W. J. Cash in a lecture on the South:

> Cracker (the southern poor white) almost completely [has] abandoned economic and social focus, failed wholly to develop class feeling, and became in his fashion a remarkable romantic and hedonist. To fiddle, to dance all night, to down a pint of raw whiskey at a gulp, to bite off the nose or gouge out the eye of a favorite enemy, to father a brood of bastards . . . such would be the pattern he would frame for himself. And if this left him a little uneasy . . . well, there was escape in orgiastic religion.[97]

One upper-class observer described the followers of a political demagogue as "ill-dressed, surly . . . unintelligent and slinking . . . the sort of people that lynch Negroes, that attend revivals and fight and fornicate in the bushes afterwards."[98] Gunnar Myrdal repeated the claims of southern "educators and intellectual leaders" who likened the "shortcomings" of "poor whites" to "Negroes," namely "violence, laziness, lack of thrift, lack of rational efficiency and respect for law and order, lack of punctuality and respect for deadlines."[99]

This characterization was not just confined to yeoman farmers of the South: northerners used the same stereotypes in their descriptions of *all* white southerners. The examples are plentiful, perhaps lending credence to Howard Odum's speculation that "propaganda on the South is one of the chief indoor sports of unstable folk in other climes."[100] Lewis Mumford said in 1931 that "the Southerners themselves are exactly like the Old Regime in Russia as portrayed by Tolstoy and Chekhov: lazy, slow-moving, torpid, imperturbable, snobbish, interbred, tolerant of dirt, incapable of making effective plans of organization."[101] Ralph Bunche offers a slightly less hostile but revealing observation of southerners of both races:

> White Southerners employ many of the same defense mechanisms characteristic of the Negro. They often carry a "chip on the shoulder"; they indulge freely in self-commiseration; they rather typically, and in real Negro fashion, try to overcome a feeling of inriority by exhibitionism, raucousness, flashiness in dress, and in exaggerated self-assertion. An air of belligerency, discreetly used when it can be done without risk, is one means of release for the individual who feels himself the underdog.

According to Bunche, this could be seen even in southern members of Congress, who "as a group are more abusive and indulge more in personalities and rough and tumble repartee than the legislators from any other section. . . . The Southerner is proficient, too, at conjuring up arguments to show how shabbily the South has been treated. Like the Negro, the white South holds out its hands for alms and special privilege."[102]

Some southerners located the origins of these depictions of the South in the North's economic conquest of southern states following the Civil War. Jonathan Daniels, a liberal journalist, suggested in 1938 that the North profited from maintaining the South "in its place," which was "a place in the nation similar to that of the Negro in the South." "The Negroes were sold down the river again after emancipation, and the price paid was a fixed economic differentiation which left the whole South in slavery to New England instead of some of the South in slavery to other southerners." New England profited from this situation "long after Lincoln in a manner of speaking set the Negroes free. Of course everybody was free in the South, free to fight among themselves for the too little that was left when tribute was paid." Daniels's dream of a "new, free, fed, housed, happy South" could not be achieved simply through "improvement" of the South; rather, a national program was needed "for the relinquishment of advantages elsewhere over the South."[103]

These examples suggest that "race" and origins have no essential connection to each other, that a society might theoretically use the categories "black" and "white" to define any random grouping of people. The category *white* referred to a skin color or area of origin, but even more to a quality: to be white meant to be civilized and independent. Whatever category was created in opposition to white referred, not to a type of person, but to the opposite quality, uncivilized and dependent. "Negroes" were *black*—the opposite of white—in their relation to *white* southerners. But poor whites were also *black*, in one sense, in relation to elite *white* southerners. And ultimately, in a limited way, the South as a region was *black* in relation to the country as a whole. White southerners clung to white supremacy. They stole the labor of African Americans daily, engaged in violence against them, and undermined them in every imaginable way to enhance their own position. And they did so in the context, not just of a region, but of a nation whose social and economic order valued whiteness and so implicitly rewarded such behavior.

The concerns of southern Democrats about ensuring that states would administer OAA and be able to maintain Confederate pension programs took place in a larger context wherein white southerners were experiencing their status to be under siege, in ways that recalled Reconstruction. With the onset of the depression, the South had experienced, perhaps for the first time since Reconstruction, an increased dependence on an expanding federal government in the midst of widespread and devastating poverty. Senator Connally likened the depression to the "Tragic Era" of Reconstruction, saying that in both periods "[o]ur economic system had almost completely broken down. Banks and credit institutions cried out for government assistance and received it."[104] Southerners also witnessed a small but significant growth in African American federal employees, agency positions created for "Negro advisors," and a first lady who greeted African Americans in public and spoke openly about their rights.[105] Although one can go too far drawing comparisons between the federal employees who went South to administer New Deal programs and those who made the same trip in the 1870s to advise and assist the freedman, such comparisons might help to explain some of the animosity expressed by southern Democrats, especially for women social workers who had no business, according to one speaker, coming in from other states and "telling the women of the country how to raise flowers and children."[106]

The question of whether the state or federal government would administer OAA was vitally important in this larger context, because to southern Democrats the Social Security Act, and OAA in particular, was a potential means of salvaging states' rights in the face of faltering southern state governments. If the depression, and the growing dependence on the federal government, recalled Reconstruction for these southern members, then a state-administered program stood for the white South's reconstruction on its own terms. As Representative David Lewis of Maryland said on the House floor, in words that were repeated by southern Democrats in both houses, the federal government needed to act on the Social Security Act to save "states' rights," because "[t]he State is incompetent to act"; if the federal government did not prop up the states, the dual government structure would collapse.[107]

The unity of southern Democratic leadership behind state administration of OAA was based on this desire to salvage the states and to prevent the intervention of the federal government in states' perceived areas of authority. In this way, they represented a broad spectrum of their white constituents. Evidence of this is seen in the resistance of liberal southerners to the federal government's intervention in lynchings; even southern-born antilynching organizations like the Association of Southern Women for the Prevention of Lynching refused to cooperate with federal antilynching legislation, and the Committee for Interracial Cooperation only reluctantly joined the federal fold in 1935 under formidable pressure.[108]

The only real moment of total southern unity in Congress in 1935 occurred during the Senate filibuster of the federal antilynching bill. For some members like Ellison DuRant "Cotton Ed" Smith of South Carolina, the main offense of the bill may well have been its intent to punish lynchers; for others, specifically Hugo Black, the bill was problematic because it posed a threat to organized labor. These southerners may have had different concerns about the bill, and their words express different positions on lynching and southern race relations. The one aspect of the bill that was unifying in its offensiveness was its allowance of federal intervention; they all agreed that the main intent of the bill was to undermine state authority.

This is seen most clearly in the testimony of Hugo Black. It has been said that Black voted against federal antilynching bills because he had no choice as a southern Democrat. But his words suggest that he stood with other southerners against federal intervention. Black easily filled his duty in the antilynching filibuster by speaking at length against the bill on the argument that it would open the door for federal repression of strikes and union organizing, just as the Fourteenth Amendment had done in an earlier generation. This argument gave him a means to save face, to refuse to support the bill without supporting lynching. So when he rose to speak in favor of states' rights, he appears to have done so from his conscience. He said, repeating a sentiment expressed again and again, "We know the object of the measure; we know its history," and asked, "[W]ith the knowledge of the iniquitous conception of [the] idea behind this bill back in the days of Thad Stevens and his group, why should it now be revived to mar the harmonious relations that exist between us?"[109]

To say that southern Democrats in Congress were not unified by the *intent* to exclude African Americans from the Social Security Act is not to say that their various positions on the Act were not motivated by their racialized positioning and interest. They sought to protect the property and value of whiteness. But they were not alone in that design, as the next chapter shows.

This chapter suggests that to understand how racial discrimination was embedded in the Social Security Act, one needs to look beyond the parameters of the South. The Act was constructed by a nation, and no region of that nation was exempt from its long history of racial discrimination. The national race system allowed northerners to locate racism in the South, to focus their efforts on reforming racism there, and, in the process, to turn a blind eye to race dynamics in the rest of the country. This had sweeping ramifications for the discriminatory policy created through the Social Security Act.

three

Colorblind Public Policy
The Staff of the Committee on Economic Security

On the evening of October 10, 1950, Edwin Witte stood before a gathering of his friends and colleagues in Madison, Wisconsin, to honor John R. Commons on the occasion of his eighty-eighth birthday. The room was filled with many of Commons's former graduate students at the University of Wisconsin, men and women who had followed him into careers serving the goals of progressive reform. Many of them were veterans of the battles that Commons inspired through the twenties and thirties to empower and improve the conditions of industrial labor in America. Witte's remarks at this event expressed his understanding of the meaning of reform that bound Commons and his former students. Witte spoke for this larger group when he said that Commons "inspired his students, particularly his graduate students, to devote their lives to the improvement of our democratic way of life and our economy of free enterprise, for which he developed in them a profound admiration." He noted that Commons's students "emerged from his classes, indeed, as men who wanted to improve what they thought was wrong, but without destroying our political, economic, and social structure."[1]

Commons was brilliant, an original and eccentric force who cast a long shadow in a number of arenas including academics, labor reform, and public policy. He was a prolific writer and an expert in labor history. Among the reformers whom he had mentored were many prominent policymakers. In addition to Witte, they included Elizabeth Brandeis Raushenbush and Paul Raushenbush, daughter and son-in-law of Supreme Court chief justice Louis Brandeis; John Andrews, who headed the American Association for Labor Legislation; Arthur Altmeyer, assistant secretary of the Department of Labor; Harold Groves, a member of the Wisconsin legislature;

and William Leiserson, chair of the Labor Mediation Board. This group had bonded through Commons's informal "Friday Niters" with graduate students and their spouses, and they had become "strong friends all round instead of breaking up in cliques" and would "help one another wherever they go."[2] This "Wisconsin group" contributed to some of the country's most important labor and social policy legislation. The most significant of these was the Social Security Act.

The previous chapter demonstrates that southern Democrats in Congress were not primarily responsible, as they have been credited, for the exclusion of most African American workers from the Social Security Act. In fact, it provides evidence that the Committee on Economic Security (CES) and its staff played a part in that exclusion, especially seen in the suggestions made by Edwin Witte and Secretary Henry Morganthau to the House Ways and Means Committee. This chapter explores the specific role of the CES in researching and drafting the Act. It pays particular attention to how the Wisconsin group influenced the process: although the CES staff was large and diverse, final authority over the Act's development rested with members of this group.

The CES Staff

In June 1934 President Roosevelt announced to the nation that America would join most of the industrialized world in the creation of a federal social welfare system under his leadership. For this purpose he established the Committee on Economic Security to present a proposal and appointed Secretary of Labor Frances Perkins to chair the committee. The staff was assembled in the late summer of 1934 and eventually grew to include over one hundred people. They worked long hours in cramped quarters through the fall of 1934 and completed the proposal in late November; the report was then sent to Roosevelt in December.

The president had indicated various criteria for the type of social welfare system he wanted to present to Congress. The system should be "national in scope" and ensure the "maximum" state and federal cooperation. It should include employee contributions, so that it would not be viewed as welfare, and it should be unified because "the various types of social insurance are interrelated, and I think it is difficult to try to solve them piecemeal." Roosevelt appears to have been genuinely convinced that Americans needed a safety net, but his papers reveal that he was not personally invested in its specific features and administrative apparatus. He entrusted the details to the CES and would be satisfied as long as its plan was generally compatible with his broad philosophy.[3]

Through Secretary Perkins, all key leadership positions on the CES were quickly assigned to members of the Wisconsin group. The most important staff job, that of executive director, was given to Edwin Witte, an economics professor at the University of Washington. Witte had been an unpolished country boy from rural Wisconsin and raised in a home that emphasized Christian service. Though he became well connected in business and political circles through his work, he lived modestly in the same small house in Madison throughout his adult life. Much of that work was done anonymously, and despite his tremendous influence over the founding of the American welfare state, he is not well known. Perkins's assistant secretary, Arthur Altmeyer, was picked to head the CES Technical Board, and he was involved in hiring many others.[4]

Whereas the CES leadership came from the Wisconsin group, the majority of staffers represented a broad array of backgrounds in academia, social service, and activism outside of the Wisconsin network; they arrived with distinct philosophical approaches to welfare systems. Two groups of staffers came from within the New Deal administration—the Federal Emergency Relief Administration (FERA), U.S. Department of Agriculture (USDA), and Agricultural Adjustment Administration (AAA)—and both groups had ties to a particular member of the CES and particular constituencies. After joining the committee, two other more loosely organized groups formed around common work and perspectives. All of these unofficial groups of staff had very different ideas about the purpose and best design of social welfare systems.

The FERA staff worked closely with that agency's director, Harry Hopkins, who was also a member of the CES. Hopkins had a close working relationship with the president, who had trusted him with the massive federal relief effort that had won much popular goodwill for the Roosevelt administration. During the creation of the Social Security Act, the main concern of Hopkins and his staff was to protect the interests of the current unemployed and prevent their segregation from more privileged workers.[5] To do so, they developed a radical proposal that would replace emergency relief with a large-scale public works program to guarantee a low-paying job to all needy unemployed Americans regardless of previous employment status. CES staffer Evelyn Burns remembered that Hopkins did not want to see the U.S. welfare state built around programs like unemployment insurance (UI) and old-age insurance (OAI): "I think the FERA chaps had the view: 'This is all very well, but it really is not touching the unemployed group.' Because what were we talking about? We were talking about unemployment insurance, paying benefits for 15 weeks: a great big bold program, you know. The FERA, who were dealing with these chaps who had not worked for months and months and months, could easily say, 'Well, this is chicken feed in relation to the problems that bother us.'"[6]

The second insider group—employees of USDA and AAA—were involved in the Act's development through the CES Technical Board and Henry Wallace, secretary of agriculture and another member of the CES. In this group was Rexford Tugwell, who often represented or accompanied Wallace to CES meetings, and Jerome Frank, who helped draft the bill on Wallace's behalf. The Technical Board was actually dominated by this group, which represented the most radical factions in USDA and AAA. Their work on the Social Security Act revealed the same concern for African American workers and the treatment of "labor on cotton farms in the South," which would lead to their termination from AAA in 1936. Frances Perkins characterized this second group, which also consisted of Aubrey Williams, Louis Bean, Victor Valgren, and H. R. Tolley, as "a team of high-strung, unbroken horses" for their independent views.[7]

A third alliance formed quickly after the staff assembled in Washington. It was led by Barbara Armstrong, a Berkeley law professor, and her colleagues Douglas Brown and Bryce Stewart, all academics in fields related to labor and social insurance.[8] Armstrong, whose background was in poverty analysis, had distinguished herself nationally for her concern for the aged and unemployed. She was brought to Washington to direct the development of the OAI portion of the Social Security Act with the collaboration of Douglas Brown, a Princeton economist, although she became involved in debates about UI as well. A strong, opinionated woman, Armstrong could be "tactless" and "make her listeners feel rather inferior"; according to Evelyn Burns, she had made Edwin Witte "cry" more than once using her "lawyer's style" of arguing.[9]

Early in the process, Armstrong advocated a "unified" system of social welfare. Essentially, this system provided benefits on the basis of *need* rather than on the specific *cause* of the need. In this way, benefits would be determined according to the number of a worker's dependents, not the amount of his or her former earnings. Armstrong argued that although there was "considerable sentiment among social workers" for differentiation between the "unemployed" (can't find a job) and the "needy" (unable to work), "[t]here is, of course, no more reason why a man who is ill and therefore unable to earn should be aided on a basis with a stigma attached than a man unable to find work."[10]

Finally, a group of women labor activists on the CES staff appear to have coalesced around their common research into European models of social welfare systems. These women were keenly concerned that workers who were marginal to the U.S. economy, including agricultural and domestic workers, be covered by any unemployment and old-age program. They surveyed dozens of countries and gathered detailed information on different kinds of welfare systems that had successfully provided for such workers and encouraged Witte to make the U.S. system consistent with more socialistic European models. They also urged that the United States collaborate internationally and participate with the International Labor Organizations' conventions for social insurance, which had been adopted by dozens of countries.[11]

Knowing that they would face opposition, the women labor activists researched creative solutions to the enormous challenge of implementing a unified system in a country of the size and complexity of the United States. For example, Olga Halsey recommended that OAI contributions be tracked by geography, rather than by industry, arguing that people tended to stay in a region more often than they stayed in a particular firm. Her system would have treated all unemployed people the same way, regardless of their reasons for being out of work. Though Halsey and her colleagues do not appear to have been affiliated with the more middle-class/professional network of women in the New Deal or the Federal Women's Bureau,[12] they were concerned about women workers. They strongly advocated in social insurance coverage for women, whether or not they worked for wages.[13]

All of these groups of CES staffers advocated a version of social welfare that was "unified," and their approach appears to have been consistent with the public directive given the CES by FDR to create a cradle-to-grave safety net. The public was clamoring for old-age pensions for all Americans, and because Social Security was intended to replace Emergency Relief, there was an incentive for creating a comprehensive program.

But the fight waged by all of these groups was over before it began. As early as September 1934, Witte drafted a Preliminary Report to the CES reflecting John Commons's vision and little of the perspectives of the non-

Wisconsin staff. Hopkins and his FERA cohorts determined fairly quickly that the CES would not be the vehicle to implement their goals and persuaded President Roosevelt to give more direct, personal attention to work relief outside of the committee. They withdrew from the CES and worked to implement a massive public works measure that was seen as a companion bill to the Social Security Act.[14] The CES Technical Board modified its fight for a unified system by working to ensure that the programs created by the Act would be federally administered, which would guarantee some equity between richer and poorer regions of the country and more equal coverage of workers. The board's members voted more than once for a strictly federal UI and OAI system, but they were overruled by their chair, Arthur Altmeyer.[15]

Witte's proposed system veered far afield from European models. His plan established separate and unequal programs for workers and the unemployed, and it did not cover women who did not work for wages and most marginal workers. CES staffers continued to conduct research and submit reports through the fall of 1934, but the final proposal given to the committee and then FDR was based entirely on the plan that Witte had written in September. Much of the research of the CES staff ended up being superfluous, because the members of the Wisconsin group had gone to Washington already knowing exactly what kind of social welfare system they would create. Their plan not only represented their philosophy of the meaning and purpose of welfare. It also would salvage the faltering Wisconsin state unemployment program to which many in the Wisconsin group had devoted years of work.

The Wisconsin Agenda

The social welfare system described in Witte's September report was, first and foremost, an expression of the economic philosophy of John Commons. Commons's reformist vision was steeped in a belief in the regenerative power of capitalism, a concept adopted by the Wisconsin group in toto.[16] He did not oppose the growth and consolidation of corporate capital, but he recognized its potential for creating economic instability and leading to the inhumane treatment of workers. Much of his work in labor reform was directed toward enhancing the bargaining power of labor in order to maintain a check and balance with the power of corporations. He believed that government had an important role in enabling the equal meeting of management and organized labor at the negotiating table. UI was a critical component of this plan, because it would increase the bargaining power of industrial labor by increasing workers' security. That benefit was widely recognized, and it could be achieved through many types of UI systems.

But Commons had an even more specific plan for unemployment insurance, one that could only be realized through the Wisconsin model. He sought to use UI to give firms an economic incentive to lower their unemployment rates. Commons's design, which was incorporated into the Wisconsin state unemployment compensation bill, required employers to set aside a percentage of their income in a designated fund that could be used only to pay benefits to their laid-off workers. Through a merit system, companies that achieved low unemployment rates would be able to reduce the percentage of their set-aside. The plan offered great incentives for businesses. It was understood that the amount of the set-aside would be passed on to the consumer in the form of raised prices, so businesses with low unemployment rates could theoretically increase profits from the combination of raised prices and the advantage secured against businesses with higher rates. This was the essence of the unemployment compensation bill passed by the Wisconsin legislature. However, the program had never actually been established due to the resistance of businesses, which feared that the set-aside tax, because it would require them to raise prices, would disadvantage them in relation to neighboring states.

The Wisconsin group went to Washington to implement federal UI as a way to salvage their floundering state program, as well as to promote their vision beyond the borders of Wisconsin. The group worked with two members of Congress to introduce a measure—the Wagner-Lewis Act—in the Seventy-third Congress that incorporated the main features of the Wisconsin unemployment compensation bill. It encouraged all states to enact unemployment compensation systems by imposing a business tax on those who did not. The bill ensured that states would design and administer their own systems. This was critical from the standpoint of Wisconsin, whose own "employer reserve" system, under which employers established individual unemployment insurance funds, would not be allowed under a federally administered system or one that required states to "pool" reserves across industries, as most European countries had done. During the Seventy-fourth Congress, the Wisconsin group arrived in Washington to lead the staff work for the CES. The plan drafted by Edwin Witte in September 1934 was based on the same model as the Wagner-Lewis Act, which John Commons had outlined in a letter to Witte and Perkins in November.[17] Thus, although he was not actually involved in drafting the Social Security Act, Commons was its "spiritual father."[18]

At a time when it seemed to many Americans that capitalism was on the brink of collapse, the Wisconsin group endeavored to shore up the U.S. economic system by instituting federal unemployment insurance. But using UI for this purpose meant that the features of the program would be determined by the needs of the Wisconsin program rather than the national needs of the unemployed. To be compatible with the Wisconsin plan that the group had worked so hard to establish, the federal program must allow individual states to construct and administer their own plans. Moreover, unemployment insurance would have to be kept separate from all other programs created for people in need—and only available to industrial workers—precluding the possibility of a more unified system like those advocated by Barbara Armstrong and others on the CES staff.[19]

This plan to use social welfare as a way to salvage the U.S. economy was strongly criticized by the most vocal of the non-Wisconsin trained staff of the CES, especially Barbara Armstrong, Douglas Brown, and Bryce Stewart. As Brown wrote Senator Robert F. Wagner: "My whole philosophy of unemployment insurance is that the first objective is to provide an effective system of financing employees when out of work for as long a period as possible. . . . To permit men to have inadequate relief in the hope of regularizing employment seems to me . . . [to be] dangerous."[20] The plan, according to Armstrong, Brown, and Stewart, was "absurd" because it left individual firms to swim or sink on their own and did not assist workers in the greatest need.[21]

Critics of the Wisconsin plan strongly disagreed with a requirement that employees under UI contribute to their coverage from their own paycheck. For the Wisconsin group, this was a necessary feature of the plan, for two reasons. First, if employees were required to contribute, policymakers could justify excluding any workers whose coverage would be inconvenient; they would not have to design the plan to fit the needs of all workers, since workers would be seen to be paying for their own participation. And second, employee contributions would give UI the appearance of an insurance program and would not be tainted by the stigma of welfare.[22] But employee contributions disadvantaged workers with marginal incomes, for whom even small reductions in their wages could be too much.

Most African American workers were excluded from UI because their coverage was not necessary to the intent of the program, which was to force industry to regulate industrial unemployment. The Social Security Act covered only regularly waged workers of large industries, whose contributions could be easily collected, who were not mobile or seasonal, and who earned enough to contribute to the program. African Americans were most often excluded by the limit on employer size. Because they were prevented—by discrimination in hiring and union membership—from taking jobs in industry, they typically worked for small employers. The Social Security Act provided UI only for employees of firms with four or more employees, which tended to be those who already had the greatest protection, including most of the 20 percent of American workers who were unionized and others employed by large companies that paid relatively decent wages. It therefore did not cover the more vulnerable employees of firms that had less than four employees, including the small homes, farms, and other establishments that hired most African American workers. In the final UI title of the Act, of the country's 10.5 million farmers and farmworkers, more than 98 percent were excluded by this restriction, as well as 90 percent of the 3.1 million domestic workers. By contrast, only 5 percent of the country's 11.4 million manufacturing workers were not covered and 46 percent of the 6.1 million trade and wholesale workers (many women fell into this category).[23] Excluded workers also tended to earn too little to contribute to UI from their paychecks. Their employment was less stable than industrial jobs, because they worked seasonally, or were frequently let go and rehired, and since UI had not been designed with their needs in mind, they were inconvenient to cover.

Farm and domestic workers, the vast majority of African Americans who were employed, were therefore not actually excluded from UI in the House's revision of the Social Security Act because they had already been excluded by the basic structure of the bill. OAI, the insurance program for older Americans, which evolved into Social Security, was developed in a very different way. Yet that program too structurally excluded African American workers as an indirect result of the Wisconsin agenda.

The Plan for Old-Age Insurance

The U.S. social welfare state was built to accommodate UI, but the system had to provide more than just that for industrial workers. Most immediately, the CES had to respond to a public that was clamoring for an old-age pension system for all older Americans upon retirement, and that put substantial pressure on Congress to act. The task of drafting a proposal for such a pension program was not given to the Wisconsin group; rather, Barbara Armstrong, the Berkley academic, was put in charge. Although she had to work within the basic structure outlined by Edwin Witte, she might have had some ability to make oAI more consistent with her concept of an equitable, "unified" social welfare system. Yet in the end, oAI was just as discriminatory as uI, because it had to be made compatible with uI.

Although she has not been officially credited, Armstrong may well be responsible for the fact that the Social Security system was actually created in 1935. She later contended—and others supported her charge—that both Edwin Witte and Frances Perkins were reluctant to include oAI in the Social Security Act.[24] The Wisconsin group, she said, did not want to create potential difficulties for uI by loading up the Act with unpopular programs, especially since the public was demanding a pension plan that was not contributory. Evelyn Burns asserted that Barbara Armstrong "of all the people I know, deserves the most credit" for the American Social Security system. Burns said that Armstrong was never acknowledged for her role and was not in any way drawn in, after the Act's passage, on "any of these subsequent developments."[25]

This lack of recognition undoubtedly stemmed in part from Armstrong's outsider status in Washington, in the eyes of both the Wisconsin group and the New Deal women's network with which Frances Perkins was well connected. Before her assignment to lead the development of an oAI proposal, she did not know anyone involved with the cES and had difficult relationships with the Wisconsin leadership. Armstrong did hook up fairly quickly with a network of woman reporters with whom she shared information. This network was instrumental in helping her to launch a national protest after Roosevelt made a minimizing comment about oAI that raised concern about his administration's commitment to the program.[26] As a woman, she was also aware of the limitations placed on her ability to maneuver in an environment dominated by men. After hearing Perkins hold her ground in an argument with Harry Hopkins, Armstrong said, "[N]o woman talks to a man like that in public who is supposed to be a man of distinction."[27]

Armstrong was not consulted about the overall structure of the Social Security Act, and she made her contribution within the parameters framed by the Wisconsin group, which segregated the insurance programs from the poverty programs. The OAI title received less attention than UI and may not have been expected to survive by some members of the Wisconsin team. It was submitted to the president and then Congress basically as Armstrong and her staff constructed it.[28]

Because she was forced to work within the larger frame established for UI, Armstrong designed OAI along the lines of an insurance-type pension program, taxing employers for the old-age security of their workers. Her original draft based the amount retired workers would receive in benefits on a percentage of their prior earnings, a feature that disadvantaged lower-income workers, including most African American workers. This imbalance was further exacerbated in the final Act by the imposition of employee contributions, in keeping with the requirement in the UI program.

OAI discriminated in different ways from UI in the original Act. The OAI title did not include some of the same limitations and exclusions that were built into UI, including the restrictions placed on employer size. But the OAI title was discriminatory—primarily by tying benefits to former earnings and establishing requirements for coverage that privileged workers with steady incomes from a single employer. The bill required that the benefits enjoyed by a retired worker be calculated according to both the number of weeks worked and his or her "average monthly wage." The average wage counted to a far greater extent in the formula than the number of weeks worked, which would tend to lower the benefits of agricultural and domestic workers and other low-wage workers.[29] As benefits for OAI ranged from $10 to $85 per month, lower-paid workers were not expected to survive on the pensions they received. In fact, to receive any benefits, workers had to accumulate a certain number of hours—$50 per employer per quarter in the final bill. This disadvantaged agricultural, domestic, and other workers who frequently had to piece together an income working for different employers.[30]

Like UI, OAI required that employees contribute to their coverage out of their monthly wages. But in the case of OAI, which was federally administered, this requirement would have a different impact on the economy than the state-administered UI program. OAI employee contributions, which had to sit in a discrete fund and could only be used to pay OAI benefits, removed large sums of money from circulation. It was acknowledged at the time that if all American workers were included in OAI, the fund would swell to unmanageable proportions. Even with only a portion of the population covered, payroll taxes did result in "untold economic mischief" and were blamed in part for the recession of 1937–38.[31] Ironically, OAI employee contributions necessitated, in a roundabout way, creating public assistance programs for the same uncovered workers who had been excluded from OAI. Edwin Witte testified that some of the excess raised through OAI could be "loaned" to pay grants for Old Age Assistance (OAA), the means-tested program for indigent older people. Witte basically argued that the dependence of a large portion of workers on public assistance was technically necessary to enable OAI to function for the rest.[32]

OAI also discriminated against the South as a region, as did UI, by benefiting industrial states, and this had an enormous impact on the majority of African Americans who lived there.[33] Employer contributions for OAI were passed on to consumers nationally through higher prices, leaving agricultural areas of the country to subsidize the better-off urban areas. In the short term, both OAI and UI discriminated by favoring those workers who would receive benefits in the first years of the programs, before they had paid enough into the system to cover those benefits. As it reviewed the draft recommendations of its staff, the CES Technical Board leveled "considerable objection" to paying pensions to industrial workers who did not need them, because they had not paid into the system long enough to cover what they would take out.[34] As taxpayers in agricultural states, farmers paid for old-age pensions to cover all of the uncovered workers in their state, but the system treated them as charity cases rather than insured workers.[35]

So African American workers were excluded from the Social Security Act because they were superfluous to the larger agenda of the Wisconsin group, which was to enhance the bargaining power of labor and regulate the economy. Most African Americans, as agricultural and domestic workers, would have fallen through the cracks, one by one, and been excluded from the insurance programs by virtue of their marginal status in the labor market. Sad as it was, it might be argued that this situation was not a direct result of the racialized interest of policymakers, but because African American workers were overlooked or were too difficult for the plan to cover as it was designed. In fact, historians have made that argument; these workers were excluded from the Act for "administrative" reasons.

But there is more to this story. To understand the deeper causes of discrimination in the Social Security Act, we must scrutinize the Act as a whole and see how the different parts relate to one another, especially the public assistance and insurance programs. We must also go back to an earlier time, to John Commons's vision and to the racialized world that it sought to create.

The Wisconsin Group and the Meaning of Race

African Americans suffered a loss of income by their exclusion from the workers' insurance programs, but they were also harmed by the exclusions in a way that was far more subtle, though ultimately maybe even more destructive. The Social Security Act did not just create programs for workers; it also established a second tier of programs for those who did not qualify for insurance coverage, as well as for mothers and children. In the process of the Act's development, both the insurance and public assistance tiers became racialized, and African American workers were relegated to a status of dependence.

The Wisconsin group, expressing fears widely shared by Americans in the 1930s, were determined to protect industrial workers from the "psychological assault" of unemployment. In the depression years, work had become a scarce commodity, and many men, including professional men, voiced great anxiety about the potential loss of their ability to be productive. More than riches, they argued, happiness was dependent on work. Richard T. Ely, Commons's mentor and colleague at the University of Wisconsin, said of "productive work" in more abundant times: "It is the road along which we must struggle to regain the vision of a Paradise presented by poets and seers. Man needs toil for self-expression and or happiness. . . . It is the road to the development of all our best faculties."[36] Members of FDR's brain trust, like Raymond Moley, were well aware of this anxiety. Moley had deliberately built Roosevelt's 1932 address to the Democratic National Convention, which secured him the nomination, around two "key words": "work" and "security"—because he believed that party delegates, virtually all white men, would respond to these ideas more than to any others.[37]

The Wisconsin members of the CES appear to have personally identified with industrial workers, but not with those who had been unemployed for any length of time, a group that was assumed to be inferior. The Wisconsin team believed, in Ely's words: "No one discharges the best employees. Even now, with exceptions, people of high-grade capacities have jobs."[38]

Edwin Witte agreed that in times of high unemployment, the economy would weed out the "less capable." But the Great Depression was so severe that many people who had always felt secure in their jobs or professions were now unemployed, and this was the group with which Witte most identified. He speculated that "the greatest suffering" was not experienced by those receiving relief, but by those who were "just above the margin" of poverty and "too proud to ask" for help.[39] Witte believed that industrial workers shared with professionals a pride in independence and self-sufficiency that was the heart of the American identity, and he sought to extend to them the level of economic security more commonly enjoyed by middle-class men.

If work was the key to happiness, then economic dependence loomed as the greatest horror imaginable. Dependence, while reasonable for women and children, was thought to be deeply destructive to men, more so than the tangible effects of poverty or even the trauma of combat. Unemployment was bad enough, as a stigma became attached to a man who had been out of work for any period of time, and he became less and less desirable to employers. Much worse, however, was the degradation of government relief, which was "humiliating" and "demoralizing." Workers who were unable to find work were vulnerable to diminished "morals" and "radical thought." Indeed, it was repeatedly pointed out that more socialist European and British welfare systems damaged workers by refusing to segregate them from the "disastrous psychological effect" of "the dole."[40]

The professionals on the CES staff were very personally affected by the assault on manhood represented by relief, as is shown in Witte's response to a letter from a man who headed a "white collar" program that provided office work for some professional men on relief. The letter said that working with professional recipients "has taught me where the 'forgotten man' is to be found. He is *not* the gutter-snipe who has never been of any service to society for he is at least kept from starving. The people who see little difference between relief and suicide are the folks that have made me heartsick in these days." Witte replied immediately, and with uncharacteristic emotion, saying that the letter had "distressed" him and referred to the pending closure of the program as "discrimination."[41] Manhood and economic dependence were incompatible, and dependence might just be worse than suicide.

The Social Security Act was designed to save not just the economy but also white manhood. To this end, the two tiers of the Act were designed each to create the other: public assistance programs were deliberately constructed to be psychologically degrading, fostering dependence, to elevate the relative status and independence of the industrial workers enrolled in UI and OAI. The first step was to define the difference between the tiers. Health was the first criterion used: "workers" were virile and healthy, "physically able and available for work," in contrast to the "aged, the sick and the disabled," who were unable to work and therefore ineligible for assistance.[42] The second criterion was need: the first-tier unemployed included workers who had paid insurance premiums to protect themselves in times of unemployment; the second-tier unemployed were poor people in need of public assistance.

The tiers would have to be segregated physically to prevent any confusion or affiliation between them. It was generally thought that any merger of UI with relief would be a "fatal error," "almost sure to be disastrous."[43] This argument was repeated like a mantra by the leaders in public policy whom Witte interviewed before the first draft of the Act was outlined.[44] It was even generally argued that UI recipients should not be required to receive benefits near a relief office, so they would avoid having to witness "the psychologically distasteful functions of the application of a means test."[45]

To elevate the status of industrial workers by dissociating them from the poor, policymakers thus consciously set out to make the receipt of relief a negative, humiliating experience. A memorandum distributed to the CES staff in December 1934 explained this strategy. The memo delineated five differences in the ways that "relief" and "contributory insurance" would be administered. First, relief, unlike contributory insurance, must be means-tested, with prospective recipients required to prove that they were poor. Second, recipients of relief would be required to take a job outside of their chosen field and be willing to work for lower pay. Third, relief must be subject to controls to prevent abuses and malingerers. Fourth, relief should be made less desirable, even including a punitive element, and recipients pressured to find work. Finally, relief should pay less than contributory benefits.[46] The meaning of "unemployed" was constructed as a unique condition for white male industrial workers, who would be eligible for UI, a condition that reflected shifts in the economy and was unrelated to their qualifications and competence as workers, one that would be survived through an insurance program to which they had contributed. All other unemployed workers would be regarded as indigent—as less qualified, less valued workers who had lost their jobs through their own inadequacies, who needed to be pressured to find work, and who depended on the government for their survival.[47]

Through this policy, the language of social welfare was altered to express, unequivocally, that "work" and "dependence" were opposite conditions. The term "dependent" was injected into the official discourse of Social Security to signify an appropriate condition for those, especially mothers and children, who were not regarded as workers. However, the word was used more expansively, even though it was considered to be dangerous to masculine independence, to refer to any man or woman who received public assistance. Administrators were instructed to replace the terms "indigence" and "poverty" with "dependency" or "need" when referring to noncontributory government assistance. The term "pauper" was to be replaced with "needy" or "dependent"; "Mothers' Pensions," with "Aid to Dependent Children"; and "relief," "dole" or "pensions," with "public assistance."[48]

Having been excluded from the insurance programs, African American workers were relegated, at least in theory, to public assistance and the stigma that it entailed, along with most white women, those who were physically incapable of performing certain kinds of work, and the elderly poor. It might appear that the assignment of African American workers to this category was just bad luck or just an extension of their placement in the job market. But by tracing the step-by-step development of the Act's discrimination of African Americans, we can see a consistent internal logic throughout the process, one that is located in the actual plan for UI to salvage the economy. To understand the roots of this discrimination, we must explore the racialized worldview of John Commons.

The men and women who created the Social Security Act said little about their understanding of the meaning of race or their feelings about African Americans—they existed in a climate where liberals strove to be colorblind. But two decades earlier the relationship between unemployment compensation and race was made explicit in the writings of John Commons, who took a great interest in theorizing about racial difference during the years that he mentored many members of the Wisconsin group.

Common's philosophy regarding the need for unemployment compensation was based on a racialized analysis of labor. Commons believed that the white male industrial worker exemplified the essential American worker, and that "Negro" workers were, because of their degradation through slavery, "unfit" for the labor of white wage earners. According to him, the key to regulating the labor market was to enhance the bargaining power of labor and force business to negotiate with workers. Labor would be strengthened in two ways: first, by making unemployment compensation available to the wage-earning class, because "[t]he future of American democracy is the future of the American wage-earner." But not all wage earners would be included in this plan. Only the "wages and standard of living" of *white* wage earners must be protected, he argued, as only they comprised the "enlightened and patriotic citizenship." "Negro" and immigrant laborers were problematic because they acted as a "reserve army of labor" that glutted the market and were "willing" to accept little pay and poor treatment. The second part of his vision was to diminish this "reserve army of labor": the "lower" immigrant workers through immigration restrictions and "Negro" unskilled laborers by uplifting themselves through education. Commons saw the continued presence of African Americans in the United States as a hardship. "Certain it is," he declared, "that had the white wage-earners possessed the suffrage and political influence during colonial times, the negro would not have been admitted in large numbers, and we should have been spared the race problem."[49]

This analysis of the relationship of the white worker to unemployment compensation reflected a contemporary understanding of racial difference, one that Commons himself had helped to pioneer and that was expressed widely by white liberals. In the first decade of the twentieth century Commons and others began to argue that although races were inferior and superior to one another, as previous generations had believed, their differences resulted from environmental and historical factors and therefore could be overcome in time. Commons's rejection of biological determinism had won him the respect of many African American activists and "race men," including W. E. B. Du Bois.[50]

But his philosophy of race relations in the United States was based on a contradiction that was still characteristic of white liberal culture in the 1930s. Commons believed that a true democracy could not exist without "equal opportunities before the law, and equal ability of classes and races to use those opportunities," and this was the kind of country he sought to help build. He also acknowledged that opportunity, oppression, and class stratification were factors in the "eminence achieved by the English race in America" that did not reflect "racial superiority" but rather "circumstances": "They got here first, they were merchants instead of farmers, the best of their classes immigrated. Class is more important than race in assessing the eminence of a people."[51] However, his argument did not challenge the view, commonly held by liberal Americans, that "Negroes" were, at least under existing conditions, inferior. As he struggled to explain this, he continually slid into justifications based on assumed biological differences. Commons contended that race "oligarchy" developed when "a social class or an entire race" was incapable of meeting the demands posed by democratic citizenship—that the root of racial hierarchy was the deficiency of African American people. Though he said that this deficiency resulted from "conditions," not biology, he saw those conditions beginning in the "primitive" cultures of Africa. The origins of "Negroes" in humid African climates produced a race of people "indolent, improvident, and contented":

> Here is the problem of races, the fundamental division of mankind. Race differences are established in the very blood and physical condition. . . . Races may change their religions, their forms of government, their modes of industry, and their languages, but underneath all these changes they may continue the physical, mental, and moral capacities and incapacities. . . . Race and heredity furnish the raw material, education and environment furnish the tools.[52]

According to Commons, "inferior races" were responsible for raising themselves to the level of superior ones. "The degraded status of blacks had nothing to do with white attitudes or practices." Rather, this status "was inevitable in the nature of the race at that stage of its development." Their poor continued development in the United States occurred in spite of the "opportunities and educational advantages . . . given the negro, not only on equal terms, but actually on terms of preference over the whites." Voting restrictions, Commons maintained, should apply to all but the few African Americans who had advanced in order that the "Negro race" eventually be uplifted to a point where it could exist on equal footing in society.[53]

By the 1930s this developmental theory of race evolved into a philosophy known as "gradualism," which was often substituted by New Dealers for more direct references to racial inequality. The Wisconsin group believed that any imperfections in the policy they created could be taken care of through the continuous progress of liberal society over time; this belief enabled them to set aside any concerns that were raised about the many Americans who were excluded from their plan. In the thirties, the concept of gradualism had not yet been drawn into civil rights discourse, as it was by the time Martin Luther King Jr. wrote his famous letter from the Birmingham jail to white ministers who had advocated patience for slow and steady progress.[54] By 1949 Aubrey Williams, a white southern New Dealer considered to be very liberal on race, had articulated this critique of a gradualist approach to social change, arguing that it facilitated discrimination because those in power would only negotiate away what they considered worthless and would retain what they deemed valuable. Gradual change thus allowed institutions time to adjust and found new avenues to maintain existing power hierarchies.[55]

In 1935 the concept was not yet openly discussed in the context of race, though it had obvious ramifications for racially defined minorities. CES staff member Wilbur Cohen later said that Commons taught all of his students

> not to try to be so global that you took on so much more than you could administer that failure would ultimately be certain. . . . [T]he men and women I worked with . . . were strongly of the belief of the inevitableness [*sic*] of gradualism. In other words, they felt it was more important to take one step at a time . . . to digest one meal at a time rather than eating breakfast, lunch, and dinner all at once and getting indigestion. This was their social philosophy.

It was a theory of "orderly evolution that is acceptable by the body politic as being practical, realistic, and one they're willing to build upon."[56] Though it was presented as a neutral strategy to ease administration, it was infused with the same developmental discourse that would determine who would be invited to the table first.

The U.S. welfare system was founded on a belief in the inferiority of African American workers. On the surface, it might appear that black workers were excluded from UI and OAA for administrative reasons, because their employers were typically too small to be of use in regulating the economy and their paychecks too small to afford contributions. However, the broader vision through which the Social Security Act was conceived and birthed was steeped in the belief in the inferiority of African American labor and the importance of white labor to the character of the country and the economic system that enabled it. John Commons developed his scheme for salvaging capitalism through unemployment compensation based on this conviction. That scheme became the core of the Social Security Act, and other programs created by the Act were made to fit around it.

Members of the Wisconsin group knew that they were creating an unequal system that would privilege some workers at the expense of others. They knew that a large proportion of those affected by the exclusions would be African Americans.[57] They knew that sharecroppers in particular were "as a class almost constantly without resources with which to meet unemployment or any other emergency," and that they "form a disproportionate number of relief cases."[58] But all of this was considered to be necessary in the context of the group's larger goals.

The Wisconsin agenda was the most influential factor in the construction of the Social Security Act as racially discriminatory. But a question remains. The Wisconsin group was organized, ambitious, and assigned leadership of the CES staff. But that does not in itself explain how this group came to have such a dominant impact on the Act. The Wisconsin plan was not popular; other social insurance experts on the CES staff were highly critical, southerners in Congress believed that the plan unfairly favored northern states, no large constituency of Americans supported it, and European countries offered working models of more unified systems that had actually been tested. How could the agenda of even the most effective group have triumphed in that context?

The Authority of the "Objective" Administrator

One answer to this question lies with the authority enjoyed by Edwin Witte, Frances Perkins, and other administrators, one derived from a general perception that they were not politically motivated, but were more like scientists, disinterested and neutral, and were able to objectively assess proposals according to universally agreed-upon truths.[59] CES staffers, like Barbara Armstrong and Douglas Brown, did not have this same degree of authority; they were seen by others and themselves as advocates for a cause they believed in. Its authority gave the Wisconsin group the power to define the issue of exclusion as one of "administration," to appropriate the issue to their own recognized field of expertise.

The Wisconsin group was, in fact, in the vanguard of a movement that sought to implement a new approach to government administration, one that had begun to permeate New Deal agencies. This approach had been developed by University of Wisconsin faculty members such as John Commons and Richard Ely. Commons and Ely trained their students to be unbiased and apolitical administrators, whose presence would ensure that administration would be governed by science, not politics. They would embody this disinterested position and "make the work of administration their life work."[60] For Commons, this new type of public servant held the promise for reconstructing American democracy. He asserted that "[t]he problem of democracy is how to make wealth, politicians, and experts the servants instead of the masters of the people." The maintenance by public servants of an "objective" posture was one answer to this quandary and would work in concert with "initiative and referendum, civil service reform, appointment of commissioners, and recall by the people."[61] No one more closely exemplified the new administrator than Edwin Witte. Witte had steered clear of politics throughout his career, "being careful not even to make a campaign contribution," and was known to be willing to prepare arguments for both sides of an issue.[62] He said that impartial analysis was possible only if administrators "are genuinely non-partisan and hold their positions free from the vicissitudes of politics."[63]

Barbara Armstrong was hindered not only by her status as an outsider, but also by her outdated ideas about the role of academics in public policy. Douglas Brown later remembered that he and Armstrong came from the tradition of "academic freedom"; "the President, the Secretary or anybody else couldn't tell us what to think." In that capacity, they openly debated and fought for what they believed to be in the best interest of the public good. But the Wisconsin people were a puzzlement. On the one hand, they claimed to have no personal positions on issues; Witte, according to Brown, saw his role as an academic as "the servant of whatever powerful person he worked for, more like a lawyer." Armstrong interpreted Arthur Altmeyer's seeming detachment as a lack of caring and of "real convictions." And yet their self-images as objective servants of the process did not square with their investment in a particular version of the Social Security Act that, Armstrong argued, they were actually "fathering."[64]

Witte and other members of the Wisconsin group had difficulty trying to be both objective administrators and visionary reformers at the same time. Thomas Eliot, discussing the "subsidy" plan for unemployment insurance, a rival of the "Wisconsin plan," acknowledged: "I have been having a hard time to appear impartial and judicially minded, and at the same time squelch the subsidy plan."[65] Witte admitted, after the House rewrote the

UI titles of the president's bill, "I have tried to look at this entire question without particularly considering Wisconsin." But, if the Wisconsin plan were not followed, "Wisconsin will have to scrap its unemployment compensation law . . . and begin all over again."[66]

Indeed, the group from Wisconsin was heavily involved in the politics behind the Social Security Act. Once the CES bill had been introduced in Congress, Witte and his Wisconsin colleagues worked tirelessly for its adoption. They used contacts in the National Consumers League and the American Federation of Labor (AFL) to drum up popular support for the CES bill, and warned these contacts about less obvious provisions in the various drafts of the bill that they might find problematic. They sought public relations assistance and "people of prominence to put their names to articles written by members of the staff of the Committee."[67] They kept the governor of Wisconsin and Senator Robert M. La Follette Jr. informed of the preliminary work of the CES, though it was to be kept strictly confidential. They used the governor's influence with and access to politicians to forward their common agenda, sometimes offering them unsolicited advice on how to vote on amendments or interpret proposals. Witte strategized ways to defeat the initiatives of lawmakers who did not fully endorse the CES bill.[68] He drafted statements for the Democratic National Committee to be used in the 1934 congressional campaigns and pulled together statements for administration supporters who were campaigning for office.[69]

These activities do not seem to have marred their reputations as objective public servants, even in the eyes of the congressmen whom they sought to persuade. Members of the Wisconsin group were continually invited to attend closed-door sessions on Capitol Hill where political motivations would be expressed off the record.[70] They were asked to help draft House and Senate versions of the Social Security Act and wrote arguments for members to publicly express opinions both for and against parts of the bill (though never against UI).[71] Moreover, Witte enjoyed significant power over policy decisions. In a "highly confidential" memo to a subordinate of Henry Wallace, Jerome Frank said that as of midnight, "Mr. Witte had not decided whether all the suggestions made by Secretary Wallace would be incorporated" in the bill.[72] The "neutral" positions of the Wisconsin group gave them, in some ways, more power than they would have had had they been elected or appointed. Katherine Lenroot remembered that Witte had a "very strategic, almost predominating, influence in the work of the Committee [on Economic Security], because he was recognized as an authority, and spoke with authority."[73] The "authority" derived from an assumption of objective expertise afforded power to men like Witte who had never won an election and were virtually unknown to the American people.

The assumption of objectivity also led to bipartisan political access and recognition. After the Social Security Act was passed, for example, Witte returned to Wisconsin a hero; he was honored by a joint session of the Wisconsin legislature, which asked him to personally walk them through the Act. The bill enabled him to further solidify his relationship with business in Wisconsin. He got the opportunity to recommend many of his friends and students for jobs in Washington, including an assignment for John Andrews to the International Labor Office in Geneva. And he was able to write the official "insider's history" of Social Security. Witte had begun to explore the possibility of writing a book about the Act's development as early as November 1934, when he began to discuss options with McGraw-Hill. Members of the Wisconsin team, most notably Arthur Altmeyer and Wilbur Cohen, went on to important careers in the Social Security Administration.[74]

The Wisconsin group also worked to influence the president to accept its plan. Witte later suggested, and others on the Wisconsin team concurred, that he had merely implemented the president's ideas for social insurance, especially in his insistence on state administration of UI. However, other evidence suggests that this is not the only possible interpretation. Barbara Armstrong claimed that Roosevelt only reluctantly went along with state administration of UI, and that he announced late in 1934 that he would not accept it if it turned out to be as clumsy as it appeared to be. If the president did support the Wisconsin plan, he may have been swayed by Justice Louis Brandeis, who, according to Raymond Moley, a member of FDR's brain trust and a confidante of Witte's, was the source of some of his "inspiration and information" about state administration, or by Moley himself. In July 1935 Witte thanked Moley for his help in convincing Roosevelt to approve the CES plan, saying that "we owe a great deal to you in connection with the President's attitude." The president apparently wanted a "simple," "cradle to grave" system that covered everyone "for every contingency of life." But Frances Perkins agreed with Witte that the system could not be simple and was "doubtful of too ambitious and large a scheme."[75]

"Colorblind" Public Policy

The Wisconsin group did not see itself as invested in a particular political agenda, but rather as a disinterested public servant. Likewise, it did not regard itself as promoting the interests of the dominant race. One of the goals of the new approach to government administration was to achieve a "colorblind" perspective, to not recognize racial difference and to acknowledge the common humanity of all people. The administration of Franklin Roosevelt embodied this perspective, which has led historians to credit the New Deal with nurturing the "seeds of civil rights." However, the quest to attain color blindness was just as problematic as the goal of attaining "objective" expertise. "Colorblind" policy did not remove power from its administration, as it was supposed to do, but instead merely masked the operation of power.

The colorblind approach had its roots in a body of scientific work that challenged the reality of "race." By the early thirties, the work of Franz Boas and others had proved that many so-called racial differences were not biologically based, and scientists began to argue that race should be dropped from the vocabulary of science. These developments led to a shift in the liberal analysis of the underlying cause of America's "race problem," which, it was now argued, stemmed from the *recognition* of racial division. White New Dealers sought to counter the economic chaos of the depression by creating a "harmony of interest" within and between classes and denying "the significance of racial divisions" so that, in the words of Paul Kellogg, "they had almost no sense of race as a public issue when World War II began."[76]

The theory that race was not "real" struck a powerful blow to the doctrine of white supremacy, but it also undermined, in the eyes of white liberals, the legitimacy of the race identification of minority groups and the reality of diverse experience and oppression. It led to the conclusion that racial antagonism and hierarchy were the products of emotional and psychological attachments to a false racial identity. It was racial *feeling*, of white supremacists and "Negro" activists alike, that perpetuated discrimination, which could be eradicated only when the drive for efficiency and profit was allowed to rule unfettered by racial prejudice. In the words of Harold Ickes, generally regarded as the most race-liberal member of FDR's cabinet, "Government should not sanction any policy which affirmed race differences or perceived black needs as distinct from the needs of other Americans."[77]

But just as the belief in the existence of objective expertise could cloud people's ability to recognize political agendas, belief in the possibility of colorblind policies could mask a culture that perpetuated a white norm. One way was through discrimination in hiring. In 1935 the civil service did not recognize "race" and had neither overtly discriminatory nor preferential policies for equal hiring. But it still required photographs of job applicants, a requirement described by one man who had been rejected for employment as "a pernicious and systematic method of excluding Negroes."[78] Especially painful for many African Americans was the neglect of patronage for "Negro" leaders who had helped FDR get elected in 1932. This was true for Robert Vann, the outspoken editor of the *Pittsburgh Courier*, the man who had admonished African America to "turn the pictures of Abraham Lincoln to the wall" and vote for Roosevelt.[79] A representative of the Democratic National Convention Midwest district claimed in 1934 that not a single patronage position had been given to a "Colored Democrat" in his region, even though "[t]he Colored vote is the balance of power in every state." He said that "[n]ot even a ["Negro"] messenger has been appointed."[80] This discriminatory treatment could not be directly challenged because it did not result from an overtly discriminatory policy, and the colorblind New Deal culture prevented any open acknowledgment that African Americans were not being hired.

The white norm was enforced in other ways as well. For example, a handful of African Americans were hired by New Deal agencies, usually as "Negro Advisers," and this was cited as evidence of the administration's commitment to counter discrimination. However, the "Negro Advisers" were typically pressured to downplay their racial identities. These few were mostly Ivy League–educated men who were hired away from black or interracial organizations like the National Association for the Advancement of Colored People (NAACP) and the National Urban League. They represented FDR's recognition of black organizations and leadership for their backing in the 1932 election and have been referred to as "window dressing" for the lack of support they received from the White House.[81]

One of the most sought-after qualities in a "Negro Adviser" was the ability to not "think black." Robert Weaver, hired by Harold Ickes as such an adviser to the Department of the Interior, was considered a "first class administrator" and a "thoroughly emancipated Negro" who "made his appeal not to the moral conscience of America but to its rationality." Will Alexander, a southern race liberal and an AAA administrator, argued that African Americans needed to be educated about the folly of "race conscious" thinking. He advocated Forrester Washington for the post of "Negro Adviser" of FERA over two other candidates because "[t]o a surprising degree, Washington seems to me to be able to view the problems of Negroes with the minimum of racial feeling."[82]

Once they were more established and less vulnerable, black New Dealers began to speak out against this policy. In the early 1940s Robert Weaver said that "[s]ocial programs initiated or supported by the Federal Government must involve racial policy." What might look like "no racial policy" was, "in fact, a most dangerous one, since it frequently implies ignoring colored Americans. The Negro is too often not considered an integral part of the body politic." Despite widespread protest from the African American leadership, Weaver had originally been turned down for the position with Interior in favor of Clark Foreman, who was white. Secretary Ickes argued that it was unnecessary for a "Negro" person to represent "Negro" affairs; a white person would be more accepted and therefore more effective.[83]

Similar pressure was experienced by Jewish New Dealers, who, in light of the racist discourse in Germany at that time, may have been particularly open to the idea that science could be the means of eradicating all racism. For instance, as Edward Berkowitz reported, Wilbur Cohen discovered that the world of public administration allowed him some reprieve from limitations that he might encounter outside. His identity as a "technician," he said, "suited a Jewish person better than did that of a frontline politician or bureaucratic manager. Voters did not want to see Jewish people as public officials." But the price he had to pay was assimilation. "As Cohen and his friends became more successful at their jobs and mixed professionally and socially with many non-Jews, they tended to downplay the Jewish content of their childhoods."[84]

Jerome Frank, a lawyer with the Agricultural Adjustment Administration and a "liberal's liberal," who stood out among New Dealers for his affiliations with black organizations, was a "proudly assimilated Jew [who] took his Americanism seriously and wore his Jewishness lightly." He told Secretary Wallace, in regard to having hired dozens of lawyers for the AAA legal staff, "I have taken such care to discourage Jewish applicants that I have gained the reputation among my non-Jewish friends at Columbia,

Yale and elsewhere, of being anti-Semitic." Frank's concern for societal perceptions led him to conclude that "a Jewish chief counsel wisely should not hire other Jews if he could avoid it."[85] His fears were not exaggerated. A member of the House Ways and Means Committee told Arthur Altmeyer, apparently with the agreement of the chair, that the Social Security Board had initially hired "too damn many New York Jews." FDR became involved, and it was determined that less than 5 percent of the board's employees were Jewish.[86]

Far from erasing race from policy, the colorblind approach had the effect of censoring public discourse about race among policymakers. It protected them from having to articulate or confront the ways that racial difference figured into their worldviews and their reformist visions. It also protected them from acknowledging their own racialized positioning.

This would have been even truer for the Wisconsin group than for other liberals living in more integrated areas of the country. In Wisconsin, middle-class reformers would have experienced little or no pressure to confront race issues. Madison's African American community was even smaller than that of Milwaukee, which in 1940 was contained within a single square mile and had a population under nine thousand; minority political organizing in Madison thus lagged behind that in more diverse parts of the country.[87] Unlike their mentor John Commons, members of the Wisconsin group did not take public stands on racial issues; there are strong indications that they were not affiliated with minority organizations or especially interested in their concerns. This was true of Edwin Witte, Arthur Altmeyer, Wilbur Cohen, and Tom Eliot, who drafted the CES version of the Social Security Act. Despite the wide circles in which they traveled, their papers include almost no correspondence with African Americans, articles by black writers, or black publications. The fact that Witte was using the lower-case spelling of "Negro" in 1936 suggests that he was somewhat removed, not only from "race liberal" thought, but also more mainstream northern race sympathizers—even the *New York Times* was using the upper-case spelling by 1934 following a national campaign conducted by the NAACP.[88]

With one exception, the research conducted by the CES staff did not refer to race. That exception was a series of reports on the number and percentage of older Americans who were "Negro" and white. The report showed that "Negroes" were growing in the younger age groups, but only whites were increasing in the older groups. "Native white elders will certainly be more numerous in 1940 and 1950 than now, and . . . will constitute a still larger portion of the total population." The report concluded that this growth necessitated an old-age pension program.[89]

Even in the rare instances where racial diversity was acknowledged, the political meaning of this difference was erased by the language used by those who sought to embody the "new administrator." Members of the Wisconsin group, like many reform-minded policymakers, tended to speak a language incapable of expressing a vision that was not driven by neutral technical considerations. For instance, in regard to agricultural and domestic workers, a report generated by the CES staff stated: "Inclusion of these groups of workers is difficult administratively and, for short time and intermittent workers, *is of relatively little value*, since they seldom accumulate any substantial benefit rights" (emphasis added).[90] In other words, the inability of workers to earn enough "benefit rights," or wages, to pay into an insurance system was not an ethical issue but purely one of the technicalities of administration. This language distanced the speaker from the topic and made it possible to discuss issues removed from their political and social context. It was a language of facilitation that reduced words like "value" to their most superficial meanings; it could not address the question, "What does it mean that we do things this way?" but only, "How can we make them work more efficiently?"

This language, which scrupulously excised all reference to "political" concerns such as justice, fairness, and equality, could only recognize the issue of exclusion as one of "facilitation." Edwin Witte appropriated the issue of exclusion early in the process. "Who should be brought under unemployment compensation?" he asked. "This is a practical question to which no dogmatic answer can be given."[91] Once drawn into this discourse, it was no longer a "political" issue. And despite all of the evidence offered that inclusion was possible, the ultimate experts were given the final word.

The perceived objectivity of the Wisconsin leadership of the CES staff enabled it to design a Social Security Act that discriminated against African American workers. But the colorblind culture of the New Deal did not allow for that discrimination to be understood as such and addressed; it was only approached through the dispassionate administrative discourse that did not recognize race as a political reality. Yet the Act's framers were very conscious of racial politics. It was that consciousness that ultimately led them to advocate the exclusion of agricultural and domestic workers.

As demonstrated in the previous chapter, the Wisconsin leaders of the CES staff were instrumental in convincing a sometimes reluctant Congress to include explicit exclusions in the House bill. But the story of their interest in the exclusions begins much earlier and ultimately reveals the racialized politics that framed the issue.

The CES and the Politics of Race

After the non-Wisconsin staffers lost the fight for the creation of a unified social welfare system, they set about, in the fall of 1934, convincing Edwin Witte to alter the Wisconsin plan so that more marginal workers, especially agricultural and domestic workers, could be covered by unemployment and old-age insurance. In a number of reports to Witte, they indicated that, although it might be more difficult to include these workers in UI and OAI under the Wisconsin plan, it was entirely possible.

Their first task was to successfully challenge Witte's insistence that UI and OAI could not, at least initially, manage the coverage of agricultural and domestic workers. In his preliminary report to the CES, Witte had stated that administrative problems had initially kept European systems from including agricultural and domestic workers.[92] This conclusion was countered by the research of these CES staffers. Natalie Jaros argued that administrative difficulties had not been responsible for the delayed coverage of agricultural workers in European systems; rather, unemployment in this area had not been significant enough to warrant coverage prior to the mechanization of farms following World War I.[93]

Second, the non-Wisconsin staff argued that administration was feasible especially with the use of a stamp book collection procedure common in European systems. This procedure, which required employers to purchase stamps at post offices and then provide them to employees per units of work, would have been cheap, efficient, and self-regulating, since employees could demand their own stamps. One plan to use stamp books involved paying laborers benefits according to some prevailing wage for farmwork in a specific area. This plan, its author pointed out, could be applied to sharecroppers, who would receive unemployment benefits if they were unable to secure a contract for the coming season. Witte and others discussed the possibility of imposing a set-aside of the UI tax as an interstate transfer fund that would be administered federally, for which some of the UI tax might be allotted. In February 1935, after the bill had been introduced in Congress, Isador Falk, a member of the CES Technical Board, presented a proposal to offer cash benefits for wage loss due to illness, and suggested that such a program could cover domestic and agricultural employees under UI since it would provide an incentive for them to comply with registration and contributions. R. Riefler of the Technical Board argued that seasonal and short-term workers could receive a "dismissal wage" when laid off without cause.[94]

More research by the CES staff was conducted on farmworkers than on domestics. One reason was that administrative problems were thought to be greater in providing OAI for domestics, especially those who worked in private homes. Barbara Armstrong advocated the inclusion of farmworkers in OAI but was more cautious about covering domestic workers. In a September 1934 preliminary report, she wrote: "There are no special difficulties in the way of old age insurance for agricultural workers. . . . The agricultural employee, moreover, is an extremely low-paid worker and has unquestionable need of old age protection . . . there would be no excuse for omitting the agricultural group from old age insurance." Armstrong acknowledged that it would be less feasible to cover domestic workers. But if domestics were excluded, "the fact would have to be faced that a group of workers in need of old age provision were being eliminated from the insurance scheme" only because of the administrative difficulty of collecting contributions from household employers.[95]

Another factor was that many professionals, especially professional women, had a personal interest in the employment of domestic servants. Married women had to fight to retain their jobs and may have felt under attack after 1932, when Section 213 of the National Economy Act barred women married to men in government service from taking government jobs. This statute led to the dismissal of 1,600 women by 1937.[96] Unlike its silence on the plight of domestic workers, the CES staff was up front with its advocacy of the right of professional women to work. Witte said that he supported the inclusion of part-time workers in UI and OAI, a category dominated by women, whose inclusion was the first legislative priority of the Federal Women's Bureau. He maintained that the CES and its network "strongly opposed" their exclusion from UI and OAI.[97]

This support for professional women may have influenced the CES network's position on the domestic servants who made women's professional work possible. Researchers at the University of Wisconsin found that 30 full-time domestic jobs were created by the employment of 64 professional women. All 64 women reported that they would have to give up their jobs if domestic service were unavailable.[98] Domestic workers were pretty much abandoned by the New Deal women's network. The Consumer's League "more or less condoned" the exclusion of domestic workers from its model minimum wage-and-hour legislation and did not fight for their inclusion in the Social Security Act.[99] Even after the Act had passed, and it was shown that including domestic workers would have been relatively easy, one justification for their continued exclusion remained: Housewives did not regard themselves as employers, and it would take a great deal of reeducation to alter that thinking.[100]

When the appropriate research was finally conducted after the Act passed, it was concluded that no justification existed for excluding domestic servants from OAI. Wilbur Cohen observed in 1938 that domestic and agricultural labor should not be treated as a unit by policymakers, because it would be "very much easier" to include domestic servants than agricultural workers. Because they tended to live in urban areas, no great "administrative problems exist with domestic workers"; the women who employed them would generally have office experience, so there would be no "educational problem" in training employers, and houses that could afford servants could afford the OAI tax. Certainly the CES was aware of the poverty of domestic workers and the fact that, as Cohen noted later, as urban workers they did not have the "recourse to other means of support" available to farm laborers. In April 1935 the CES had seen a study finding that 76 percent of women in New York City almshouses were former domestic workers.[101]

Unlike domestic workers, farmworkers had natural advocates through the involvement of Henry Wallace and CES staff who had been borrowed from the USDA and the AAA. The research on agricultural laborers was initiated in September 1934, when the CES instructed Louis Bean, with the help of H. R. Trolley and Joseph Viner, to conduct a study on the feasibility of including agricultural employees in the insurance programs. Witte later stated that nothing ever came of this research, and it was not included in the report sent to Roosevelt and Congress. In fact, however, in November, Bean presented a comprehensive report on the inclusion of agricultural workers in the insurance program, which was written under the direction of Josiah Folsom of his staff. The report gave ample evidence that farmworkers were in great need of social insurance and that their inclusion was feasible using the stamp collection method.[102]

The conclusions of Bean and others were validated within a few years of the Act's passage. One 1939 report prepared by the Bureau of Old-Age Insurance pointed out that only 300,000 of the country's 6.8 million farms employed enough workers to fall under the Social Security Act, and that "[t]he farms hiring labor are among the largest and are most likely to keep records." It claimed that agricultural workers were included in European old-age insurance systems without any major difficulty, and that they could have been included in the U.S. system with relative ease.[103]

The inclusion of agricultural and domestic workers was given even more support by the National Council on Social Security. The council was established late in the process (its first meeting was held on November 14, 1934) mainly for "publicity purposes"—to generate "geographic" support for the president's bill.[104] However, that plan backfired on the Wisconsin leadership of the CES when the council came out strongly in favor of including agricultural and domestic workers in the Act. In its recommendations to the CES on December 7, the council urged that UI be "compulsory for all employers with six or more employees, including those engaged in agriculture and in domestic service." It also advocated greater federal control of UI after its chair, Frank Graham, was lobbied by his old friend Evelyn Burns.[105]

Despite all of the support for a more inclusive system, the Wisconsin approach was adopted in the final report. Witte's recommendation to exclude agricultural and domestic workers was not based on staff research. The highest-ranking consultants hired by the CES to develop the specifics of the UI and OAI titles came out in favor of inclusion, with some hesitation by Barbara Armstrong regarding domestic workers. The Old Age Security Committee of the Technical Board argued against specific exclusion. But Witte himself acknowledged that staff work did not have much impact on the process.[106] As Evelyn Burns remembered: "I do think that the staff on that committee did feel after a while that there was an effort to put everything into a box that was already a preconceived box, and substantially the box was something that the Wisconsin boys wanted, and that Miss Perkins wasn't going to buck the Wisconsin boys and Arthur Altmeyer, as chairman of the technical advisory committee, wasn't going to buck Wisconsin. He was Wisconsin."[107]

Once the draft report was prepared on November 27, 1934, it was submitted to both the CES and the Technical Board for review. That report recommended that agricultural and domestic workers be excluded from the insurance programs in the Social Security Act. In a series of meetings that followed, the CES approved the main recommendations of the staff, except for the specific exclusion of agricultural and domestic workers. Witte credited Harry Hopkins with insisting that the explicit exclusion be removed, and Barbara Armstrong credited Frances Perkins, though it is also likely that Henry Wallace also favored its removal. The CES then submitted the amended report to the president on January 16, 1935, and it was released to the public the following day. FDR approved the report, including the theoretical coverage of agricultural and domestic workers, and a bill was drafted and introduced in the House and Senate. Roosevelt made only one change to the report to indicate that this was only one of the proposals that Congress might consider.[108]

There is some evidence that the AAA and USDA camps worked behind the scenes with Henry Wallace to eliminate the language excluding agricultural and domestic workers. Wallace requested that a different collection method for agricultural workers, such as the stamp book system, be specifically mentioned in the bill, presumably to undermine arguments against inclusion based on "administrative difficulties." This language was retained in the CES's original bill regarding OAI, and similar language was retained in the final bill. Wallace also asked Witte to speak to a member of his staff on the subject of inclusion versus exclusion.[109]

As head of the CES, Frances Perkins would have had the last word on what to recommend to FDR. Barbara Armstrong said that Perkins insisted on taking the language out because she was "sick and tired and fed up with always leaving out the domestic and the agricultural." Perkins publicly supported the inclusion of commercial agricultural laborers in UI, declaring that they were "probably the most submerged class in the United States." She was obviously aware that agricultural laborers were predominantly African American, Hispanic, and Asian.[110]

But Perkins's sensitivity to the plight of agricultural laborers was inconsistent, and her position on agricultural and domestic labor probably did not reflect a stand against racial discrimination. She had not established a track record defending agricultural laborers. In fact, she argued strenuously that they were not "workers" and that their problems were not under the purview of the Department of Labor.[111] Years later she still revealed herself to be out of touch with the sharecropping system, defending it for its paternalistic care of the laborers.[112] Secretary Perkins also did not fight for the inclusion of agricultural and domestic workers once the bill went to Congress. On February 25, 1935, she sent a list to FDR of the things that really mattered to her in the Social Security Act, and inclusion of these workers was not on her list, though she did remind the president of her interest in protecting the features of the Wisconsin UI plan.[113] Perkins has been described as one of Roosevelt's more race-liberal cabinet members, and she is remembered for hiring African American clerical workers in the Department of Labor and conducting studies on discriminatory hiring in government. But contemporaries remembered her timidity. Will Alexander said that Perkins "dread[ed] very much to deal with the racial problem in the South." She complained that "[e]very day brings a group of demands from a group of Negroes to be appointed to something or other."[114] Apparently it was commonly understood among those considered to be "race liberals" that she hired a "Negro Adviser" out of fear, rather than a desire to build bridges with African American workers.[115]

The pieces of the CES positions on this issue add up to a puzzle. Why was Edwin Witte so insistent on excluding agricultural and domestic workers from the Social Security Act in the face of so many reasons why those workers, at least those who were not already excluded for structural reasons, could be included? Why did Secretary Perkins overrule Witte and insist on including them in November, only to abandon the cause with such apparent ease once the Act went to Congress? There is an answer to the puzzle; the pieces make sense when seen through the politics of race.

The reason that Witte worked to keep agricultural and domestic workers out of the Act was because he believed—wrongly it turns out—that it would be impossible to gain southern support for the measure if it covered African American workers. Witte promoted this assumption among other members of the CES and worked hard to discourage them from discussing the issue of inclusion directly with the congressional leadership. He repeatedly warned Harry Hopkins against making an issue of the exclusion of agricultural and domestic workers because the Ways and Means Committee "will not reverse itself on agricultural workers and domestic servants," and "[a]ttempts to compel them to do so may lead to votes against passage of the bill by some of the administrative members of the Committee." Witte cautioned Hopkins a third time, noting that "it is doubtful whether it is wise to press the members to restore the original provisions."[116] In an internal report distributed in February 1935 he blamed the exclusion of agricultural and domestic workers entirely on Congress. He wrote: "Unquestionably, it is desirable to include commercial agriculture and large domestic establishments, but as realists we must recognize that legislative bodies will probably prefer the traditional complete exemption."[117]

Yet the House leadership claimed that this was not the case. The Senate Finance Committee was highly critical of the exclusions, and House members had to be convinced by New Deal allies that they were administratively necessary. The decisive moment in Congress followed Secretary Morganthau's testimony before the House Ways and Means Committee during which he argued for the exclusion of these workers. Morganthau's statements demonstrated he knew so little about the issue of inclusion that he was unable to give a basic description of the stamp tax system of collection. When asked about coverage of domestic servants in England, he said, "I am not familiar with the experiences of Great Britain," though he had access to ample staff reports on that subject. Morganthau based his argument, not on the depth of his knowledge of the subject, but on his authority, as chief expert on such matters, to make the call. Apparently, Perkins had publicly objected to excluding agricultural and domestic workers when called on to comment during the same hearing. When asked about Perkins's disagreement, Morganthau replied, "I want to make it clear that Miss Perkins and I are in complete accord, but this particular matter is purely one of administration," suggesting that her opinion as secretary of labor did not match his expertise in administration as treasury secretary.[118]

Frances Perkins, in agreement with Witte's assessment of congressional priorities, fought to keep agricultural and domestic workers in the original Social Security Act to give the administration bargaining power with Congress—that is, as an item to trade for support of the Wisconsin plan for UI. For example, she wrote the following memorandum, apparently intended for FDR to use as talking points in phone conversations with House Ways and Means leaders Jere Cooper of Tennessee and Fred Vinson of Kentucky and possibly others:

> The Economic Security Bill is taking a long time in Committee. Is the Unemployment Insurance Title holding it up? . . . If you feel that it is absolutely imperative for you to vote to exempt all agriculture, still you will not feel that you must vote for any further exemptions. . . . I am sure, too, that you will not object to allowing the States to adopt plans somewhat like that of Wisconsin. . . . I should be sorry to see

agricultural labor exempted from unemployment insurance, but I understand the political difficulties which result in rural districts if you vote against such exemptions.[119]

Perkins seems to be suggesting that Congress support the Wisconsin plan in exchange for administration support to exclude agricultural workers. A copy of this memo was found in the papers of the Act's sponsor, Robert Wagner, suggesting that it was circulated among at least some lawmakers on Capitol Hill.[120]

If Perkins's exchange was, in fact, offered, House leaders did not bite. They excluded agricultural and domestic workers per Morganthau's instructions. But they also undermined the Wisconsin plan for UI by prohibiting states from allowing individual employer UI accounts, on which the Wisconsin plan was based. Witte claimed that the AFL and "social workers" such as Paul Kellogg and Abram Epstein had been able to persuade the House to side with the detractors of the Wisconsin plan. The Wisconsin plan was restored through a floor amendment offered by Wisconsin's Senator La Follette, and the final bill created an unemployment compensation program "more conducive even than the original bill to the individual employer reserves that businessmen favored almost universally."[121] The fate of agricultural and domestic workers—the majority of the country's African American wage earners—was not raised again.

Richard Ely once said that the work of administration was the improvement of "human welfare." As he explained, "We wish to make this a better and happier world than it is."[122] This was, no doubt, the intent of John Commons and his students as they struggled to construct and then implement the first pillars of the American welfare state. But these were the same people who ended up using the economic welfare of African Americans as a pawn in the worst kind of political maneuvering. They did not go to that place because of identifiably "racist" agendas. Rather, their worldview, saturated as it was with a belief in the reality of their own whiteness, masked the fact that their vision of a happier world rested on systems of inequality.

four

Shaky Ground

Black and Interracial Organizations

Speaking at the Twenty-fifth Annual Conference of the National Association for the Advancement of Colored People (NAACP) in June 1935, Josephine Roche declared that the Social Security Act was "one of the most historic measures . . . to be passed by Congress, because it writes into our national law the principle that human beings' welfare is the first charge on government." The measure had just been approved by both House and Senate and was awaiting reconciliation by a conference committee. The NAACP, by then the country's largest and most politically influential interracial organization, had been working for over two decades to promote the civil rights of African Americans. Roche, a long-standing friend of the NAACP, had served the Committee on Economic Security (CES) in different capacities through the fall of 1934. In her address at the 1935 gathering, she made no mention of the exclusion of African American workers from the Act but instead emphasized the "economic and social justice" that it embodied.[1] Later in the program, Roche, a white woman, helped Mary McLeod Bethune to her feet to accept a bouquet of flowers. NAACP executive director Walter White, in describing the moment to a congressional aide, recalled that "the two women stood there with arms about each other. When I tell you that Mrs. Bethune is dark of skin, you will understand how Josephine's action was obviously an unconscious expression of that human brotherhood of which she had just spoken."[2]

This scene raises obvious questions. As demonstrated in previous chapters, the creators of the Social Security Act did not protect the "welfare" of the vast majority of the "human beings" who were not white men; African American workers were denied the "economic and social justice" that the Act was said to embody. So, why did the NAACP celebrate the Act through its conference's keynote address? And why did White and other NAACP leaders applaud Roche's comments? Could they possibly have been unaware that most black workers were excluded from the Act? Or did they not grasp the significance of that exclusion?

This chapter tells the story of the participation of the NAACP in the development of the Social Security Act, as well as that of the other two interracial/black organizations represented in Washington in 1935: the National Urban League (NUL) and the Joint Committee on National Recovery (JCNR). It explores the nature of white liberalism in the 1930s from the vantage points of these organizations and the ways that liberal perspectives on race defined what could and could not be changed through policy.

African Americans in Washington

Of the myriad organizations lobbying in the nation's capital during the Seventy-fourth Congress in 1935, only the NAACP, NUL, and JCNR, represented by a handful of individuals, were dedicated to protecting the interests of the country's 11.9 million "Negroes," or 9.7 percent of the U.S. population. African Americans were not represented by the largest labor, business, and agricultural lobbies; they were denied membership in most affiliated unions of the American Federation of Labor (AFL), and, as workers, their interests were usually at odds with the lobbies of agricultural and business employers.

The NAACP, NUL, and JCNR were represented in Washington by their top leaders, mostly educated, relatively young African American men.[3] The NUL, which was founded in 1911 to protect and ease the transition of southern African Americans who were migrating to northern cities, emphasized economic assistance, job training and placement, and housing assistance to urban blacks. It worked mainly through branch offices, rather than its national office. The JCNR was an umbrella organization established by a small group of Ivy League–educated black men with leftist politics to act as a watchdog for the interests of African Americans in New Deal policies. The Joint Committee, which existed on a shoestring budget raised from its member organizations, was a consistent and energetic, though peripheral, presence on Capitol Hill through the Seventy-fourth Congress. Lobbyists from black and interracial organizations could generally count on information and assistance from African Americans in the administration. They especially sought the aid of Mary McLeod Bethune, a member of FDR's unofficial "black cabinet." Others, most if not all of whom were men, were "Negro Advisers" to the more progressive departments and programs.[4] Many "Negro Advisers" had been hired away from the NAACP or the NUL, both of which expected them to pursue the goals of these organizations from the inside.[5]

But such an agenda was very difficult if not impossible. "Negro Advisers" worked for an administration in which many African Americans had rested their hopes; they did not see themselves as spies in a hostile enemy camp, but rather as fortunate participants in efforts to integrate government. Their loyalties were often divided. When the Social Security Act was first introduced, for example, Robert Weaver, "Negro Adviser" for the Department of the Interior (DOI), worked behind the scenes on behalf of African Americans, reaching out to those who were closer to the bill to counter its discriminatory impact.[6] But as a New Dealer himself, Weaver, when called upon, also defended New Deal programs to African American communities by denying or downplaying their discriminatory effects.[7]

Unlike "Negro Advisers," many white friends of interracial organizations wielded considerable power in the Roosevelt administration. Some of them were what John Kirby has called "white race liberals," those who advocated the New Deal style of reform and saw in it a means to achieve racial progress. Those most willing to advocate African American rights tended to be grouped in the DOI (Secretary Harold Ickes had once directed the Chicago chapter of the NAACP) and in a radical arm of the Agricultural Adjustment Administration (AAA). The AAA group included Jerome Frank and Gardner Jackson, both of whom fought for the inclusion of farmworkers in the Social Security Act; they were driven out of AAA, according to Walter White, in part because of their advocacy of "Negro sharecroppers." However, even these friends often could not be relied on when challenges to the New Deal administration were raised. For instance, although he was a member of the NAACP legal committee, Felix Frankfurter repeatedly refused to give Walter White a legal opinion on the Costigan-Wagner Anti-lynching Bill, because it might embarrass FDR, who did not publicly support it.[8]

The sensitivity of Jerome Frank, Gardner Jackson, and Felix Frankfurter to racial inequality was not representative of white New Dealers, who more typically expressed sympathy for "Negro rights" but were neither invested in nor well informed about issues of African Americans. This broader group included members of the CES, especially Frances Perkins and Henry Wallace.[9] Outside of government, it was connected to white liberal reform movements and organizations, but not substantially affiliated with interracial organizations and issues.

The three black/interracial organizations that lobbied Washington during the Seventy-fourth Congress had different degrees of access and experience. The NUL was represented by T. Arnold Hill, who had become its acting executive director in 1934, when executive director Eugene Kinckle Jones was "loaned" to the Department of Commerce. Though the Urban League was large and well established, its small New York–based national office had little authority over the forty-two branch offices and no national program. Under Hill's leadership, however, it became active in New Deal lobbying; Hill spent every other week in Washington through the Seventy-fourth Congress. Aside from Jones, Hill's allies in the capital included Mary McLeod Bethune, head of the National Youth Administration, who was the NUL's vice chair; Hill also knew Frances Perkins and Harry Hopkins from joint work on settlements and health services in the 1910s and 1920s. Nevertheless, the NUL did not enjoy much influence in either the White House or Congress.[10]

The second lobbying organization in Washington, the JCNR, better defined as "black" than interracial, was small, with only two salaried staff members in 1934–35: John Davis and Robert Weaver. To give their venture more legitimacy, they approached George Edmund Haynes, who was then representing the Department of Race Relations in the World Council of Churches. Haynes became a very active chair of the JCNR board of directors. Davis served as executive director throughout the committee's three-year existence, at the end of which he and others more openly pursued their radical political agendas through the National Negro Congress (NNC). The JCNR lobbied for twenty-six national associations, including the NAACP, but not the NUL.[11]

Of the three organizations, the NAACP had access to the most resources and exercised the greatest clout with Congress and the Roosevelt administration. Unlike that of the NUL, the NAACP's national office—which was located in New York City and in September 1935 employed sixteen people, including two professional women—wielded substantial control over its branches. Throughout its history, the national office had maintained that it was "the expositor of policy, with local branches as instruments of action";

this enabled it to generate a more unified approach to the issues than the NUL.[12] Also, the NAACP benefited from a more solid funding base than the other two organizations, as 80 percent of its budget was provided through membership dues.[13] The Urban League depended on white philanthropy, and the JCNR received half of its budget from the NAACP.

The NAACP had developed relationships with Congress and the administration through its executive secretary and chief Washington lobbyist, Walter White. Still, White's position in the nation's capital was always tenuous. Born in Atlanta in 1893 and raised in a middle-class home on the border of segregated white and African American neighborhoods, he had been named James Weldon Johnson's successor after over a decade as assistant secretary in the NAACP's national office. White was a "pale-skinned, blue-eyed, blond black man" whose ability to pass for white enabled him to make a name for himself investigating lynchings in the South during the 1910s and 1920s.[14]

He enjoyed limited access in Washington, and even that was always circumscribed by race. White had particular influence with Eleanor Roosevelt, who enabled him to meet with FDR several times. He trusted the first lady and Louis Howe, the president's personal assistant, and engaged in regular correspondence with FDR's staff after 1932. He had the ear of Senator Edward P. Costigan and his staff, especially Costigan's secretary Lee Johnson, and used Costigan's office as a base camp at the capitol to send telegrams, write letters, and receive messages. White had also developed contacts with "Negro Advisers" in the DOI, AAA, and other federal departments.[15]

In recent years Walter White had led the NAACP to legislative victories. The greatest of these was the successful fight in 1930 to prevent the nomination to the U.S. Supreme Court of Judge John J. Parker, of North Carolina, who had made public racist statements and denounced black suffrage "a source of evil and danger." The outcome of this battle reflected its importance to the NAACP, as well as the association's growing influence in Washington. The *Christian Science Monitor* called this triumph "[t]he first national demonstration of the Negro's power since Reconstruction days." W. E. B. Du Bois wrote that, after careful review of all the facts, he believed that the vote defeating the Parker nomination "was due more to the influence of the Negro than to any other single factor."[16]

Still, the NAACP's position was never secure. In a virtually all-white professional environment, where African Americans typically ran elevators, pushed brooms, or served food, and where lobbyists for organizations with little political pressure were virtually invisible, African American lobbyists faced the constant possibility of insult and disregard. Charles Houston, legal counsel for the NAACP, expressed anger and frustration when, while denying him and his colleagues an appointment with the president, a White House staffer referred to them as "boys." "Negro" lobbyists were easily ignored and had little or no recourse.[17]

These lobbyists were always dependent on the goodwill of their white supporters, because they teetered on the brink of offending by seeming too "aggressive" or "arrogant." This problem surfaced in the NAACP's campaign to integrate the Senate and House cafeterias. The association pursued legal redress on behalf of men and women who had been refused service or in other ways had suffered discrimination. After Representative Oscar DePriest, an African American, was denied service in the House cafeteria when he tried to host a darker-skinned companion, Walter White introduced a House resolution to integrate the cafeterias. The NAACP then mobilized its branch offices in an attempt to get the resolution passed.[18] Steven Early of the Democratic National Committee tried to use White's involvement in the cafeteria issue to undermine his standing with Eleanor Roosevelt. Early was frequently irritated by what he considered to be White's insulting lack of appropriate deference toward the president. He told the first lady's personal secretary, Malvina Scheider, that he had been "advised" that it was White who "went into the restaurant within the Capitol Building and demanded that he be served, apparently deliberately creating a troublesome scene." Early said that "[t]he belief in some quarters is that he did this for publicity purposes and to arouse negroes throughout the country through press accounts of his eviction from the Capitol," and that he was known to be "one of the worst and most continuous of troublemakers."[19]

Eleanor Roosevelt defended White, saying that she knew him well, that he was a "fine person, with the sorrows of his people close to his heart." Yet her answer also revealed the shaky ground on which he stood: "I do not think he means to be rude or insulting. It is the same complex which a great many people belonging to minority groups have, particularly martyrs." The first lady suggested that "the type of thing that would make him get himself arrested in the Senate restaurant" was "an inferiority complex which he tries to combat and which makes him far more aggressive than if he felt equality. It is worse with Walter White because he is almost white."[20] Like other "Negroes," White could not be seen, even by his "white" friends, outside of the box in which he was trapped by his racial identity.

But Walter White was not just contained within the borders defined by the dominant society. He and other African Americans defined for themselves the meaning of race, what it meant to be "Negro" or "white." Unlike white policy-making circles, black and interracial organizations had no choice but to work to understand the meaning of race, and that thinking influenced all of their organizational goals and strategies. To comprehend the involvement of these groups in the Social Security Act, therefore, it is necessary to appreciate their different understandings of the meaning and significance of "race."

Race, Class, and Integration

The three black or interracial groups that lobbied Washington in 1935 expressed very different ideas about the meaning of race, the specifics of what racial justice might look like, and the best means of achieving equality. The miniscule staff of the JCNR did not even share a perspective internally. George Haynes argued that issues that inordinately affected African Americans were race issues, regardless of intent. He was inclined to promote "Negro unity," arguing for "group solidarity which requires group consciousness of internal worth and perception of values in Negro life and experience."[21] On the other hand, John Davis and Ralph Bunche saw class as the primary social hierarchy. Davis believed, in the words of a contemporary, that "the superexploitation of Negroes" arose from "economic and not racial causes," and he sought to promote solidarity among all workers.[22] Davis and Bunche envisioned, not the assimilation of black people into white society, but a revolutionary dismantling of the social and economic hierarchy, because, they contended, racial prejudice did not result from ignorance or retarded development, but from economic exploitation. For a brief period Haynes, Davis, and Bunche found common ground, though their differences did not sustain the JCNR much beyond the passage of the Social Security Act.

Notwithstanding their differences, Davis and Haynes were extremely critical of the New Deal, discerning a link between its discriminatory policy and the racial and class interests of the Roosevelt administration. Davis regarded the New Deal as a "middle class attempt to reconcile conflicting class interests of capitalists and workers." Bunche believed that it could do little for African Americans "within the existing social structure."[23] Though this was not Haynes's view, he did share with Davis an identification with lower-class African Americans. This common ground enabled them to work together in their challenge to discrimination in the Social Security Act.

The position of the National Urban League in the mid-1930s deviated both from that of the JCNR and from the NUL's historical position. Under the new leadership of T. Arnold Hill, the NUL determined to join the efforts of the most segregated African Americans—those who moved between work in segregated shops or occupations, homes in segregated neighborhoods, and segregated churches—in opposing discrimination. The league thus turned to the "Negro masses" to accomplish change, rather than the white liberals and philanthropists on whom it was financially dependent.

But the perspective that had the most potential to influence the Social Security Act was that of the NAACP. The first thing to recognize about the association's identity was that it considered itself more radical on the issue of racial justice than other organizations: it fought for nothing less than a guarantee of the legal rights of African Americans as citizens. William Pickens said that concern for day-to-day living was the "business of Howard University, of Tuskegee Institute, of the colored Masons, of the Colored Women's Clubs, of the Negro Baptist Church, of the Negro Hotel, of the Negro card party, of the Negro family." The role of the NAACP, he said, was to seek the "ultimate goal of unqualified equality."[24]

The most important thing to understand about the *racial* identity of the national office and board of the NAACP in the mid-1930s was that it was interracial. For many of its white and black members, the mere existence of the association served the cause of civil rights through its embodiment of an integrationist philosophy. They viewed segregation as the root problem of the "Negro condition" in America; African Americans had undergone "spiritual atrophy" from being cut off as a separate race from the rest of American society.[25] The interracial identity of the NAACP's national office and board was primarily influenced by those of its members, including Walter White, who represented what David Levering Lewis has called "extreme cultural assimilationism." The ultimate consequence of this approach, for the small group of African American and Jewish political elite who adhered to it, was the "abandonment of [racial] identity."[26]

Maintaining the association's interracial identity was very important to some of its white members, especially in the mid-1930s. As Mary White Ovington remembered, at the NAACP's founding in 1909 "the number of white and colored was about even," but by the time of its 1935 annual conference, "Negro members" had taken over the branches and "whites are not one in a hundred." She claimed that "[o]nly at the meetings of the Board do we have decisions that represent interracial discussion." She appealed to the largely African American membership: "You don't want to be segregated. You want to be Americans. . . . How is it possible to get this except you win the whites to your cause?"[27] At the same conference, Joel Spingarn claimed that white members of the NAACP "were men and women who have gone out and fought the battle side by side with their colored brothers, taking all the chances." Although African American listeners may have winced as he likened the insults he had suffered to theirs (being walked out on as he spoke, being refused a place on a conference program), he clearly did not feel that his whiteness prevented him from doing the core work of the association.[28]

Many white members of the NAACP, including Spingarn, were Jewish, and this was important to their commitment to interracialism. Hasia Diner has argued that during the twenties and thirties "two of the most blatantly anti-Semitic decades in American history," Jewish identity was constructed, in part, through identification with black Americans. "[T]he imagery of Black life . . . resonated to Jews as Jews." This resonance stemmed from common enemies and discrimination, and a shared vulnerability in a racist white Protestant country. Jewish interest in African Americans intensified following the lynching in Atlanta of Leo Frank, a northern middle-class Jew. Jewish philanthropists gave generously to the NAACP as well as provided legal talent; much of the work of the NAACP and the NUL would not have been possible without this support. Jews might easily have sought to elevate themselves through differentiation from African Americans; instead, many Jews used much of their own limited clout and resources to express solidarity with them.[29]

The interracial identity of the NAACP was also important to some of its African American leadership. This was especially true for Walter White, one of the most ardent believers in cultural assimilation.[30] Necessarily embedded in the concept is an understanding of the relative value of blackness and whiteness. Assimilationists understood race through the contemporary developmental discourses that treated the category "Negro" as inferior. They sought to move African Americans up and away from that category into a race-free society, which meant a white society that did not acknowledge racial difference.

The goal of assimilation was obviously affected by the literal color of a person's skin and other physical features that suggested ancestry; whether for the length of a train ride or for a lifetime, the category "Negro" might, literally, be escaped by some but not others. Skin tone mattered to African Americans, though in different ways depending on gender, region, and class. Gunnar Myrdal observed that "many individual Negroes will be found, when speaking about themselves, to rate their own color lighter than it actually is, but practically none to rate it darker." African American women supported a huge industry for products to straighten hair. Myrdal reported that lighter-skinned women were highly valued by black men, which is why, he suggested, fewer women passed than men.[31]

Skin color was a factor in NAACP internal political and personal dynamics as well. Many felt that Walter White's ability to pass for white (ironically signified by his name) intensified his interest in assimilation and resistance to race pride and identification. This perception hampered his leadership. Joel Spingarn asked White to move cautiously in his defense of the integrationist policy of the NAACP, "suggesting . . . that you realize that hundreds of Negroes think you are really a white man whose natural desire is to associate with white men."[32] W. E. B. Du Bois made a more subtle argument, recognizing race as an identity not fixed and essential: White's understanding of the meaning of race, he wrote, was inevitably a product of his *positioning*, often, as white. According to Du Bois: "Walter White is white. He has more white companions and friends than colored. He goes where he will in New York City and naturally meets no Color Line, for the simple and sufficient reason that he isn't 'colored.' . . . It naturally makes Mr. White an extreme opponent of any segregation based on a myth of race."[33]

White responded to Spingarn's concern by asserting that if the accusations were true, he could easily have "stopped living as a Negro and passed as white when I could associate exclusively with white people. As you know, I choose my friends and associates, particularly the former, not on the basis of their race but wholly on mutual points of interest."[34] But his words supported Du Bois's point. White's 'whiteness' meant that he could *choose* whether or not to consider race a "mutual point of interest."

Assimilationists like White focused solely on racial inequality and did not challenge the U.S. class structure. Their goal was assimilation by class

— middle-class blacks absorbed into middle-class jobs and neighborhoods, for example. But that focus created painful gaps in understanding between them and many African Americans who were not easily assimilatable. The NAACP had to deal with the perception of many blacks that the association was a "hightoned" organization that existed primarily for the benefit of "upper class Negroes."[35] But even as the NAACP sought to rebuke such perceptions, it revealed a lack of identification with the African American working class. In a draft article titled "Is the NAACP Highbrow?" which attempted to address these charges, the authors contended that the association was not out of touch with the "masses," though they had difficulty determining how the "masses" would want to be referred to. The first draft used the word "common" repeatedly to describe the target audience, but others expressed concern that this would be offensive. Roy Wilkins and George Bagnall suggested that "ordinary" or "plain" be substituted; none of the NAACP staffers who worked on the piece seemed comfortable talking about and to the African American working class. All of the examples given in a memo arguing that the NAACP was not highbrow involved its work on behalf of "the friendless, the poor and the helpless," juxtaposing them to the professional class. The piece spoke a language of paternalism, not collective, joint action by the association and working-class organizations and individuals. At least two board members approved a final draft of the article. Bagnall said that if it was used as a pamphlet, it would need to be condensed because the "masses will not read a solid type article of this length."[36]

Both its integrationist philosophy and middle- and upper-class culture created distance between the NAACP and the "Negro" Church, which constituted the primary mass organization of the nation's African Americans.[37] The Reverend J. Raymond Henderson urged these disparate groups to recognize their common missions. He said that the church was an organized, potentially willing mass of activists who just needed to be educated about the association's program, but who regarded NAACP "officials" as "being a cloistered lot, caring only for the fat salaries, the society of the literate, and atheistic because they do not regularly appear in their Sunday congregations." NAACP leaders had not shown support for the "Negro" Church and did not attend services themselves because "the minister has nothing to tell them."[38] Beneath the divide between the NAACP and the church was a deeper schism over the "voluntary segregation" practiced by the "Negro" Church and other organizations of working-class African Americans and the assimilationist practices of the NAACP. Walter White argued that segregation of all kinds "perpetuates and increases" the "chasm of misunderstanding, of suspicion, of hostility" and delayed solving the "race problem."[39] He believed that as individuals and groups developed—black and white alike—they would come to see the fallacy of the color bar and would be drawn to greater integration.

In the minds of the NAACP leaders, nothing undermined integration as much as the illegal practice of lynching, and passage of a federal antilynching bill was their highest legislative priority. The association drafted the Costigan-Wagner Bill, an antilynching measure that would have allowed federal investigation and prosecution of lynching when local and state governments refused to act. Walter White doggedly pursued members of Congress to vote for this bill; indeed, counting votes and distributing evidence of congressional support consumed much of his time in Washington. And White used his precious few minutes with the president and the first lady to lobby on behalf of it. While the Social Security Act was under consideration, the NAACP sent an antilynching memorandum to FDR and to every governor, 229 mayors, 231 university and college presidents, and roughly 1,000 others, including religious leaders, heads of women's clubs, judges, and editors. It also sponsored a traveling exhibit of photographs depicting lynching in all its graphic horror, which reached more than 2,000 people in seventeen cities. In addition, the NAACP held mass meetings on lynching and distributed pamphlets, one that showed a young white mother holding a little girl up to witness a hanging over the heads of the crowd, the caption reading "Her First Lynching."[40]

The antilynching campaign was not only consistent with the association's philosophy but also emotionally effective, thus generating support for the NAACP. It was especially useful in gaining the advocacy of Jewish philanthropists. White privately told one donor that a provision had been slipped into the proposed legislation to allow the prosecution of vandalism and other crimes directed against Jewish communities. He said, "We are giving no publicity to this, because it would stir up all of the Fascist groups. However, we have in mind reaching through the Costigan-Wagner Bill Fascists, anti-Semitic, anti-Catholic and other repressive groups."[41] The campaign was more broadly effective with northern liberals who may not have recognized or acknowledged racial segregation and discrimination in their own backyards (and in many of their kitchens) but were affected by photographs of charred bodies and bloodthirsty mobs. Lynching had become a modern spectacle by the 1920s, as postcards and remnants of such executions were sold as souvenirs, and the NAACP made use of this popular interest. The association knew that the existing federal code was sufficient to permit federal intervention in state and local responses to lynchings, and so the Costigan-Wagner Bill was technically unnecessary. But even if the measure did not pass, it was worthwhile merely for the purpose of "raising hell."[42]

Although the Costigan-Wagner Bill was the NAACP's highest legislative priority, most African Americans did little to promote it. Walter White noted that "[m]ost of the volunteer lobbying done at Washington was done by white people, only a few colored people, even in Washington, being interested enough to help." This lack of visibility made it hard to use the "political threat of revolt by Negro voters against senators who did not persistently and faithfully fight the [southern antilynching bill] filibuster to the limit."[43] Further, the antilynching fight did not generate financial contributions by NAACP members. Interest was transitory and unpredictable, even though African Americans of all classes had access to information about the Costigan-Wagner Bill through the black press, which White claimed gave ample and "unparalleled support" to the proposed legislation and to the "significance of the fight." One cannot overstate the historical significance of lynching to the economic oppression of African Americans in the South and to their psychological oppression throughout the country. But in 1934 fifteen people were lynched, compared to the millions of blacks facing job discrimination, poverty, and insecurity. To many, lynching may not have seemed to be the most pressing concern.[44]

But the NAACP's campaign had a purpose beyond the actual battle against lynching. It sought to use the issue to create an alliance of the educated, liberal classes and in doing so to dissolve the line dividing black from white and North from South. The association passionately argued that lynching was no longer an issue of race or region: "No longer can the rest of the country point the finger of scorn at the South. . . . Forty-four white persons have been lynched since 1919. . . . Lynching, therefore, is no longer confined to Negroes."[45] On one level, deemphasizing race was a strategic move, because the lynching of whites generated more financial support than did the lynching of African Americans. Walter White told John D. Rockefeller that fund-raising was difficult, though lynchings had been increasing, "due to the fact that all of the seventeen victims (this year) have been colored. . . . The fact that no white people have been lynched this year and that most of the lynchings of Negroes have not been spectacular ones results in there not being much general interest or indignation."[46] But on another level, as Roy Wilkins said in a memo to White, "the whole strategy [for the Costigan-Wagner Bill] was to remove the campaign from a racial basis, and most particularly to remove it (in the publicity at least) from the direct sponsorship of the Association."[47]

In White's view, progressive, enlightened southerners were natural allies of the NAACP, and he worked tirelessly to build alliances with them.[48] Liberal southerners, such as Jesse Daniel Ames of the Association of Southern Women for the Prevention of Lynching and Will Alexander of the Committee for Interracial Cooperation, had been waging their own fight against lynching, but they steadfastly refused to support legislation that would allow federal intervention. Southern liberals typically expressed "disdain" for the NAACP and Walter White, viewing them, in the words of Howard Odem, as a well-meaning but "unscientific agitation agency that did more harm than good."[49]

But White persisted. He maintained that lynching was no longer about race or region but a common problem for all enlightened people, because he rested his hopes on building that relationship. Like John Commons, NAACP leaders believed that some groups were more civilized than others. Unlike Commons, however, they insisted that civilization was not a function of race.[50] Whites and blacks had their lower and higher elements, and racism was caused by the lower elements of both races. To end racial injustice, society would have to educate those lower elements, to teach lower-class blacks to have self-esteem and stop confirming racist stereotypes, and lower-class whites to become tolerant and civilized. In fact, lower-class *southern* whites represented the most undeveloped stage of "emotional and mental retardation limited to racial prejudice."[51] White was "heartened" by the "swiftness of the growth" of feeling against prejudice and bigotry among younger southern whites; within "a few years" they would "replace in positions of power the narrow, and bigoted older generation who have fattened on race hatred and bigotry."[52] Racial hierarchy would be eradicated, not by assaulting its economic base, but by educating and civilizing white southerners.

Lynch mobs provided the NAACP with its best evidence that lower-class whites were the least evolved constituency in America. The association described lynch mobs using the same primitive, sexualized stereotypes employed more generally throughout the country to depict African Americans. In reality, white people of all classes supported or participated in lynching, for a variety of political, psychological, and economic reasons. From the time of Reconstruction, lynch victims tended to be, not black males accused of raping white women, as commonly assumed, but African American men who owned property or businesses, or in other ways challenged the economic injustice of racial hierarchy. To the NAACP, lynch mobs consisted of lower-class whites who were driven by primitive impulses like lust and sadism. An article in *The Crisis* described lynching as a sexual perversion, a form of "lust murders" seen only in uncivilized peoples. "One is forced to conclude that a large section of our southern whites are nothing but primitive sadists forever lurking for new victims."[53]

This offers one explanation for the NAACP's conflict with Communist organizations during this period. Communist circles were among the few white-dominated spaces where race was discussed.[54] With the advent of its Popular Front position, the Communist Party called for "self-determination for Blacks in states where they were the majority," as well as "anti-lynching, anti-Jim Crowism, trade unionism, Black and white workers' unity, and anti-fascism and anti-imperialism."[55] Lenin went beyond the position of the Socialist Party that the "Negro question is a pure labor question"; he considered black America to be a colony, a "subject nation" that pivoted on the southern sharecropper.[56] In March 1935 the Communist Party organized the Provisional Committee for Defense of Ethiopia in New York City led by the League of Struggle for Negro Rights. Ethiopia, the "last remaining independent Negro country in Africa," was, according to the *Daily Worker*, held as the "haven of the oppressed Negroes throughout the world."[57]

In spite of the close attention that Communists paid to racial hierarchy, middle-class African Americans usually rejected their overtures for collaboration, fearing that the ultimate goal of Communist organizing was to replace the rule of upper-class whites with that of the lower classes. This sentiment was expressed in a NAACP poll of the leading editors of the country's black press.[58] Though somewhat sympathetic, William Kelley, editor of the *Amsterdam News*, expressed concern that communism would bring "dictatorship under a propertyless white proletariat . . . the same ignorant white working class which forms the backbone of every lynching mob."[59]

The NAACP's commitment to class-based assimilation had recently been reaffirmed through a crisis that led to the departure of W. E. B. Du

Bois from the association. The crisis was initiated by Du Bois's advocacy, in early 1934, of "voluntary segregation." This stand has typically been viewed as an aberration, a departure from his life's work to that point. But from another angle, it was entirely consistent—a challenge to the association's professional-class, assimilationist identity. He disrupted the impossible paradox of "two-ness" that he himself had articulated in *The Souls of Black Folk* (1903), the divided identity of African Americans, by acknowledging the fractured meaning of both "American" and "Negro."

The fight was instigated by an editorial written by Du Bois that appeared in the January 1934 issue of *The Crisis*. Here he argued that African Americans considered "voluntary segregation" as an alternative to either acquiescing to segregation imposed from above or seeking integration into a rejecting white society. "Negro" people should seize control to the extent that they were capable and turn toward union with one another for empowerment. The editorial provoked an immediate and outraged response from the NAACP leadership. Walter White in particular frantically worked to dissuade the board and the reading public from taking the commentary seriously. He wrote: "If the Association's attitude is not one of opposition to segregation, then I have misinterpreted it for nearly twenty years."[60] A struggle for control of the NAACP ensued, ending with Du Bois's resignation in June 1934.[61]

In the mid-1930s the word "segregation" had connotations, not generally associated with Du Bois, of political conservatism, which was at odds with both the NAACP's more radical constitutional focus and the emerging liberal colorblind consensus. Though by this time African American intellectuals had begun to grapple with the concept of racial *separatism*, the word "segregation" was never used in this context.[62] Among blacks, the word signified Booker T. Washington's accommodationist strategy, which accepted inferior treatment in exchange for limited economic opportunities. William Hastie declared: "For fifty years prejudiced white men and abject, boot-licking, gut-lacking, knee-bending, favor-seeking Negroes have been insulting our intelligence with a tale that goes like this: Segregation is not an evil. Negroes are better off by themselves." Even if segregation led to better conditions for African American people, it was still too great an insult to bear: "A man does not resent being spit upon because saliva does him bodily harm." Hastie likened Du Bois's position to "the safe but overcrowded 'amen' corner with 'good,' 'sound,' 'conservative' Negroes."[63]

Despite the heat in Hastie's charge, Du Bois's challenge fundamentally differed from Booker T. Washington's brand of accommodation. Washington accepted the fact of the U.S. class structure and sought to integrate African Americans into its bottom rungs, positioning themselves to eventually move up within it. Du Bois, on the other hand, called on African Americans to reject this hierarchy. He argued that the combination of "outside pressure and a lack of social control within the race compels a class structure among Negroes which tend[s] to copy that among the whites."[64] If any real progress was to be made in establishing racial equality, the opposing class interests of different groups of African Americans had to be broken down. Those class divisions, Du Bois maintained, rested on a fundamental acceptance of the inferiority of the "Negro" identity that blacks sought to escape through "rising."

In a flurry of subsequent editorials, Du Bois attacked the NAACP leadership for inconsistency regarding segregation, contending that its integrationist philosophy served professional African Americans but not the lower classes. The association treated as a necessary evil, and did not protest, segregation in universities or hospitals, for example, which provided many black professionals with a livelihood; instead, it focused on hotels, theaters, restaurants, and transportation facilities, sites of employment for the African American working class. In light of the critical situation caused by the depression, Du Bois sought to concentrate resources in a way that would economically benefit lower- as well as upper-class African Americans.[65]

He also charged the NAACP leadership, in effect, with internalized racism. The "Negro" identity had been so indelibly linked with slavery that "there grew up in the minds of the free Negro class a determination and a prejudice which has come down to our day. They fought bitterly with every means at their command against being classed with the mass of slaves."[66] A rejection of "segregation" might mean "utter lack of faith of Negroes in Negroes, and the desire to escape into another group, shirking, on the other hand, all responsibility for ignorance, degradation and lack of experience among Negroes, while asking admission into the other group on terms of full equality and with [a] full chance for individual development."[67] Du Bois sought to challenge the widespread understanding among the black middle class that its responsibility was to "lift' the lower classes "as we rise," to educate and ultimately help lower classes to assimilate. This philosophy of uplift reinforced the division of African Americans who were better able to assimilate from others who, because of skin color, occupation, and region, were not. He called for a repudiation of uplift and challenged the ways that the approach worked to divide African Americans at the expense of the lower classes. He called for the "Negro" people to love themselves and each other, and for those who had the benefits of "uplift" to turn around and embrace those who did not.[68]

The urgency of his argument stemmed from a concern about two things: the immediate and deteriorating economic situation of most African Americans, and the inferior place that the New Deal was establishing for them in the economic order. Du Bois was convinced that all NAACP efforts should focus on economic issues.[69] He said: "Economically, the Negro is on the whole losing ground. This is partly due to the current depression, but more especially due to the fact that the present organization of industry is changing, and while the Negro had an insecure place in the former organization, he has a much more questionable place in the new organization which seems to be coming."[70] Forced segregation complicated this picture, because its purpose, "confessed or semiconscious," was "to so isolate the Negro that he will be spiritually bankrupt, physically degenerate [*sic*], and economically dependent."[71] He suggested that such economic dependence was being solidified by the New Deal, and it could be fought only by "economic co-operation carried out by Negroes of education and intelligence who regard their education not simply as an open sesame to a privileged position, but as [the] means of a service to a disfranchised and disinherited group of workers."[72]

Du Bois's analysis offered a radical interrogation of the operation of racist segregation. But it also represented a desperate, heavy-hearted concession to it. His proposal for voluntary segregation sought to rally support for black inclusion in New Deal largesse, even if granted on a "separate but equal" basis. During those critical months when the blueprints for the American welfare state were being drawn, the issue of equal *distribution* of federal assistance was considered to be separate from whether funding would be provided through segregated institutions. Du Bois believed that securing proportional funding for African Americans was the highest priority.[73] He was persuaded "from wide knowledge of present conditions throughout every part of this country that unless the Negro unites for the intelligent guidance of his economic and industrial interests, he is going to be left out of the New Deal and the future re-organization of society. This is no pipe dream. I know what I am talking about."[74] William

Pickens wrote that there were "thousands of evidences of the truth" of Du Bois's argument about segregation. Referring to the National Recovery Act, which had included unequal wage scales for African American and white workers, Pickens asserted: "I find that the NRA is the greatest robbery against colored people's rights and property in my life time. . . . [I]t is clear: That better organization on the part of colored people themselves, and more cohesion in their own ranks, would have prevented millions of dollars of this robbery from being taken from them, and would have made much of the accomplished injustice impossible."[75] Du Bois wondered, "[A]re we going to stand out and refuse the inevitable and inescapable government aid because we first wish to abolish the Color Line? This is not simply tilting at windmills; it is, if we are not careful, committing race suicide."[76]

One of the issues to which Du Bois undoubtedly referred was a pending administrative decision about whether to allow Homestead Subsistence projects—that is, rural housing communities—to be created on a segregated basis. Southerners in Congress fought against integrating the projects (and, in fact, they used Du Bois's promotion of voluntary segregation in their defense).[77] The NAACP, however, opposed the establishment of separate projects for African American families, jeopardizing their receipt of any government aid. The association gathered its strongest allies, including John Hope of Emory University, Charles Johnson of Fisk University, Dr. Mordecai W. Johnson of Howard University, and Crystal Byrd Fauset of the Quaker Committee on Race Relations, and spent nearly three hours convincing Eleanor Roosevelt not to support the creation of "Negro projects" on a segregated basis.[78]

Du Bois lost the fight over the direction of NAACP, and that outcome determined the relationship of the association to the Social Security Act. The African Americans most affected by the Act were the sharecroppers, tenant farmers, domestic workers, and unskilled laborers who made up the "Negro" working class, those who lived segregated lives, and so the class conflict within the NAACP would bear heavily on its position on the Act.

THE NAACP, NUL, AND JCNR all had different perspectives on race, ranging from Marxist class analysis to assimilation. One might think that, especially for the NAACP, the inclusion of African American workers in the Social Security Act could not compete with existing priorities; it was less clearly defined as racially motivated, less dramatic, harder to capture in a photographic exhibit. Budgets were tight and hard choices had to be made. Yet, regardless of their thinly stretched budgets, overworked staffs, and the plethora of issues that required their attention, all three organizations considered the inclusion of African American workers in the Social Security Act to be of great importance and all three became involved in the Act's development. Regardless of their differences, all three organizations saw in Social Security an opportunity to advance their larger agendas.

The Social Security Act

For different reasons, the NAACP, NUL, and JCNR all had to stretch beyond their established agendas to battle discrimination in the Social Security Act. The JCNR tended to focus on programs created in the first round of New Deal legislation and had its hands full fighting discriminatory National Recovery Administration (NRA) codes and wage scales. Before 1935 it had not paid much attention to agricultural or domestic workers, concentrating instead on the rights of African American industrial workers. Also, the small size of its staff ensured that any project taken on would displace an equally pressing issue.

But the JCNR board saw in the Social Security Act an opportunity to extend its critique of New Deal discrimination into a new arena: social welfare. Through its mere existence, the Joint Committee trumpeted the fact that not just southern states but also the liberal federal government created discriminatory public policy, and the Act enabled it to further develop that claim. But the decisive factor in the JCNR's decision to become involved in the fight was the passionate interest of board chairman George Edmund Haynes.

Haynes was of an older generation of activists than Davis and Weaver; he was an original member of the NAACP and cofounded the forerunner of the NUL, the Committee on Urban Conditions among Negroes. He later became the first executive director of the NUL (1910–17). Since 1921 he had been executive director of the Department of Race Relations of the Federal Council of Churches in Christ. His wife, Elizabeth Ross, was the first African American national secretary of the YWCA. Because of his commitment to cooperation with white organizations and the education of white America to overcome prejudice, some have described Haynes as "old school." Yet one biographer argues that he was much more complex and visionary than his conservative label suggests. This view paints a picture

Through the Social Security Act, African American and white workers were segregated into different tiers. John Commons, the "spiritual father" of the Act, believed that America's future rested on its ability to protect the character and independence of white male industrial workers such as these. (National Archives)

One of many cartoons produced by the Social Security Board to generate support for UI by contrasting it with negative images of welfare. This cartoon suggests that welfare programs, but not UI, posed a financial burden on society, masking the fact that the cost of UI was footed by the American public through increased prices. (National Archives)

opposite page
African American men, such as these waiting for work in an employment office around 1930, were denied UI and OAI and funneled into welfare. (National Archives)

Recipients of welfare programs like OAA were typically shown in promotional photographs with heads bowed, in postures that signified dependent need. In this photograph, Governor Chandler of Kentucky presents the state's first OAA checks to needy citizens, August 24, 1936. (National Archives)

opposite page
This advertisement, one of a number produced by the Social Security Board to promote OAI (Social Security), is typical in that it depicts an OAI recipient as proud and independent. (National Archives)

Under the Social Security Act, families headed by women were divided on the basis of race. White mothers and children who met the standards of the "worthy widow" provision were far more likely to receive aid from the ADC program than African American mothers and children. (National Archives)

As President Roosevelt signs the Social Security Act on August 14, 1935, he is surrounded by Democratic Party supporters. The two men on the far left are Rep. Robert Doughton (D-NC) and Rep. Frank Buck (D-NY). Sen. Robert Wagner (D-NY) is standing immediately to Roosevelt's right. To his left, in the white suit, is Sen. Robert La Follette Jr. (Progressive-WI), and directly behind him is Frances Perkins. To her left is Sen. Pat Harrison (D-MS), Sen. William King (D-UT), Rep. John Boehne Jr. (D-IN), Rep. David Lewis (D-MD), Sen. Joseph Guffey (D-PA), and Sen. Alben Barkley (D-KY). (National Archives)

of a man who compromised with white society for strategic reasons but who was firmly committed to organizing African American people for the purpose of demanding their civil and economic rights.[79]

Haynes offered the most direct, incisive assault on the argument that exclusion of African Americans from the Social Security Act was necessitated by "administrative difficulties" by pointing to the larger racial hierarchies through which "administrative difficulties" were constructed. Soon after FDR's bill was introduced, Haynes submitted a twenty-page memorandum to the Senate itemizing ways that the bill discriminated and proposed amendments to most sections. He wrote to members of the House and Senate, issued a press release urging African Americans to contact their representatives, and apparently also sent out a mass mailing.[80]

In his testimony before the House and Senate fiscal committees on the original CES bill, Haynes argued that the discriminatory features of the Act could be eliminated through language that ensured equal distribution of federal money, and that conditioned receipt of federal money on the equitable administration of programs by state governments. He gave many examples to back up his claim that without such language, African Americans would not receive an equal share of federal funds, as well as instances where federal antidiscrimination language ensured equal access. His most powerful example was the Morrill-Nelson Fund, which provided relatively equitable funding for colleges across the country, following an 1890 amendment that prevented discriminatory distribution. The Smith-Hughes Act, on the other hand, did not include such language and grossly discriminated in its distribution of vocational education funds: African Americans should have received $2.3 million of the total state and federal funds according to their percentage of the population, but instead got only $78,000. He used these figures to stress that discrimination through state administration was a danger outside of the South.[81]

Haynes also attacked the bill for differentiating between categories of workers, since discrimination ensured that most "Negro" workers were excluded from all but the most vulnerable jobs. For instance, in supporting documents for his congressional testimony he argued that the limitation of UI to employers with four or more employees "affect[s] a larger proportion of Negroes gainfully employed in the United States than any other class." Though he ended the sentence there, in an earlier draft, it continued, "and amounts therefore to racial discrimination, not intentionally I am ready to concede, but practically it works out that way."[82] In addition, he contended that, because "Negro" workers generally earned less money for the same work done by white workers, their UI contributions should be equalized, and employers should pay a greater share for their "Negro" employees so that they could draw the same benefits as their white counterparts.[83]

Haynes's analysis of the Social Security Act recontextualized the bill within the history, not of social welfare or economics in America, nor of administrative issues, but of racial injustice. During his testimony before the House Ways and Means Committee, he framed the Act with a lengthy discourse on the history of legislative discrimination against African Americans rather than the discriminatory aspects of that specific measure. Even after being advised to return to the Act by the acting chair, he continued to speak to the history. When his allotted five minutes was exhausted, and he had not yet discussed the bill, he demanded additional time and threatened to withdraw all support for the Act of the JCNR's member organizations; his demand was granted. In this way, he momentarily seized discursive control of the hearing, insisting that the bill be addressed through the eyes, not of dispassionate technicians or politicians, but of the people against whom it would discriminate.[84]

The JCNR waged a proud fight for inclusion in the Social Security Act, but the battle was cut short by a crisis in the organization's funding base that grew throughout 1935. That crisis resulted from a withdrawal of support of white philanthropists as well as of the NAACP. The JCNR had been established with a start-up grant from the Rosenwald Fund, which continued to pay John Davis's salary until 1934. At that time, funding was discontinued, which left the Joint Committee dependent on the contributions of its member organizations, of which the NAACP was by far the largest.[85]

But the NAACP became engulfed in a growing swell of concern about Davis's leftist politics, and Haynes's fight against discrimination in the Social Security Act was a casualty of that fear. The association had begun to lose sponsors because of its endorsement of the JCNR, and NAACP board members, especially Frances Williams of the YWCA, concluded that Davis should either be reigned in or cut out. Walter White began to circulate rumors that Davis was angling to turn the organization "over to the Communists" in order to undermine support for the JCNR among black leaders.[86] Despite evidence of continued backing by other NAACP leaders, funding was eventually eliminated.[87] The JCNR, minus Haynes, quickly reorganized as the National Negro Congress, which openly promoted a leftist political agenda.

The National Urban League had a larger leap to make than the JCNR: it had no lobbying agenda in Washington before the mid-1930s and had shown virtually no interest in federal policy-making. But it became involved in the Social Security Act as a part of a larger change in the NUL's philosophy and mission that occurred in 1934 and 1935. Eugene Kinckle Jones had led the league for many years, and his departure to a well-paid position with the Department of Commerce in 1934 reflected the traditional NUL strategy that prioritized gaining access to administrative jobs. Under Jones's leadership, the National Urban League had played a conservative role as a "diplomatic go-between, operating behind the scenes and speaking in public in polite terms, if at all, while it met in offices and council rooms with the power structure to open new opportunities to Black workers."[88] But under the leadership of T. Arnold Hill, the NUL briefly departed from its more accommodating approach and moved into the organization of African American labor. Hill set out to change common perceptions that the New Deal was not an "Urban League program."[89] The league began openly critiquing New Deal programs, especially the Civilian Conservation Corp, the Public Works Administration, and the Federal Emergency Relief Administration (FERA), and lobbying the federal government for equal treatment for African Americans. The NUL's first priority in 1935 was relief for the unemployed.[90]

But Hill's vision reached beyond lobbying; he believed that equal treatment could be achieved only through organized pressure. Under his leadership, the league took steps to transform a fledgling network of NUL-sponsored Emergency Advisory Councils (EACS) into a mass movement. In 1933 it created EACS to respond to local discrimination through FERA. The EACS operated through 201 local councils that were formed to ensure that African Americans were getting their share of relief and jobs through public works. Hill saw in EACS an opportunity to create a movement that would make African Americans "a potent force for national and racial development."[91]

A second prong of Hill's strategy was the organization of African American workers through a federation of all black labor unions, which broke with the former league strategy of seeking inclusion through the AFL. This move was made in the face of a growing awareness that "Negroes" would be left out of the new society created by the New Deal *as workers*. Hill said: "The future of Negro workers will be unprotected under any plan without adequate representation of their case. This they have not now in the A F of L nor in the machinery of the NRA. But they do have it among 5,000,000 Negro workers whose organized resistance could not possibly be ignored."[92] Hill realized that this change might alienate some of the NUL's white membership and jeopardize the base of its funding, which was provided mainly by white philanthropy. A third prong of his agenda was to circumvent the white members' influence on the organization by shifting the league's funding base from philanthropy to the "Negro" middle class.

Under Hill, the National Urban League showed a keen understanding of the significance of the Social Security Act to African Americans and took action to address its discriminatory features. Hill was critical of the plan for UI because it left control of the funds in the hands of employers and states, observing: "One has but to remember with what unfairness too many employers have dealt with their Negro workers, and how unsatisfactorily states have administered benefits for Negroes."[93] Hill participated in the president's Conference on Economic Security in November 1934, and the league sent telegrams and letters to policymakers in Washington denouncing the discrimination in the Act.[94]

The priority the NUL's national office and branches assigned the Social Security Act was evidenced by the attention they gave the issue at the league's regional conference, held in Pittsburgh in February 1935. At that meeting, participants were mobilized by a speech in which Reginald Johnson presented a detailed analysis of the merits of the Lundeen Bill over the president's Social Security Act. Central to his argument was the fact that the Lundeen measure covered agricultural and domestic workers. "After considerable discussion," participants voted to endorse the Lundeen Bill. Later that day the endorsement was retracted and replaced with more general language "urging the inclusion of agricultural and domestic workers in the provisions of any unemployment insurance act to be passed by Congress and urging Federal rather than state administration of insurance funds."[95] This appears to have been a compromise solution, though it is unclear who opposed the original endorsement.[96]

The promise of the EACs and workers' councils exceeded their reach; they never generated a mass movement of any size, certainly not one powerful enough to challenge the wide-scale discrimination against African Americans in New Deal programs. The NUL's national office continually expressed concern that EACs were not active. It measured success in small victories: four people employed here, a person appointed there. And although unemployment relief was the NUL's highest priority in 1935, the league did not accomplish much. Its brief list of achievements in that year was topped by the establishment of a "Housekeeper's service" in New York City, where relief funds paid domestics to care for the households of sick housewives, and the maintenance of one lobbyist in Washington for several months.[97]

Hill's hope that this new "militant" approach would expand the funding base of the NUL was not realized. The league's financial problems became desperate; many times it could not meet its payroll and was forced to reduce staff. Much to Hill's chagrin, the African American middle class did not move in to replace the philanthropic support for a program "which they themselves admit is necessary." He blamed the failure of his mass organizing strategy on the middle class's lack of involvement in the needs of black workers. Toward the end of his brief tenure, Hill became "disillusioned" about the potential for real change through mass movements.[98]

In different ways, both the JCNR and the NUL challenged discrimination in the Social Security Act by contesting the larger economic structures through which the Act had been conceived. Both sought to lessen their dependencies on white philanthropy and to create coalitions between the African American working and middle classes. For both, involvement in the Social Security Act was curtailed by diminishing financial support; their agendas were simply too radical. This led to the collapse of the JCNR and a change in the NUL's leadership, which returned to a less proactive position and a diminished involvement in federal policy.

ALTHOUGH THE NAACP had developed a more comprehensive legislative agenda than the National Urban League, under normal circumstances it would not have considered the Social Security Act of primary concern. First, the NAACP's legislative agenda was very narrow and focused almost entirely on achieving a federal antilynching bill. Second, the association had long considered social welfare issues to be within the purview of local governments and charities concerned with establishing neediness, not defending *rights*. It had not become involved in the movement for social welfare and showed no interest in the development of the Social Security Act through the late summer and fall of 1934.[99]

But subsequently the NAACP did take an interest in the Social Security Act. This turnabout resulted from intense pressure from within the membership to become more involved in "economic issues." The term "economic issues" described a spectrum of concerns. It referred to the desperate poverty of lower-class African Americans during the depression and the New Deal services that might more effectively relieve some of the misery if discriminatory features were addressed. It also had more blatantly ideological connotations for those who argued for greater involvement of integrationist organizations in labor organizing, black/white labor unity and/or leftist politics, or even economic separatism. Generally, the term connoted some form of economic organization that would involve the African American working class. Roy Wilkins told Joel Spingarn, NAACP board chairman, that "[a]mong the liberals and radicals, both Negro and white, the impression prevails that the Association is weak because it has no economic program and no economic philosophy." This "clamor" for an economic philosophy came from "isolated places out in the country," including the Cleveland and Columbus branches. "Of course," Wilkins continued, we know that in New York City the overwhelming opinion among "the colored people who think about the Association at all is that it needs more radical economic philosophy."[100]

The challenge to become involved in "economic issues," and specifically in New Deal discrimination, came primarily from an emerging generation of African American academics and organizers, but it expressed a more general consensus that had been developing among "Negroes" of different classes and regions.[101] The importance of the New Deal to African Americans is evident in various interracial conferences, beginning in mid-1933, that emphasized the "primary importance" of New Deal politics.[102] It is seen in the minutes of meetings and conferences of the NAACP and the National Urban League and local branches, the formation of the JCNR and the National Council of Negro Women, in December 1935, the black press, and letters from sharecroppers and other laborers to the president and the first lady.[103] New Deal programs provided many African Americans, for the first time, genuine and substantial federal support through emergency relief, while excluding them from major restructuring of agriculture and industry through discriminatory policies of other major programs like those administered by AAA and NRA. Black leaders understood both the immediate and long-range significance of the New Deal to African Americans of all classes, rural and urban, men and women. They believed that the New Deal was reordering society and would to a large degree determine the place of African Americans within it.[104]

The NAACP was compelled to listen to these voices, because the only potential it had for real power in the legislative arena lay with organized electoral pressure. But the demand was even more immediate. The NAACP had withstood a recent attempt, led by a handful of board members including W. E. B. Du Bois, to democratize its structure and change its focus to economic issues. This movement culminated in a report titled "Future Plans and Programs of the NAACP," referred to as the "Harris Report," written by Abram Harris, an economics professor at Howard University and author of *The Black Worker* (1931), a classic volume.

The Harris Report sought to shift the attention of the NAACP from legal cases to the "real condition of the great mass of Black men." The highest priority of the Association, it asserted, should be "economic issues." This would involve collaboration between branch offices and black churches and interracial agitation around labor issues such as old-age pensions, unemployment insurance, and widows' pensions.[105] Harris agreed with Du Bois that no plan for economic emancipation would succeed until a "Negro intelligentsia" was able to challenge the "political and social values" assigned to the "Negro masses" by white philanthropists and by the NAACP's own leaders Walter White and James Weldon Johnson.[106]

Though it carried Harris's name, the report apparently reflected a wide consensus among a large segment of the association's black leadership. L. B. Granger of the NUL Workers Bureau claimed that "[s]uch a program has been discussed so often by so many persons that it would be difficult for any person or organization to state definitely that he or it was the first to conceive a workable plan."[107] Despite its ultimate rejection by the board in June 1935, it took over the 1935 NAACP Annual Conference, which pivoted around New Deal discrimination.[108]

Both the significance of the Social Security Act and the pressure to expand the NAACP's legislative agenda set the stage for the association's decision to become embroiled in a fight against discrimination in the Act. Yet it did not engage in this fight right away. When the original CES bill was first introduced in Congress in January 1935, the NAACP understood that the measure would create discriminatory policies. Walter White told board chair Spingarn that, if black workers were excluded from the Act, "it would be one of the most severe economic blows the Negro has ever suffered, and would unquestionably create more utter despair than almost anything which could be done."[109] Nevertheless, the NAACP refrained from becoming seriously involved. Its staff analyzed the bill and marked it up for possible amendment. This marked-up copy noted that, although share-croppers were not specifically excluded, they would not be covered by UI or OAI if they were not considered to be "contract labor." The staff added language to the child welfare section requiring federal oversight of funding in "jim crow states" and in other places inserted, "with adequate safeguards against discrimination on account of creed or color."[110] In testimony before the House Ways and Means Committee, Charles Houston said that the bill was discriminatory, but the association did not lobby individual members. Walter White sent a telegram to Senator Robert F. Wagner, the bill's sponsor, with whom White had collaborated on antilynching legislation, and asked for his assurance that the measure contained "adequate safeguards against discrimination on account of race." On the same day White sent a copy of the bill to be reviewed by a lawyer.[111]

The NAACP's reserve changed abruptly, however, following rumors circulating a few weeks later that the House Ways and Means Committee might pass out a bill that was even worse than the CES version. These rumors anticipated Secretary Morganthau's testimony before Ways and Means, in which he suggested that the committee consider specifically excluding agricultural and domestic workers. Shortly before that testimony, White telegraphed Senator Wagner to confirm a report that the administration had agreed to exclude these workers, but there is no record of a reply. This rumor had apparently originated in an Associated Press dispatch on February 2, 1935, stating that the administration was preparing to trim the cost of its economic security bill by excluding farmers, domestics, and casual workers.[112]

The threat that Social Security might exclude domestic and agricultural workers provided the NAACP with what had been lacking: a means to attack the Act without attacking its supporters. The association entered the fight because, initially, it did not accept the explanation that these exclusions were about "trimming costs"; it believed that, instead, they signified the administration's concession to the southern Democrats who controlled Congress. On February 5 Charles Houston sent a frantic wire to Walter White from Washington with the news that the rumor had been verified by Morganthau's testimony, and that this represented a "direct blow at Negro workers and surrender to South."[113] Houston pleaded with White to become involved, and Frances Williams chided White to "get into the thick of the fight on the Economic Security Bill."[114] Roy Wilkins went so far as to suggest that the NAACP consider supporting the radical Lundeen Bill.

White concurred, and a flurry of activity followed, as the association blanketed the capitol with telegrams and letters. In letters to Frances Perkins and Harold Ickes, he referred to "this gross injustice to this large body of helpless workers."[115] At its February 11 meeting, the NAACP board agreed that the association should "put up a strong fight" to get these workers included, and a committee was appointed, under the leadership of William Lloyd Imes, to determine concrete actions that might be taken.[116]

The NAACP received less-than-satisfactory responses from the administration. Arthur Altmeyer replied to White's letter to Frances Perkins, and Edwin Witte answered his telegram to the president. Altmeyer sent only a brief acknowledgment, but Witte claimed that the CES agreed with White that agricultural and domestic workers should be covered by Social Security but had been overruled. Secretary Morganthau sent a slightly longer reply, claiming that he "did not recommend that farmers or any others should be excluded from the benefits of old age pensions" but pointed out the difficulty "at the start of the system" if those workers were included.[117] White was not convinced, and asked John Davis to analyze the letter.[118]

Those who pressured the association to fight for inclusion stressed the opportunity it provided to appeal to the "Negro masses." Frances Williams declared that the proposed legislation was of critical importance because "so much of the NAACP's work has had to be work which directly benefited individuals and only indirectly benefited the Negro group. This situation has led to lack of interest on the part of many Negroes who are not very farsighted. The Act . . . could directly affect a large number of Negroes, and to champion something that involved a large group directly, seems to be strategically important at this time."[119] Williams persuaded YWCA leaders to write detailed letters to both Senator Pat Harrison and Representative Robert Doughton arguing that women would be hard-hit if agricultural and domestic labor were excluded from the Act. The letters identified farmers' wives and daughters and domestic servants as YWCA members. The YWCA was also the only organization other than the NAACP to offer public testimony on behalf of farmers and others left out of OAI. And in a move that was equally unusual, they framed their argument in the context of *racial* discrimination, calling for "provisions against discrimination on account of race, creed or color in the administration of all benefits."[120]

Though the YWCA was dominated by "white liberals," it did not participate in the colorblind approach common to policy-making circles. In the YWCA, race ideologies were shared and discussed, as evidenced by frequent reference to race in *The Womans Press*, its official organ. Some of the articles reflect ignorance of the privileges afforded white Americans and subtly affirmed "Negro" inferiority. Yet even as these attitudes and beliefs were expressed, they were also analyzed and challenged, and writers genuinely struggled to address their own participation in racist systems of power. For example, Marion Cuthbert exhorted white Americans to look at the economic and political realities that lay beneath the surface of prejudice. "[W]hites" could address their fears of "Negroes" through "get[ting] to know Negro people to that degree that sincerity in friendship cannot be questioned." Though not many "white people" were "willing to run the risk of some loss within their own group" to move beyond the color line, Cuthbert called for the courage to make this sacrifice.[121]

A second source of pressure on Walter White to make the Social Security Act an association priority came from its legal counsel, Charles Houston. Houston never accepted the argument that the Social Security Act could not serve African Americans because of "administrative difficulties." He identified the Act's discriminatory structure well before agricultural and domestic workers were specifically excluded. In his testimony before the House Ways and Means Committee in February 1935, he argued that the bill perpetuated discriminatory treatment by distinguishing between organized (industrial) and unorganized workers. He asked why OAI and Old Age Assistance (OAA) were created as separate programs, making one a "direct federal right" and the other dependent on state action. He said that not nearly enough money was appropriated for OAA, so many people would not be covered and that "many" would include "Negroes." Moreover, UI would only be available to waged labor as "a gesture to organized labor." He saw black workers being squeezed out by the interests of southern Democrats and the AFL.[122]

Morganthau's suggestion that agricultural and domestic workers be excluded was just one more piece of bad news about a bill that was already profoundly discriminatory. Houston's testimony shows that the NAACP had no illusions about the original CES bill; most African American workers would be ineligible for social insurance under that legislation because of the exclusion of employers with fewer than four employees. What specifically triggered the NAACP campaign against the bill was Houston's assumption that southerners in Congress were behind the new exclusions.

The NAACP had learned long ago that it could challenge southern Demo-crats without losing the support of liberal New Dealers. It therefore fo-cused its legislative agenda on *southern* race hierarchies and institutions.

For a brief moment, then, the Social Security Act appeared to provide a perfect opportunity for the NAACP to become more involved in trying to prevent New Deal discrimination, while still targeting the South and avoiding a direct attack on the white liberals who were the Act's main supporters. In fact, the CES bill could not be challenged without challeng-ing the vested interests of the network behind the proposed legislation. Its most discriminatory features, especially state administration, exclusion of employees of small employers, and differential treatment of different groups of workers, were all necessary to the Wisconsin plan for federal UI. To fight discrimination in the president's bill, the NAACP would have had to wage a battle against its white liberal friends. Yet after Morganthau's testimony, the exclusion of most African American workers seemed to be an issue that could produce an alliance of black, interracial, and white liberal groups against the southern-controlled Congress.

That moment was short lived, however. It appears to have been brought to a close by a longtime friend of the NAACP, Abraham Epstein. An old-age pension advocate and expert, Epstein was not personally involved in cre-ating the Social Security Act; in fact, he had opposed the Wisconsin plan (he was critical of individual employer accounts) and had been shut out of the development of the federal Act. Although he shared a long history with the Wisconsin group through their mutual membership in the larger social welfare reform network, Epstein traveled in very different circles. He was a Russian Jewish immigrant with a history of working-class activ-ism who had worked on a farm for a brief period in the 1920s following a "physical breakdown." Epstein's first book, *The Negro Migrant in Pitts-burgh* (1918), reflected his awareness that African American migrants from the South were poor because they were underpaid. His wife remembered him for "always denouncing poverty, evil, destitution, racial discrimina-tion, all these things that existed in this country, that he hadn't thought existed in this country." After his book was published, she said, the "Negro community" called him "doctor" though he had never earned a PhD.[123]

Epstein recognized that the Social Security Act, as drafted by the CES, structurally discriminated against African Americans. After its passage, he explained to black readers of *The Crisis* that they stood to lose ground in relation to white Americans because the insurance programs were financed by employer and employee taxes. These taxes would be passed on to consumers:

> As a consumer the Negro will be forced to bear a full share of the indirect sales taxes imposed. Being largely in the lowest wage-earning group, his share will be all the greater. . . . Had the Social Security Act not been based merely on the principle of sales taxes, Negroes would at least not have to lose directly by it. As it is, they stand to lose a great deal by the unemployment and old age insurance systems provided in the Social Security Act.[124]

Despite his criticism of the Wisconsin approach, Epstein was a mainstay of the larger social reform network that included the Wisconsin group. He and Josephine Roche were the NAACP's most important contacts in that network. So when he withdrew support for the NAACP's challenge, that challenge disintegrated. Epstein met with Roy Wilkins in early March 1935 and persuaded him to give up the fight to cover agricultural and domestic workers in the Act. Epstein insisted that the exclusion of agricultural and domestic workers was necessitated by administrative issues, and that neither the administration nor the CES would advocate other safeguards against discrimination.

According to Wilkins, though Epstein "has known of the work of the Association for many years and . . . is familiar with most of the problems of Negroes," he said "frankly that he was interested, first in social insurance and that he did not see how we can solve the Negro problem through social insurance; in other words there are realities existing with respect to Negroes and whites in this country which no program of social insurance can undertake to correct." Epstein believed that the NAACP should not trouble itself with exclusion, since the issue was driven by the "difficulty of collecting and administering these contributions."[125] Wilkins stated more bluntly that after he had pointed out that "Negroes" would not receive much aid under OAA, because not enough money had been appropriated, Epstein told him that the Wisconsin group "did not draw a bill with the idea in mind of speeding the solution of the race problem."[126]

Epstein advised the NAACP to abandon its fight against exclusion and focus on retaining the "reasonable subsistence" language in the OAA and ADC sections of the bill. He acknowledged that this language was problematic, because in southern states, standards for "decency and health" are generally considered to be below those for "whites." But he said they could do a lot worse, noting that Virginia's Senator Harry Byrd had criticized the language for implying federal control. "Dr." Epstein, because of his racial positioning, could afford to see the race problem as separate from the problem of social insurance.[127]

Wilkins reported on his conversation with Epstein at the March 11, 1935, meeting of the NAACP board. Immediately after, the association abandoned its fight for inclusion of agricultural and domestic workers in the Social Security Act—long before the bill had even left the House Ways and Means Committee on April 5 for review by the full House and then the Senate. Walter White continued to loosely monitor developments and gathered some materials with the intention of writing an article on the Act. He obtained a copy of the Act after its passage in August and considered drafting amendments to include agricultural and domestic workers that would be introduced in the 1936 session of Congress. But for all intents and purposes the NAACP's involvement was over, at least for the time being.[128]

The NAACP was not swayed by Epstein's argument. Rather, the conversation with Epstein revealed that a fight against the Act would ensure a conflict, not with southerners in Congress, as Charles Houston had originally believed, but with the northern reformers who created the bill and, beyond them, with the large network of white liberals within and outside the New Deal administration on whom the association relied for its access in Washington. At the March 11 meeting of the NAACP board, when its members decided to drop the fight, they agreed "the Association's position on this bill ought to be identical with the very carefully put together testimony of Mr. Houston before the Senate Finance Committee."[129]

The exchange between Wilkins and Epstein exemplifies the ways that the liberal adherence to colorblind social policy circumscribed the NAACP's legislative agenda. Whiteness afforded some people the perpetual option of retreating into a justification of policy that did not account for race, that did not look below the surface of "administrative difficulties" to acknowledge the racial hierarchies on which the policies were constructed. Of the administration representatives that responded to Walter White's letters and telegrams regarding the Social Security Act, not one referred to his point that the Act was *racially* discriminatory—his perspective was simply ignored, rendered invisible.

The NAACP encountered the same resistance in the second attempt to expand its legislative agenda. Immediately following the decision not to pursue the Act, Walter White and the board began working, with the help of John Davis, on an investigation of the "Status of Negroes under the New Deal." White estimated that such a study could "result in corrective action that would mean many hundreds of thousands of dollars in the pockets of Negroes."[130] Charles Houston drafted a resolution, to be introduced in the House by Representative Joseph A. Gavagan, and persuaded Representative William P. Connery Jr. to have the Labor Committee hold a "friendly" hearing. White set out to raise the estimated cost of the investigation—$2,500—and contacted local Urban Leagues to find people to testify about discrimination they had experienced, including "sharecroppers from Arkansas and other southern states, domestics, steel workers, [and] victims of the [NRA] laundry code."[131]

Though the NAACP put a great deal of time and effort into initiating the investigation, as in the case of the Social Security Act, it dropped the issue in less than two months. Though the association proceeded with caution and took care to keep friends informed, it became clear that its hands would be tied to too great an extent. For one thing, to keep the resolution from being sent to the Ways and Means Committee, where it would probably die without a public hearing, it had to be drafted in such a way that it did not deal with actual funding. Representative Connery, the main congressional supporter of the proposed investigation, agreed that the resolution was not expected to pass but that the goal was to "agitate" through a public hearing. The NAACP sought the support of its friends in the Roosevelt administration, asking many of them to testify at a Labor Committee hearing. To give evidence would, of course, be difficult, since they would to some extent be pointing fingers at themselves. Of the dozen people whom the NAACP asked to appear—including Harry Hopkins, Henry Wallace, and Frances Perkins—there is evidence of only one acceptance. Harold Ickes agreed to testify about his efforts to combat discrimination, as well as the areas where it had not yet successfully been addressed. Generating financial support proved to be a problem, though White went to all of his best funding sources.[132]

Finally, Senator Costigan suggested that such an investigation might hurt the fight for an antilynching bill. He claimed, rather unconvincingly, that the proposed study might represent one more example of "persistent personal hostility to [the] south." Walter White disagreed, saying that the investigation "could not possibly be construed" that way, because "unhappily, there is a vast amount of discrimination to be uncovered in the North."[133] Work on the resolution continued for a couple of weeks after Costigan's warning, but his words undoubtedly had an impact. The resolution was never introduced in the Seventy-fourth session. The issue was raised briefly again in the late summer and then died down.[134] The NAACP continued to flounder in its attempt to address New Deal discrimination without alienating its base of support.

Even if the investigation had gone forward, it is unlikely that public hearings on the resolution could have offered a forum to express the depth of analysis of structural racism presented by Charles Houston in regard to the Social Security bill. Any study that involved New Dealers would necessarily have focused on individuals and specific programs that discriminated; it could not have illuminated ways that the colorblind culture of the New Deal perpetuated racial hierarchy without indicting friends of the NAACP. The real message about New Deal discrimination expressed in Houston's testimony—that any "new" deal built on existing, racially inscribed categories of labor would only re-create racial inequality—could not be communicated in a colorblind environment.

five

Gender and the White United Front

The Women of the Federal Children's Bureau

On a warm September day in 1936, Ruth Cushman, a field worker for the Federal Children's Bureau, found herself in Lowndes County, deep in the rural black belt of Alabama, clapping and singing in the hot midday sun with the thirty local midwives—all African American—who comprised the backbone of the country's health care system. The Bureau had sent Cushman to help establish the state's Maternal and Child Welfare (MCH) program, one of three programs for children created by the Social Security Act. By traveling to this county as a representative of a federal agency, she inevitably waded into the messy racial politics that were obstructing African Americans nationwide from access to adequate health care. In a detailed report, for example, she wrote that the county did not have a sanitary officer for "political" reasons, as "the plantation owners do not take kindly to having sanitary measures instituted." Cushman was hosted by the Lowndes health officer and two nurses, "one colored, one white." She began the day attending a class for midwives, which was held in the home of a friend of one of the trainers, with the thirty students "assembled on the porch and in the yard." The meeting "was opened with two songs and a prayer" and "closed with a bag inspection" followed by more singing. Later that day she accompanied a "colored nurse" on home visits to six families.[1]

This scenario represents the best of the work of the Federal Children's Bureau in the years following the passage of the Social Security Act. It depicts a federal agency that did not huddle in its offices in Washington but stretched itself to form relationships with local programs, with health care providers and the women and children they served in all regions of the country. It also reflects a sensitivity to race and class divisions, as well as a desire to bridge those gaps through experience, to collaborate with local communities, and to treat even the poorest constituents with respect.

A very different story has been told of the first years of a second program created by the Bureau through the Social Security Act: Aid to Dependent Children (ADC). The previous chapters have described how Unemployment Insurance (UI) and Old Age Insurance (OAI) structurally discriminated against African American workers. But the Act did not just create a safety net for white, male workers; it also established the country's first permanent federal poverty assistance programs, including ADC, which evolved into Aid to Families with Dependent Children (AFDC), the core of the American welfare state for over sixty years. From the beginning, ADC sharply contrasted with Maternal and Child Health: to receive aid, the caretaking adult of a dependent child had to travel to a welfare office to apply for assistance, bring paperwork proving that he or she was poor enough, and be prepared to answer questions about the applicant's most personal behavior. In this way, program administrators acted more as watchdogs than collaborators in the lives of single mothers. They went into communities to check on the moral qualifications of women receiving aid, to make sure that they did not keep "unsuitable homes" that might result in a denial of benefits.[2] And ADC served mainly white women and children in the southern states, where most African Americans lived.

ADC and MCH, though both created through the Social Security Act, represent two very different views of federal welfare. This chapter describes the development of these programs, especially ADC, and their distinct approaches to the treatment of African Americans. It also explores how different groups of policymakers thought about the racialized meaning of motherhood and the contest over meaning that was embedded in ADC. The Federal Children's Bureau was assigned the task of establishing both programs, and so the story begins with that agency.

The Women of the Federal Children's Bureau

Grace Abbott and Katherine Lenroot stood at the helm of the Federal Children's Bureau in the mid-1930s. Abbott had recently stepped down after thirteen years as chief due to failing health, but she continued to reign with her successor, Lenroot, from her new home in Chicago, where she lived with her sister Edith and taught welfare administration at the University of Chicago. A charismatic figure, Abbott had been a powerful force in the Bureau. A coworker remembered that "[w]henever Grace Abbott walked down a hall, you always had a feeling that a galley in full sail was passing by because everything seemed to come alive in her wake. She just infused a kind of spirit into the whole Bureau. It was an extraordinary place, an exciting place to work in those days."[3] After Abbott's departure, Lenroot sent her pages of single-spaced letters on the Bureau's inner workings and political problems, as often as several times a week, and Abbott traveled to Washington periodically to offer advice, attend meetings, and testify before congressional committees. Abbott and Lenroot worked closely on every detail of the children's titles of the Social Security Act and together responded to the changes those titles underwent during the Act's construction.

Abbott's involvement in the Social Security Act was informed by a tight inner circle of friends who had worked together in the Chicago settlements. This group, which included Edith Abbott and Edith's companion, Sophinisba "Nisba" Breckinridge, had developed a shared worldview and sense of mission.[4] The collaboration between these three women was so complete, according to Lela Costin, a biographer of the Abbott sisters, that it is frequently difficult to tell who wrote what. Both Edith and Nisba signed articles written by Grace during her tenure with the Children's Bureau that "articulated points of view that Grace as chief of the . . . Bureau felt she could not say publicly." With one manuscript draft, Grace wrote to Edith, "You may think this is too hot to use," but "these things need to be said." Edith and Nisba sent Grace their more promising students to work with the Bureau, while Grace found ways to follow up or publicize research conducted at the University of Chicago. The two sisters wrote, interchangeably, the "Notes and Comments" column for the *Social Service Review*, the journal they had jointly established.[5]

Katherine Lenroot was not a member of Grace Abbott's close circle of friends, but they appear to have maintained a trusting professional relationship. Lenroot had taken a different path to the Children's Bureau. Her father had been a progressive voice in the Wisconsin legislature, and she had grown up playing "almost daily" with the children of Governor Robert La Follette. At the University of Wisconsin Lenroot was an undergraduate student of John Commons, who took a special interest in her, involving her in his own work outside of class. In 1913 Commons found Lenroot her first job—with the Wisconsin Industrial Commission under Edwin Witte.[6] Though her future as a member of the Wisconsin team may have seemed secure, she altered her career path a year into that work by following her mentor and later companion, Emma Lundberg, to the Federal Children's Bureau over Witte's objections. Lenroot's relationship with Grace Abbott may have been somewhat inhibited by her closeness to Lundberg, who had resigned from the Bureau over a personality conflict with Abbott and only returned after Abbott had departed and Lenroot was named chief.[7]

The conflict between Lundberg and Grace Abbott was atypical for the Children's Bureau; in the mid-1930s a sense of shared purpose generally pervaded the Bureau and tended to overshadow interpersonal discord. The Bureau's network resembled the Wisconsin group in this way: Raised in the settlement movement and affiliated with the University of Chicago, the Bureau's network was driven by a reformist vision and the personal relationships that grew up around it. Some of this cohesiveness may have reflected the common vulnerability of at least some of the women in this network, whose woman-centered lifestyles were often maligned. Whether or not they privately identified themselves or their relationships as lesbian, they were treated with suspicion for living independently of men. This is reflected in the often-cited example of the Senate's mockery of the unmarried women of the Children's Bureau during the Sheppard-Towner Infant and Maternity Act debates in the 1920s. One senator had called them "women too refined to have a husband," characterizing their ilk, to laughter, as a "bespectacled lady, nose sharpened by curiosity: who longed to invade other women's homes because she had no babies of her own."[8]

Some of this critique, if not its cruel tone, has been incorporated into history. Scholars have portrayed Grace Abbott's circle, at its worst, as a group of elite women intent on creating career opportunities for themselves by promoting motherhood and housekeeping among the poor and immigrant women they served. This characterization stems from the Abbott sisters' days in the settlement house movement in the 1910s and 1920s; because of their deep involvement in the establishment of mothers' pension programs, Abbott's group has been credited with conceiving the punitive, moralistic treatment of mothers for which those programs are known.[9]

But in her study of the Chicago mothers' pension program, Joanne Goodwin found that its moral qualifications resulted from local politics and were not championed by the Abbott sisters and their associates. Goodwin recovered an important but forgotten aspect of the Abbotts' work that adds to our understanding of their relationship to women of other classes. She concludes that the Abbotts challenged women's forced economic dependence and that their advocacy of mothers' pensions must be understood in that context. The sisters' philosophical justification for mothers' pensions rested, not on the assumption that women had a natural duty to be mothers, but on women's unrecognized and undervalued domestic work.[10] The most radical aspect of their perspective was the recognition that motherhood is work, work that deserves the same benefits and protections as industrial labor. Nisba Breckinridge said that "[i]n exchange for economic support, [a women] offered her husband and children the value of her reproductive and domestic labor. Society had an investment in upholding the terms of support in the marriage contract and had enforced legal obligations that recognized a widow's right to inheritance and a wife's right to support."[11]

In the 1930s the women of the Children's Bureau made basically the same argument. They regarded motherhood as women's most important work, necessary for the good of society. As Katherine Lenroot wrote in an article titled "What America Expects of Her Daughters": "[T]he biggest job that confronts [women] — the job upon whose success the success or failure of our civilization rests — is to become such wives, such mothers, such teachers and such citizens that the children of tomorrow will be brought up in full realization of the interrelationship and the interdependence of all life." But their vision of motherhood did not condemn lower-class women to economic dependence. In the same breath, Lenroot said that America "expects of her daughters that they shall become healthy, sturdy, self-reliant, full-fledged individuals," able not only to "manage a home" but also "to earn a living, to participate intelligently in the affairs of community, State and Nation." Motherhood constituted important work, but women should not be trapped by it.[12]

This is shown in the Bureau's attitude toward marriage. At least for some of the many women in this group who chose to forego marriage, this reflected an awareness that marriage involved a sacrifice of a woman's work and economic independence. Apparently Edith Abbott was so "opposed to marriage" for her women students that they hid their engagements from her rather than risk her disapproval.[13] But Bureau women sought independence not only for professional women; in some cases they also encouraged rural, poor, and working-class women they served to leave their marriage if it was not in their best economic interest. An administrator of the Louisville, Kentucky, mothers' pension program wrote to the Bureau asking whether the program should keep providing mothers' aid to women whose husbands had been released from prison. In a thoughtful, lengthy response, Florence Hutsinpillar told him that such a wife should be kept in the program while her husband looked for work; if he refused to support his family after he found a job, she could continue receiving aid only if she obtained a legal separation and pursued his financial support through the courts.[14]

According to Bureau leaders, all single mothers deserved compensation for their work in the home regardless of the propriety of their relationship to their child's father. Before passage of the Social Security Act, most state and local mothers' pension programs only covered widows who were deemed morally upright; pensions were a form of charity, not an earned benefit. But Grace Abbott claimed that all mothers whose labor was not compensated by their child's father deserved a pension, including those who never married. She said that social workers "generally agreed" that mothers' pensions should be available to unmarried mothers on the same basis as other single mothers. The Federal Children's Bureau consistently showed concern for unmarried mothers, though it could have easily disregarded them due to their small numbers—twenty-eight out of every thousand births in 1927—and marginal status. Katherine Lenroot and Grace Abbott also sought legal protections to keep unmarried mothers and babies together, to help them get established as a family within their communities, and to remove the "discriminations" to which such families were subjected.[15]

The fact that the Bureau's leadership had developed some understanding of the destructive effect of economic dependence on all women and children enabled it to empathize with the even greater vulnerability of African American women and children. This sensitivity seems to have applied only to its constituents; the Bureau had not prioritized racial equality in regard to African American workers. When it came to hiring staff and to relating to black professionals through their shared work, Bureau leaders tended to speak the same colorblind language employed by the Wisconsin group, referring to race to identify individuals, but not to recognize the larger political dynamic. They almost always identified professionals as "Negro," as in "Negro doctors" and "Negro midwives"; if not labeled as such, professionals were assumed to be white. For Bureau women, professional identity could not be fully expressed without a racial signifier, but race was only rarely referred to in the larger socioeconomic context as a cause of inequality. In contrast, Bureau staff rarely referred to individual mothers and children as "white" or "Negro," and insisted that "the types of care necessary for negro children do not differ from those for any other children."[16] But, in regard to their clients, race was frequently discussed in the context of social and political issues, such as the difficulty in obtaining funds for "colored" orphanages or discrimination against "colored" mothers who were pension recipients.

Though sympathetic in theory, the Bureau had not historically prioritized the hiring of African Americans or other minorities, and as of October 1935, it had no "Negro professional personnel." Lenroot remembered that "[i]t was not easy then to find a negro who was highly qualified in our field and with broad experience for top responsibility."[17] But Bureau files contain evidence that qualified African Americans were not considered. For example, Lenroot received a letter in 1933 from a "young colored lady (light) single 35 years old" who had traveled extensively in the United States, claimed to have many excellent references, had completed high school and two business courses, had taught normal school for ten years with two additional years of nurses training, and was "assistant Superintendent of girls" for three years. Her "hobby" was ethics. Desperate to work with "Negro children" in some meaningful way, she stated that "[s]alary isn't the most important factor." But Lenroot dismissed her with a brief letter and did not encourage further contact.[18]

The Bureau's concern for the well-being of African American mothers and children, and its desire to reach across cultural divides, led it into situations that exposed the prejudice of its leaders; sometimes that prejudice clouded their judgment. This was especially evident in the management of African American midwives who practiced under the MCH title of the Social Security Act. Despite their admirable efforts to cross the color line and collaborate with health professionals in the rural South, as illustrated by the scenario that opened this chapter, Bureau leaders held prejudicial opinions about the competence of the women, and some men, who provided health care to African American communities in this region.

Many factors were involved in the high infant and maternal mortality rates experienced by African American communities in the South. The leading cause of death was puerperal septicemia, a bacterial infection that was complicated by excessive bleeding after birth. Most southern "Negroes" could not afford maternity care at hospitals, and because hospitals were segregated, even those who could lacked access to adequate medical care. Midwives typically had received little training; in any case, they were unable to provide the type and level of care available in hospitals. The Bureau's own studies had suggested that the ministrations that comprised prenatal care were much less decisive to the survival of mother and child than the quality of the mother's diet, her ability to avoid physical labor during pregnancy and immediately after birth, and discrimination in hospitals and clinics. One report argued that "deaths in the practice of midwives were no more frequent than in the total colored population so that the midwives should not be particularly blamed for the higher colored maternal mortality rates."[19] Yet, despite the findings of its own research, the Bureau pinpointed the inadequate skills of "Negro" midwives as the primary problem and sought to replace them.[20]

Since the Bureau's own studies determined that these midwives did not lose more mothers and infants than other health care providers, its leadership may have blamed the midwives because it was unable to value any contribution the midwives made to the communities they served that deviated from the Bureau's scientifically based model of care. As healers practicing traditional medicine passed down through families, midwives perhaps delivered a type of care that Bureau medical personnel did not recognize. But Bureau leaders viewed midwives as entrenched and untrainable. They brought in Felix J. Underwood, M.D., a Mississippi state health officer, to testify before the Senate Finance Committee on their behalf. Underwood told the lawmakers that "[m]ost of the midwives in Mississippi are ignorant women who cannot be expected to know the first principles of obstetrics" and could not absorb much training "since their lack of education and previous mode of living cannot guarantee great results."[21] The Bureau did make limited gestures to enhance the training of midwives, but the gaps appear to have been too wide to cross, and they ended up seeking to replace African American midwives with white professionals.

The Federal Children's Bureau did make the training and hiring of African American nurses and doctors a top priority under the MCH program. By December 1936 Lenroot claimed that "[p]ractically all southern states have Negro nurses on staff and Negro nurses in counties."[22] The Bureau did not challenge segregated practices, agreeing that these women would exclusively "minister to their own people."[23]

There was limited collaboration between the Children's Bureau and interracial organizations. The Bureau openly shared information with the National Association for the Advancement of Colored People (NAACP) and the National Urban League (NUL), both of which appear to have been considered a friend. Grace Abbott, in particular, was, according to one correspondent, "individually so friendly to the Colored race."[24] The Bureau maintained relationships with the Rosenwald Fund and the Tuskegee Institute and responded quickly and enthusiastically to requests from interracial organizations for assistance and information. Nevertheless, neither the Bureau nor interracial organizations seem to have prioritized collaboration with each other. The NAACP did not pursue contact with the Children's Bureau as it did with other federal agencies; as late as 1929, Walter White apparently did not know that Grace Abbott was the Children's Bureau chief.[25] The lack of collaboration between the Bureau and the NAACP was most likely a result of different priorities and limited resources on both sides, as well as differences in the gendered cultures of the two organizations. The NAACP was dominated by men who had no policy or program that recognized the differing impact of segregation on African American women, or that sought to promote women to leadership positions within the association or establish joint priorities with women's organizations such as the National Council of Negro Women (NCNW). The Children's Bureau's focus on services for mothers and children would have appeared more soft and feminine to the NAACP than its own civil rights agenda, more similar to the historical service-oriented approach of the NUL, the "Negro" church, and social clubs, none of which concerned the NAACP leadership.

Although Bureau leaders did not consistently challenge discrimination in the professional world, Grace Abbott, Katherine Lenroot, and others took bold steps to expand the services of the Federal Children's Bureau to African American mothers and children. In the context of mothers and children, it is clear that they thought deeply about the operation of racial inequality, challenging their own prejudiced assumptions, and therefore had something valuable to offer.

Bureau representatives repeatedly claimed that race was irrelevant in any attempt to understand people or design services to meet their needs. In this area Grace Abbott was the driving force. Her childhood and young adulthood had been filled with the kinds of contradictions that would have forced her to make sense of racial difference. Though raised in a white segregated community, singing "darky" songs and being cared for by "Negro" house servants, she was also exposed to her parents' Quaker beliefs and family history of abolitionism. The Abbott family stressed, according to Edith, that "the rights of women belonged with the rights of the Indian and the rights of the Negro. Everyone must be free and equal and everyone should be dealt with on the basis of equality and justice." Though originally abstractions, these beliefs were tested during Grace's settlement work, as she came into contact with European immigrants and migrants from the black belt South.[26]

Later Grace expressed her developing appreciation of racial injustice in the "Notes and Comments" column of the *Social Service Review*, which she coauthored with Edith. The Abbott sisters argued for racially mixed juries, in response to the Scottsboro trial, so that a "universally shared prejudice may not prevail."[27] The *Review* also published a few articles about racial injustice. For example, "Family Support and Dependency among Chicago Negroes . . ." assumed that the special problems faced by black Chicagoans were entirely the result of job discrimination, not cultural issues or attributes. The piece supported economic independence for African American men and women, and assistance for "Negro" mothers.[28] Grace Abbott was usually invited to participate in conferences and other events sponsored by interracial organizations, such as the Annual National Interracial Conference, led by George Haynes and Mary Van Kleeck among others, and the Rosenwald Economic Conference of 1933, but by the mid-1930s illness frequently limited her involvement.[29]

Abbott's sensitivity to race issues was greatly enhanced by her experience in working with mothers and children, all of whom, she believed, shared common needs. She asserted that "racial differences are fewer and less important from a social welfare standpoint than the differences between individual white and individual negro children"; particularly for those who were neglected, handicapped, or delinquent, "there must be great individualization" in meeting their needs. Like all children, "Negro" children needed "regular employment for their fathers; they need good homes in attractive neighborhoods, they need progressive schools." The differences between the needs of white and "Negro" children stemmed from "the position which the negro has occupied in American life . . . [belonging] to the lowest paid economic group." Also, "[w]here there is segregation in provision and treatment of negro and white children[,] adequate public funds necessary for the care of negro children is more difficult to secure than for white children [stricken: And *how* difficult that is child welfare workers know well.]"[30]

Following a less-than-impressive record during the years of the settlement movement, Grace Abbott, as chief of the Federal Children's Bureau, began to devote time and resources to African American children and families, recognizing that little could be done to equalize service until the nature of the inequality was better understood. The Bureau had a very limited scope in those early years; except for its brief administration of a child labor law in 1917–18 and its seven-year supervision of the Sheppard-Towner Act, the Bureau was merely "an agency for research, publication, demonstration, and consultation."[31] Still, it made serious efforts—first, to gather statistics on women and children by "race," by their cultural assignment as "white" or "Negro." The Bureau asked states to record and report on the race of mothers' pension recipients in 1931–32, but this task was extremely difficult because the Bureau had no central reporting authority and was forced to rely on the willingness of typically overworked administrators. It had better luck in other places and discovered, for example, that in some cities, including Baltimore, Philadelphia, and Washington, greater percentages of mothers' pension funds were paid to "Negro" women and children than their percentage of the population might warrant. The Bureau was surprised that this was not also the case in Wilmington, Delaware, and proceeded to investigate by gathering application and refusal rates by race.[32]

The Bureau's ambitions were hampered by the absence of information and the authority to demand it. It received regular requests for statistics on black children from interracial organizations and service providers. It sent book lists, lists of Bureau publications, and any pamphlets that even mentioned "Negroes," though aware that this offering was inadequate. An untitled report, apparently written by Children's Bureau staff and edited by Grace Abbott, noted that "[b]ecause the reporting of social statistics is as yet little developed, we are lacking the factual basis we need in discussing the social problems of the negro and of negro children. In recent years the . . . Bureau has made a beginning in the attempt to get uniform statistics in a number of fields."[33] The report noted that the available figures were not national and included inaccurate comparisons; thus they were of limited value. Abbott's handwritten notes express her concern with drawing conclusions from data for which there was no solid evidence. The Bureau looked for studies on racial minorities conducted by others. Katherine Lenroot exchanged several long letters with E. B. Sarreals, of New York University, giving him feedback and identifying contacts related to his study of Puerto Ricans in East Harlem. She was "very deeply interested" in his project, and it was "extremely helpful to have such concrete and definite materials available."[34]

But in the face of limited resources, the Children's Bureau persevered. Race was one of the key issues explored in the crowning glory of the research conducted by the Bureau during Abbott's tenure: a component of the Sheppard-Towner Act. Between 1915 and 1932 the Bureau engaged in a study of maternal and child mortality, gathering data by cause of death, age, rural or urban residence, and race ("colored" and "white"). Its most significant findings were unreasonably high mortality rates in the United States, compared to other countries, and much higher death rates among "colored" women than among "white" women. Grace Abbott was personally involved with the project and made some of the statistical calculations herself. The researchers showed sensitivity to the importance of understanding the causes of the gaps revealed by the data.[35] The study also looked into "the distribution of doctors, white and colored," and "the distribution of midwives, white and colored in the various states." As the most recent and comprehensive study conducted by the Bureau, its findings became the primary supporting documentation for the Children's sections of the Social Security Act.[36]

Because of the hands-on aspects of the Bureau's work, some of its employees were forced to leave the protection of their white worlds and confront the economics of race, and even to create connections beyond their own comfort zones. Administering the Sheppard-Towner Act required Abbott and six other staff members to travel extensively through the poorer sections of the country, including black belt regions of the South. They observed local health programs, met the families served by them, and developed relationships with doctors, social workers, and local administrators. To some extent, Bureau policy was determined by these connections, as state and local administrators told them the kinds of services and standards that were needed.[37]

Bureau staff received a lot of mail from state and private programs for children. They responded warmly to messages that expressed the Bureau's own perspective on equality but remained aloof from paternalistic attitudes. Katherine Lenroot personally answered an inquiry from a white woman associated with a settlement in Houston with "two trained Negro women in charge." "[I]mmediately" after she became involved with the settlement, the woman "realized that I must rid myself of any race prejudice; this I have done & the deeper I go into the work the more serious and interesting it becomes. But Oh! I am so in need of advice and train-ing." Lenroot was "exceedingly interested" in her work and in her "attitude in approaching the problems with which you are dealing." She sent her materials, put her in touch with other settlement organizations, and en-couraged her to write "from time to time."[38] But a woman who did charity work with the children of "mountain Negroes" in North Carolina received a less enthusiastic reply. Her duties involved feeding and caring for needy children in exchange for farm chores, laundry services, and other menial labor. At her camp, "boys too poor to pay the price of an education could come and work out their destiny" and receive "Christian education and vocational guidance." Grace Abbott suggested that she try the Department of Interior; she did not encourage further contact or express support.[39]

The Bureau also rejected eugenics-based ideas about biological differ-ences. In the mid-1930s the eugenics movement was still somewhat re-spectable, as states continued to pass sterilization laws and the American Eugenics Society sponsored conferences featuring prominent speakers, sometimes including New Deal administrators. The discourse of eugen-ics, which had infused American culture, occasionally appeared in Bureau speeches and correspondence. But the attitude of the Children's Bureau can best be characterized as indifference to the work of eugenics groups and the problems they tried to solve. For example, it ignored a request for help from the Tennessee Children's Home Society in determining whether a child, "a decided negro" in a family of children who were "undoubt-edly white," could have been a "throw back," "or is the strain definitely cleared of the possibility of negro blood after a few generations of white blood?"[40] The whole eugenics approach, using biological determinants to control parenthood, flew in the face of the Children's Bureau's emphasis on environment, behavior modification, and training. Bureau publications commonly reflected the discourse of the behavioral sciences, such as the pamphlet, "Training Your Child to Be Happy."[41]

The Bureau's commitment to the belief that all children were the same led it to reach beyond the United States to build and maintain relation-ships with children's service providers and programs in Latin America. Work with children easily crossed national borders because, as Katherine Lenroot observed in her presidential address to the 1930 Pan American Child Conference in Lima, "[t]he love of parents for their children, the de-pendence of the state upon the quality of its ever-renewed citizenship, are the same from Nove Scotia to Punta Arenas, from Bahia to Trujillo. . . .

Study of the child . . . inevitably forces us to consider the most fundamental problems of our political, economic and social organization." In
the United States those problems included racial prejudice, which de-
prived children "of that equality of opportunity which was the dream
of [Thomas] Jefferson and of all who have visioned the development
of democratic institutions in this hemisphere." Lenroot expressed "mea
culpa" on behalf of the United States for "many sins" and linked care for
children to "[t]he task of abolishing war, poverty, ignorance, and racial
prejudice," which was not "only a Utopian dream," but also would take
generations to accomplish.[42]

In the fall of 1934, the leadership of the Children's Bureau sat down
to construct a proposal for the nation's first federal welfare program for
mothers and children, to be incorporated in the Social Security Act. To
that task they brought unusual sensitivity, both to women's need for the
security offered by economic independence and to the injustice of segregated and unequal treatment of African American mothers and children.
Yet the program established in the Act reflected none of their sensitivity.
ADC was designed to provide only poverty-level subsistence to the caretakers of dependent children, and these caretakers would be required to
pass means tests to prove that they were poor enough to qualify for aid.
Moreover, the program was funded far below the need and contained no
protections against the discrimination of African Americans.

There is a reason for the discrepancy. The Bureau's program, which reflected the Bureau's sensitivity and did not discriminate, was not the program incorporated into the Social Security Act as ADC. In fact, ADC was
inserted in the Act as a substitute for the Bureau's proposal. The Bureau's
program was radically different from ADC's. It would have established a
welfare system based on an understanding of the rights of mothers to compensation for the work of motherhood. More important, it offered a whole
new perspective, not just on the meaning of motherhood, but on the relationship of government to citizens.

The Bureau's Proposal for Mothers and Children

In September 1934 Grace Abbott and Katherine Lenroot were exuberant.
After years of leading a somewhat marginal federal agency, they suddenly
found themselves positioned to have a strong influence on the creation of
a bold new arena of public policy. As associates of Frances Perkins through

the network of New Deal women, they were thrilled with her appointment as chair of the Committee on Economic Security. They also identified
Edwin Witte early on as a friend of the Children's Bureau and a potential
source of support. They believed that their agenda for women and children
would now receive serious attention.[43]

Once assigned to develop recommendations for children's services under the Social Security Act, Abbott and Lenroot seized the opportunity
to implement an ambitious plan for restructuring the relationship of the
federal government to children, families, and communities. They submitted their definitive 38-page proposal for an expanded mothers' pension
program, titled "Security for Children," to Edwin Witte on November 21,
1934, with a second proposal for children's health services to follow.[44]
Throughout the drafting of the initial report to FDR in December 1934,
Lenroot and Abbott collaborated with Witte, Arthur Altmeyer, and other
CES staff, confident that their vision would be represented in the president's bill.

Their plan had two main prongs. First, they would seek to salvage the
most "clearly distinguishable" group currently suffering from the degradation of long-term relief—mothers and children—and wring from the federal government a commitment to provide adequate, long-term support
to women raising children on their own. They would accomplish this by
expanding mothers' pension programs throughout the country. Second,
they would make inroads toward the creation of permanent health and
welfare agencies in every state in the country through federal funding to
establish maternal and child health and child welfare programs.

The expansion of mothers' pensions was the most important part of
the plan. It topped the list assembled by Katherine Lenroot, and approved
by Grace Abbott, of legislative priorities for the Bureau for the 1935 congressional session, a list that included child welfare funding to establish
a national network of local, permanent health departments; a new federal child labor bill; and "federal control of home work through legislation under the commerce clause of the Constitution."[45] Lenroot drafted
proposed language for the children's titles, gathered a great deal of supporting information and statistics, and put together a committee of advocates for child welfare. The Bureau's report, "Security for Children," was a
thorough, well-argued proposal that drew on the best statistical information generated by the Bureau to date. It described, in different sections,
the need for federal mothers' pension and child welfare programs, cur-

rent state laws regarding mothers' pensions, estimated costs, and "social values" that would be promoted through the proposal.

The basic premise of "Security for Children" was the collective responsibility of society to all children in the United States. The care of children was considered to be a duty shared beyond the privacy of the family. In words and tone, the report did not express the sentiment that "we, as good people, should help the less fortunate" but rather that "all children have a right to decent care, and this should be ensured through law." It stated boldly that "[t]he Federal Government has a responsibility which it shares with the States and the local communities to see that no group of families or children shall be forgotten or neglected."[46]

This report, not surprisingly, conceptualized this collective responsibility in heavily gendered terms. Ideally, mothers fulfilled their duty by raising their children and fathers by providing for them financially. However, the necessity for collective responsibility was supported by the fact that most single mothers had to work outside the home but were segregated economically in low-paying jobs and were unable to be the main breadwinner. A mother's economic value to her children depended on her earning power: unless a single mother with "young children to support belonged to the highly skilled or professional group, her contribution in the home was greater than her earnings outside the home."[47] The Bureau's proposal acknowledged that a disproportionate number of mothers and children excluded from existing mothers' pension programs—those the proposal sought most to help—were "Negro" women, especially domestic workers, who were relegated to the vagaries of relief. This was true even in large northern cities where mothers' pension programs at the state level were relatively well funded.[48]

The Bureau's plan sought to ensure that all mothers would have equal access to mothers' aid. This was to be accomplished, first, through an expanded definition of both "mother" and "child." With one exception,[49] the proposal consistently defined mothers who would be eligible for support as those whose children had no "male breadwinner," "whose fathers were dead, incapacitated or had deserted," not as women who had no husband. It emphasized the economic responsibility of adult men to their children without raising the question of the moral correctness of a woman's relationship to her children's father. The proposal noted that this definition was not universally adopted by states, as all state laws covered widows, but only twenty states had "very liberal" laws that applied to "any mother with dependent children." The more limited definition would lead to the exclusion of large numbers of women and children, as only 44 percent of urban families that would be eligible for mothers' pensions were headed by widows. The proposal also broadened the definition of "child": an eighteen-year-old could still be considered a child if he or she stayed in school.[50]

The Bureau's proposal sought to further expand the reach of mothers' pensions through a radical approach to redistribute funding between wealthier and poorer states and counties. Grace Abbott had apparently come up with this idea.[51] Based on the equalization formula used to allocate funds for public schools, it assumed that the right of every child to an education superseded the "rights" of individual states and counties to care for their own. Under this plan, one-fifth of federal funds for state mothers' pension programs would be redistributed to states that otherwise were too poor to match federal funds. It also required states to equalize funding between richer and poorer counties and to cover all of the counties in their state.[52]

The point of equalization funding was to get mothers' pensions to the families that needed them most, specifically African American families. Counties were the critical unit to ensure fair distribution to African Americans because states were typically segregated by county, especially in the South. In 1930, for example, 56 percent of Alabama residents were identified on the census as "Negro," all of whom were clustered within the 26 counties of the black belt region of the lower middle half of the state. More than 70 percent of the residents of eleven counties in the black belt were classified as "Negro," but only 10 percent in the northern counties.[53] Because state mothers' pension programs had relied on local funding and had not required statewide coverage, "[g]reat variation exists among the States, and in the different counties in the same State, in the extent to which mothers' aid . . . was reaching all families which would be eligible under a fairly liberal law."[54]

The implications of this plan for the formation of the welfare state in America were profound. It treated economic security as a birthright, like education. It assumed that children were the charge of the larger society, not just the individual family, and that a taxpayer in upstate New York had an obligation to provide for the well-being of a child residing in the poorest rural southern county. State coverage coupled with equalization would also ensure that state mothers' pension programs would be able to compete with other social service programs for state funds, something they had been unable to do successfully in the past. In 1934 state governments had paid a little over 50 percent of the total cost ($32,177,603) of OAA programs and 48 percent of the funds ($6,711,905) spent for aid to the blind, yet they paid only 15.5 percent of the cost (ca. $37,487,479) of mothers' pensions.[55]

Equalization funding might have made a tremendous difference in the ability of African American women and children to get assistance through mothers' pensions, as it appears to have done through the MCH and Child Welfare Services (CWS) programs. The equalization formula for MCH emphasized coverage of all counties in a state, which led to disproportionate funding for smaller states and for poor states that did not have existing programs in all counties. In the 1920s the South had made impressive efforts to establish welfare services: Emma Lundberg found in 1930 that all but three southern states had functioning welfare departments and that more southern states had structures in place to monitor dependent children than states in other regions. The problem was simply a lack of money to fund the programs.[56] The funds for small states were needed to establish social welfare systems; one reason was that the rudimentary infrastructure of small state systems impeded the Bureau's ability to assess problems through research. As one public welfare administrator in Virginia wrote a Bureau staff member:

> I am sure that you will not construe this reply as any indication of our unwillingness to cooperate in [a Mothers' Pension] survey. . . . I went into the office of one of the welfare superintendents a few days ago and found her struggling with questionnaires on crime, social trends, drought, rural economics, juvenile delinquency, and others. When it is remembered that few of the county workers have secretarial assistance and that they are [a] poor relief officer, probation officer, school attendance officer, child welfare officer, combined in extremely large counties with as many as 40,000 or 50,000 people, we will appreciate the burden imposed on them.[57]

Equalization formulas also favored states that could not meet federal matching fund requirements without help.

The MCH funding scheme represented a significant reallocation of federal money to address that problem in poor and small states. For instance, New York State, with a population of 12.6 million, ranked second to last in per capita MCH funding, receiving only $82,904, or $0.66 for every 100 New Yorkers. But Arkansas, with a population of only 436,000, was allotted $31,000, or $7.06 for every 100 people. Southern states ranked very high in per capita funding, whereas states in the Midwest and on the East Coast ranked very low. If the eighteen states with one million or less inhabitants are discounted, southern states ranked higher than any other region. The same pattern is evident in the distribution of federal funds for CWS. Again, small states led in per capita funding, followed by southern states, with eastern and midwestern states grouped at the bottom of the list, with significantly lower funding.

Once the measure was in Congress, the Children's Bureau managed to enhance equalization in MCH and CWS even further than in the original bill. In the original bill, one-fifth of the funds allotted for these two programs would be distributed through the equalization formula, and an additional $20,000 would be granted to each state. The remaining funds would be divided among the states according to the number of live births. This "live birth" formula would have benefited larger states most, of course. However, the Bureau successfully fought to have that formula replaced in the House bill with a second equalization formula, one that relied on maternal and infant mortality rates, enabling the poorest states to get much larger shares. Lenroot lobbied Edwin Witte for his help, arguing that southern states would not be able to take advantage of the federal money unless the distribution formula was changed; otherwise, only northern states would benefit. It is no surprise that the southern-controlled House of Representatives followed up on the Bureau's suggestion to increase equalization.[58]

Redistributing funding to southern states, and even requiring it to be spent in all of a state's counties, would not *necessarily* lead to equal access to services for African American southerners. But equalization worked in concert with other safeguards built into the MCH and CWS titles of the Act, which we can assume would also have governed mothers' pensions. The most important of these safeguards was the administration of the programs by the Children's Bureau. Lenroot made it clear to state administrators that she intended to reach "Negro" mothers and children through MCH and CWS. In July 1937 she stated that equal service for "all races" was a priority of the programs and that "summaries of state plans approved for the fiscal year ended June 30, 1937, contain significant indications of a trend toward consideration of the special needs existing among the Negro population."[59] T. Arnold Hill, the Bureau's primary African American contact in the months following passage of the Social Security Act, expressed a great deal of comfort with Bureau policies regarding race. In a rare period of "frequent conferences" and correspondence between the Bureau and the NUL, Lenroot and Hill hashed out certain points of administration. Hill assured the Bureau that he was not "fearful that Miss Lenroot's practices and policies will exclude Negroes" and he was less concerned about government discrimination "as long as policies are entrusted to you." But he still felt that "definite care will have to be taken to insure fair and impartial treatment on the part of the specific individuals charged with carrying out these policies."[60]

The Children's Bureau took advantage of its position to work closely with states on their state plans and on the minutia of their budgets. For example, Alabama submitted revisions to its 1937 fiscal year budget for the third quarter, itemizing every salary change of five dollars or more and every new hire, and deletion of position, by county. The state had already sent the Bureau a map showing percentages of white and black populations by county, which indicated that the changes were made statewide, with no obvious preference to either population. The Bureau sent teams of social workers into states to investigate local abilities to build structures to administer the Act, and the field reports of the teams in southern states made frequent references to race. One MCH staffer, describing a trip to North Carolina, noted that the state nurse, identified as "white" and generally "excellent," would not address a black teacher as "Mister" and refused to make the necessary visits to homes of "Negro" children.[61]

It also appears that the racial divide in counties was a factor in the Bureau's approval of state plans for locating MCH demonstration projects. Demonstration projects were created under the Social Security Act for "needy areas and among groups in special need," language that appears to have been interpreted, for southern states, as areas with large "Negro" populations. Southern states were required to report on the racial demographics of proposed sites, and they seem to have complied.[62] For example, a prenatal clinic was approved for M Street in Washington, D.C., "because of need, particularly among colored people." Alabama's project was intended to include "substations" for both "colored and white patients" to be located at "strategic points" in the city and country, Maryland and Georgia located their demonstration projects to serve African American women and children, and North Carolina selected an area that was one-third African American.[63]

With the expansion of the Bureau's program through MCH, hiring African American nurses and doctors became a higher priority, and the Bureau relayed its interest to southern states. For instance, Martha Eliot told a Bureau staffer working with southern states that a recent visitor from the National Tubercular Association "is naturally very interested in persuading the states to employ some colored nurses and hopes that we will encourage this. I am sure you will."[64] In an article published in July 1937, Katherine Lenroot wrote that "[p]ractically all of the states having large Negro populations employ Negro nurses on state and county staffs."[65] Six months earlier she had noted that, under the MCH program, postgraduate courses or institutions for "Negro physicians and dentists" were being started, "in some cases under Negro leadership."[66]

There does not appear to have been significant resistance from southern states to sharing the federal largess with African American mothers and children. This could be attributed to the authority of the Children's Bureau and the attitudes of its contacts in state health and welfare departments in the South, which ranged from progressive to paternalistic. Some local administrators watchdogged the federal funds to make sure that African Americans received equal service. A doctor in Alabama informed the Bureau that MCH funds earmarked for a "colored" clinic were being diverted to a "white" clinic by doctors who were opposed to the competition generated by government-paid doctors doing preventative care. The physician noted, "People are not obstetrically minded in this locality." The Bureau promised to ensure that the funds were returned.[67] The state health officer for Alabama, George M. Cooper, had submitted his initial request for federal funding under MCH by arguing that African American mothers and infants needed the most help. He submitted a great deal of information on the racial distribution of the state, highlighting the black belt counties that received no public health services. His proposal required that all services provided by clinics under the Social Security Act "be available to any indigent female of any race, creed, or nationality," including prenatal, natal, and postnatal assistance, and assistance in the prevention of breast and uterine cancer.[68]

This lack of resistance may also have reflected an awareness of local administrators that they could solidify relations with the Children's Bureau by showing progressive attitudes about race. This was clearly Cooper's assumption. He asked the Rosenwald Fund to intercede with the Bureau on his behalf, because he feared that his political enemies might have given the impression that he was not interested in extending services to African Americans and had therefore alienated the Bureau's "good opinion."[69] Previously, Martha Eliot had told Cooper that she was particularly interested that MCH funding go to women in "rural areas," and let him know that the Bureau would have discretion in distributing equalization funds for poor states to match federal funds. In this way, equalization offered the Bureau a hammer to ensure state compliance with policies that were not specifically required by the Act.[70]

All of these features of the Children's Bureau's November 21 proposal for mothers' pensions were consistent with the final point that it made, which was that all mothers and children must be saved from the demoralizing effect of relief. To the Bureau, relief was necessary in emergencies, but damaging in the long run because it provided inadequate, stigmatized, temporary assistance that marked recipients as separate from the larger society and kept them always at its mercy. Poor children no more belonged on a welfare program for unemployed adults than delinquent children belonged in adult prisons; they required a completely different kind of help. This was what the concept of mothers' pensions, at least in its truest expression, was all about. Unlike relief, mothers' pensions as envisioned by the Bureau, was not a poverty program that required recipients to continuously prove that they were in need, but a guarantee of *permanent*, *earned* income throughout childhood. This approach would save women and children from the stigma of relief, "not only the insecurity but also the feeling of dependency which frequently results from a relief status."[71]

As Katherine Lenroot and Grace Abbott argued, relief harmed mothers and children because it could never provide adequate assistance. They asked for something approximating adequate grant levels—an average of $40 per urban family and $20 per rural family, but in "large urban areas" average grants would be $60 or more per family. During the first year of operation, before state laws were liberalized to include more families, 300,000 families currently eligible for mothers' pensions would receive grants totaling $120 million. In theory, one-third of this amount was to be paid each by federal, state, and local governments, though the federal government would pick up a much larger slice of the pie since states would be unable to make their end of the match. This figure would increase with the addition of more families. These amounts were "below standards of adequacy but somewhat above present prevailing averages."[72]

The grant levels in the Bureau proposal may seem low until they are compared with grant levels approved in the Social Security Act for ADC: $6 per month for the first child and $4 for each additional child. These limits were set in the House version of the Act, and Edwin Witte called them "penurious and illogical."[73] However, the limits reflected regional politics and, sadly, were very logical in that context: ADC included no equalization across states, and so poorer states, including most southern states, were left to sink or swim on their own. The grant limits were established by southern leaders to prevent a disproportionate percentage of the insufficient federal funds available for ADC from being consumed by northern states before southern programs were even up and running, thus preventing northern states from emptying the pool before the southern states could even find their way to the water's edge.

The Bureau plan offered poor single mothers the opportunity to keep their families together outside of marriage, as the purpose of mothers' pension laws was "to end the separation of mother and child on the ground of poverty alone." Construed this way, the Bureau pension policy assumed that poverty was the fault of society, not of individual mothers. For a woman without a decent income, "it frequently and even usually happened that either her children were taken from her and cared for at greater cost in institutions or foster homes, or she was encouraged to make the attempt to be both homemaker and wage earner and the children were taken away from her after she had broken down and the children had become delinquent or seriously neglected."[74]

The only reference in the Bureau's plan to restrictions on the behavior of mothers receiving pensions was a statement that mothers' aid programs consider "the character of the mother and her competency to give proper care to her children."[75] Elsewhere, Abbott elaborated: "Social workers have generally agreed that the dependent children . . . are best cared for by their mothers . . ., assuming always the reasonable competence of the mothers to perform the duties of housekeeper and mother."[76] Abbott did not suggest that women had to meet standards of morality in their personal lives to qualify for a pension. They only had to be single, a mother, and qualified for the work of motherhood.

The Bureau's proposal for federal aid to women and children was a bold attempt to reconstruct both the relationship of government to citizens and society's understanding of the meaning of motherhood. It was not based on a maternalist desire to push motherhood on poor women, or to punish mothers who did not meet the standards of the worthy widow. Rather, its premise valued the work of motherhood and intended that society be committed to raising all of its children in decent, secure environments. But the Bureau's plan was not the one that ended up in the Social Security Act. The proposal that was actually adopted reflected the opposite vision of motherhood, one that sought to protect an entirely different constituency.

FERA and the Racialized Politics of the "United Front"

Instead of the Children's Bureau's plan for mothers' pensions, a proposal for Aid to Dependent Children was inserted in the CES bill at the request of Harry Hopkins, a member of the Committee on Economic Security and director of the Federal Emergency Relief Administration (FERA). The switch did not occur until very late in the process. The report that the CES submitted to President Roosevelt in December 1935 had clearly used the Children's Bureau's proposal as a model for its children's aid title; indeed, Katherine Lenroot wrote Edwin Witte: "I want to say again what a grand job you did in summarizing our report." That report, though extremely brief, advocated equalization funding, coverage of unmarried mothers and their children, and the other main features of the Bureau's plan.[77]

But between the drafting of the president's report and the introduction of the Social Security Act in Congress in January 1936, FERA leaders put forward the plan for ADC and succeeded in gaining the backing of the CES. The Children's Bureau was kept in the dark about why this decision was made. Tom Eliot, who drafted the Act for the CES, told Lenroot that at the last minute the bill gave FERA responsibility for the administration of ADC "for convenience in drafting" but "no final decision had yet been made as to administration." Apparently, both Josephine Roche, with FERA though a member of Grace Abbott's inner circle, and Arthur Altmeyer agreed with this assessment.[78] In fact, the decision appears to have been firmer than Eliot implied, for at its January 7 meeting, the CES agreed to put all welfare activities under FERA. The action was taken in response to Hopkins's argument that such assistance should be coordinated by a single federal agency, but with the understanding that "matters involving insurance on a contractual basis should not be considered welfare activities."[79] Initially, FERA staffers denied that they had either written the

ADC revision or lobbied for its inclusion in the bill but later admitted that was not the case. Abbott said: "Of course, the F.E.R.A. are fundamentally dishonest in what they say about not raising a hand to get [their version of ADC in the bill], and when Aubrey Williams told me that it was nothing that they were responsible for, I told him that I knew they wrote it, and he then admitted it."[80]

FERA had developed its own plan for social welfare that it endeavored to incorporate within the larger framework created by the Wisconsin group. Like the Wisconsin group, FERA had devised a strategy for reviving the economy through social welfare. Its plan was based on a "trickle up" theory that relied on pumping cash, through emergency relief, into the lowest "economic strata," which could be counted on to keep the money in circulation rather than putting it into savings as other classes might. However, FERA also recognized the debilitating impact of relief: it "destroys the desire to earn one's own living . . . puts a premium on shiftlessness . . . [and] reduces the standard of living of millions of families to a level just above starvation."[81] Harry Hopkins and other FERA administrators sought to protect the interests of the long-term unemployed, to prevent them from being shamed and isolated from other Americans. Hopkins was also known to be more sensitive than most to the discrimination faced by African Americans.

At first FERA's answer to this contradiction was to divide everyone who would be ineligible for UI, and without a means of supporting themselves, into two basic programs. The backbone of its plan was the establishment of a Public Works Administration (PWA) program, funded at $5 billion per year, that would guarantee a job to all needy unemployed able-bodied persons. Two classes of jobs would be funded: "unskilled" workers would earn $7–$11 per day and "skilled" workers, $14–$20. The public works program would work in conjunction with farm loan programs through the Agricultural Adjustment Administration in rural areas, so that the unemployed in both rural and urban areas would, theoretically, be taken care of. The program would cost twice the $2.5 billion in federal, state, and local funds spent on relief in 1933, but most of it would be paid back through self-liquidating projects.[82]

The public works plan was only intended to help those deemed fit to work; all others would be categorized as "unemployable" and, in the initial FERA proposal, turned back to the care of state and local governments with some federal help. This "unemployable" category included 20 to 40 percent of those in need of assistance—the aged, the physically and mentally disabled, and "widows with dependent children."[83] But FERA agreed to a compromise that would combine the two categories, lumping together everyone who was ineligible for UI. During the fall of 1934, FERA joined with the American Association of Social Workers (AASW) to develop a "generic approach" to welfare, one that would, in Katherine Lenroot's words, "knot everything together" so that all poor and unemployed people could be treated through one comprehensive program. The problem with this plan, in FERA's view, was that the PWA workers, already cut out of UI, would have their status lowered further through association with the "unemployables." The remedy that FERA found was to raise the self-image and public perception of those in the most stigmatized categories through their association with others considered more worthy, especially widows and their children.[84] ADC was the product of this idea.

Not surprisingly, the Children's Bureau had serious problems with FERA's proposal. Under the FERA plan, women and children had been cast into the dreaded, ultimately stigmatized category of "unemployable" along with others who had been rejected by the labor market.[85] The "unemployable" tended to be defined by the individual inadequacies of its members, rather than by the failure of the economy to provide them with jobs or to recognize their unpaid work. In addition, people were categorized as unemployable according to fixed characteristics—such as disabilities or advanced age—when those factors might only have prevented certain kinds of work. Grace Abbott complained loudly to Frances Perkins about categorizing women in this way. She said that the "unemployable" status was particularly harmful to women because "[i]t is so difficult to provide public work for unemployed women that a large number of them as well as many, many men will be certain to be unjustly classified as unemployable and their availability for work in the future will be less. . . . To label [women] 'unemployable' is of course to misbrand them and injure them very much."[86]

The primary concern of the Children's Bureau was to keep mothers and children from being classified as unemployable and therefore stigmatized through association with others in that category. Lenroot and Abbott denounced FERA's plan for placing both employment services and welfare in the same federal department; instead, they argued, UI and employment services should be administered, along with the Bureau, under the umbrella of the Department of Labor, leaving other unemployment programs in FERA. Grace Abbott maintained that relief and employment services, "though closely related, can be better handled by two different agencies" because they each dealt with a different "type of person." Work relief should not be administered by the relief agency because "[t]he psychological effect of that is very bad." The work required to help a worker get a job "is quite different from the administration of needs tests and giving assistance in working out the various problems—physical, mental and social—of the unemployed person."[87]

The Children's Bureau proposed to align single mothers and children with workers' insurance rather than relief so that their assistance was not based on their status as poor—it wanted something similar to "the psychology of the insurance provision" without the recipient contributions. Lenroot later said that the Bureau wished to protect mothers and children from "the vagaries of relief" and from "the criticism that we foresaw would come when the public would feel that here were people who could work if only they weren't too lazy. . . . These would be a class of people that the public could see and understand."[88] But in forcing this differentiation, the Bureau also reinforced the stigmatization of the other groups that were most discriminated against through the Social Security Act, including African American workers, some of whom, ironically, were also mothers.

The ADC title of the Social Security Act looked radically different from the Children's Bureau proposal for mothers' pensions. FERA got the definition of the mothers' aid recipient broadened to include any single relative responsible for a dependent child, basing the assistance on the family's ability to show that it was poor, rather than that it was headed by a single mother. No equalization formulas were included, which would have the effect of privileging wealthier northern industrial states that could match federal funds. The amount per family was decreased, and the total federal appropriation provided was $25 million. This was much less than the $120 million called for in the Bureau's proposal, a large portion of which would have come from federal funds. Martha Eliot told Grace Abbott that "[i]t certainly is futile to appear at a hearing thinking that the section on Dependent Children has to do with Mothers' Aid."[89] In response to the FERA version of ADC, a local director of mothers' pension programs in Ohio said, "Twenty-five years ago, these mothers and children were taken out of the general relief picture and this step, at this time, would put us back where we started." She argued that "placing us in general relief in order to raise the standards of general relief to our standards" was an absurd strategy, because "with the badly equipped personnel (federal, state and local), their lack of funds, their political problems, etc., the Mothers' Aid standards would drop to their relief level."[90]

BECAUSE ABBOTT was in danger of losing what she held most dear, she did not join forces with more radical factions of the social work community that called for full, government-guaranteed employment and even economic redistribution, which sought to provide for all in need without segregating them into categories. Through her membership on an AASW committee since August 1934, she had the opportunity to outline a national social welfare program with Mary Van Kleeck and Dr. Isidore Rubinow. The committee was headed by H. L. Lurie, director of the Bureau of Jewish Social Research and apparently at least a friendly acquaintance of Abbott's. Lurie sought to use the committee to rally disparate factions of social workers behind an all-or-nothing demand for universal coverage; beyond that, he supported Van Kleeck in her public attack on the profit system that maintained inequality in America. Though he mistrusted both FDR and Frances Perkins, he had been delighted with Abbott's appointment to the Children's Bureau and obviously believed that they shared common ground.[91] Abbott, however, gave priority to the Children's Bureau proposal over the work of the AASW committee and distanced herself from Lurie when his draft proposal called for rejection of the Social Security Act. She insisted in February 1935 that although she was truly sorry that the effort had collapsed, Lurie had "undertaken not only an impossible but a relatively useless task" in his attempt to forge a radical unified social work front. By March she had dropped the committee, which had wasted "very valuable time . . . in provoking disagreement instead of reaching agreement as to gains that might be made here and now."[92] The Children's Bureau contributed to an explosive 1935 AASW conference in Montreal, in which Mary Van Kleeck's radical address was met with prolonged applause, by arranging for Frances Perkins to attend and defend the Social Security Act.[93]

The Bureau's response to the replacement of mothers' pensions with ADC was to engage in a full-tilt battle to be assigned the administration of ADC. The leaders of the Children's Bureau believed that even though the structure of the ADC title did not represent their vision, they could direct money to the poorer states and build up local networks without specific legislative authorization. In that fight, the Bureau had to contend with Congress as much as FERA and the CES. The House version of the bill left Maternal and Child Health and Child Welfare Services exactly as the Children's Bureau had designed them, but it did make significant changes to ADC, including the removal of administration from FERA to the Social Security Board, an independent federal body that would also oversee the operation of Old Age Insurance. The House version also removed all federal controls over the administration of ADC and the requirements for standards of care, "compatible with decency and health." It was apparent that the Senate would be just as hostile toward federal standards, which were widely viewed as a sectional issue, euphemistically referred to by Bureau leadership as "legislative acceptance."[94] Some powerful southern members of the House of Representatives, especially Fred Vinson, were comfortable with federal oversight as long as it was in the hands of the Children's Bureau, as they had found common ground with the Bureau's historical support of state/federal partnerships for children's services. This was also true of certain senators who had been lobbied by the children's services networks in their districts, the same networks on which the Bureau had expended so much effort to build working relationships.[95] But others, particularly Senators Pat Harrison and William King, were very troubled by the issue and insisted on state authority over hiring, grant levels, and program operations.[96] The Bureau was disturbed by rumors that the Senate might break up the measure into different bills, further jeopardizing federal control.[97] Both the Children's Bureau and FERA expressed great concern about the removal of standards, and each fought to retain administration of the program.

In its fight for control of ADC, the Bureau activated its larger network. Nisba Breckinridge notified her most important contacts on behalf of the effort, and the Bureau secured the support of many local Women's Trade Union Leagues, the General Federation of Women's Clubs, and numerous child care providers, all of whom lobbied the House Ways and Means and Senate Finance Committees. The Bureau also believed that it had the staunch support of Frances Perkins and Edwin Witte. Perkins appears to have genuinely worked behind the scenes, beginning by at least mid-January 1935, to have ADC located in the Children's Bureau, and Witte voiced public support.[98]

But the price of securing the backing of Witte and Perkins was Grace Abbott's advocacy of the CES bill as a whole, including the Wisconsin plan for UI. Witte was convinced that Abbott's endorsement was critical to the bill's passage. In January 1935 he pleaded with her to go to Washington, writing: "I know that you carry great weight with members of Congress and we very much need you."[99] The trade was solidified when the bill began to flounder in the House in early March. Lenroot telegraphed Abbott: "Important bring as much pressure as possible on house committee and house member immediately for entire bill including . . . social insurance board in department labor. . . . [A]dministration mothers aid in children's bureau will have administration support but whole bill urgently needs expression outside interest and support."[100] Facing Senate threats to break up the bill, the Bureau realized that its only chance to get control of ADC was to support the entire package.[101]

Grace Abbott endorsed the Social Security Act out of political expediency, not because she shared the vision of the Wisconsin group. Her circle was known to have "little faith in social insurance," because it segregated people into different government programs. Witte initially had tried to win Edith Abbott's support, aware that it would be a difficult task.[102] Edith Abbott advocated a unified approach to social welfare, one that would treat all unemployed people, though not mothers and children, through the same services, using all available government resources to reemploy and assist people in need, rather than establishing insurance programs for some and relief for others. She denounced employee contributions and opposed any program that required contributions in any form from the working poor.[103] In the "Notes and Comments" column of the *Social Services Review*, the Abbott sisters rejected contributory social welfare systems because they were based on a "tax on those least able to bear it." They argued that more of the cost of social welfare should be paid by "the large income tax payers." Health care also should not be managed through an insurance system. "What America wants in the way of security is *universal provision* of certain health services that will reach *everyone in need*, and not a system that reaches only the contributing group."[104] In November 1934 Grace Abbott had expressed the fear to Katherine Lenroot that the CES Advisory Council, in whose composition the Children's Bureau network had little say, would be dominated by pro-insurance experts. "I hope that the unemployment crowd are not all 'insurers'—EA [Edith Abbott] has not been invited."[105]

Despite her fundamental differences with the larger Social Security Act, Grace Abbott stood by her bargain with Witte. She took the lead in the massive lobbying effort to pull all the disparate factions of social work agencies and welfare advocates into a "united front" to promote the Act's quick passage. For six weeks in March and April, the "most crucial stage" in the Act's passage through Congress, Abbott worked tirelessly on behalf of a bill that had very little resemblance to her own vision of a social welfare system. She lobbied many different agencies personally and presided over a summit held in Washington in mid-March. Her efforts culminated in a petition supporting the Social Security Act with seventy-four signatures, some of them by prominent Americans, offering unconditional support for the Act. During Congressional hearings on UI, she set her reservations aside, even testifying that only the minimum federal standards need be applied to the program, a virtual heresy in Children's Bureau circles. And she took steps to organize a private conference of governments in industrial states to put pressure on them to enact UI legislation.[106]

One of the most difficult aspects of this bargain for Grace Abbott, especially, affected her where she lived: the Social Security Act excluded from OAI, not just agricultural and domestic workers, but also employees of charitable organizations, a category that included most social workers. This omission was one of the most contentious for social workers, many of whom had worked for years to implement a safety net for their clients, only to find themselves excluded. The House bill shut out charitable workers following a tidal wave of protest from the leadership of mainly Catholic and Protestant churches, who insisted that churches and charities had their own, superior, pension systems. The Federation of Protestant Welfare Agencies, Ministers of the Presbyterian Church in the U.S.A., and Southern Baptists all supported the exclusion, as did the National Association of Goodwill Industries and the Museum of Natural History in New York City.[107] Though the pension systems of these church and charities generally covered ministers and professional employees, primarily men, they did not provide for social workers, caretakers, and clerical workers who were mainly women.[108] Several dozen organizations lobbied against the exclusions, including many local Jewish Welfare Federations and Associations, Jewish Social Service Bureaus, YMCAS, settlement houses, employment bureaus, and clinics. The letters from these groups expressed common sentiments: that charity workers were marginal themselves and unable to pay for their own pensions—most listed salaries of less than $250 per month—and that exclusion of these workers amounted to a betrayal. The groups fighting the exclusions appear to have comprised the Children's Bureau's main constituency, as, for instance, Jacob Kepecs, superintendent of the Jewish Home Finding Society of Chicago, a strong ally, friend, and costrategist of the Bureau.[109]

The logical place for the Bureau to stand, of course, was with the social workers. But Grace Abbott showed a willingness to sacrifice even this group in hopes of retaining control of ADC. Abbott was heavily lobbied by Owen Pence of the National Council of the YMCA, who sent long, friendly letters asking for her help, but she evaded his requests.[110] She responded more directly to the AASW's Walter West, who questioned her refusal to stand up to the exclusions. She wrote: "I am, of course, entirely for including the Social Agencies. I think, however, that there is little chance that it will be done. I am sorry that the Association finds itself under the necessity of picking out small items which it is either for or against, and cannot lend its support to a measure of such importance as the Security Bill."[111] Abbott's position showed her pragmatism and the degree to which she was willing to fight for ADC, as she aligned the Children's Bureau with employers against their powerless and underpaid workers. But in this case the exploitative employers included, not factory owners, but some liberal professionals in her own circle. Even John Andrews, head of the American Association of Labor Legislation (AALL) and a member of the Wisconsin group, quietly supported the exclusion of charitable institutions from OAI, as long as the exclusion extended to his own AALL employees.[112]

If the "united front" that Abbott spearheaded did not include underpaid Jewish social workers, it also neglected representatives of interracial organizations. Abbott's files include long, detailed lists of people and organizations contacted to support the Social Security Act by state and organization within states, but interracial organizations are noticeably missing.[113] This should come as no great surprise; the Act offered very little to most African Americans, and their support would not have been expected. The united front sought to unify all those who could live with the "imperfections" of the bill, those whose most cherished constituencies were protected by it.

And though it continued to fight for administrative control of ADC, the Bureau also sought collaboration with FERA, or to be more accurate, with some women in FERA, on ADC standards for hiring and the adequacy of grants that they could lobby for together regardless of the eventual placement of the program.[114] Josephine Brown of FERA was thought to be especially receptive. Bureau leaders encouraged their larger network to "throw" itself into collaborative efforts on standards to salvage whatever it could of their original plan.[115] In the end, however, the effort failed. Congress continued to resist standards that would, the lawmakers feared, tell them who to hire and establish grant levels that would funnel federal money to northern states.

ADC was thus established as a public assistance program modeled after FERA, and all of the worst nightmares of the Children's Bureau came to pass. Small and southern states received no funds for years, and when they did, they had to pass regressive taxes in order to raise the state match.[116] Katherine Lenroot later reflected that ADC employees were overloaded with work, undertrained, and underpaid; moreover, they resented the better-paid and respected workers at Child Welfare Services, with whom they shared clients. She said that

> [r]ecipients have been subjected to all of the "stigma" or questioning of public assistance in general as to whether they were deserving, whether they were really eligible, whether we were subsidizing dependence. All these things have developed in the administration of ADC. Now, this is not to say that we would have succeeded in this tremendous problem. . . . I am claiming that we were motivated, and the friends of the Bureau were motivated, by these considerations.[117]

In the first years of the American welfare state, the main problem was that little money was distributed to many states, including most southern states, because, without equalization, they were unable to match the federal funds. The Social Security Board acknowledged, less than a year after the Act's passage, that the distribution of funds was "the most vital in the field covered by the Bureau of Public Assistance."[118] States made older, indigent people their highest priority and used their limited resources to apply as quickly as possible for OAA grants. In April 1936 Jane Hoey of the ADC program "deplored the inadequacy of grants shown in plans submitted by the different states . . . she regrets that due to the activity of the old-age group, the selections of services which are being made give preferences to old-age, with blind second place, and aid to dependent children last."[119] In fiscal year 1938–39, federal grants to states to meet the needs of OAA recipients totaled $208 million; however, only $30.5 million of federal money was distributed for ADC. At that time, eight states—among them Mississippi, Texas, and Kentucky—had not yet received any federal funds for ADC. Most other southern states with large

African American populations received much less federal funding than their percentage of the national population warranted. Virginia, Florida, Georgia, Alabama, South Carolina, and North Carolina all obtained between $3.88 and $17.35 per one hundred residents in the state, though the average amount distributed to other states was $36.80.[120] Between 1937 and 1940 African Americans were much better represented on ADC rolls nationally than their percentage of the population, but, not surprisingly, they were extremely underrepresented in the rural South.[121]

One of the chief means of discrimination was the set of moral standards imposed by states (for example, that parents be "proper people" and homes be "suitable"), which could be used arbitrarily to exclude applicants for assistance.[122] The Social Security Act did not require that mothers meet moral and "suitable home" qualifications, but such standards adopted by states were officially sanctioned by the Federal Bureau of Public Assistance in 1939.[123] Southern states used these standards to ensure that the limited available funds for ADC would be distributed to white families.

The lost fight waged by the Children's Bureau had far-reaching consequences, none more significant than the loss of the Bureau's understanding that work provided outside the marketplace had value and therefore should be compensated and secured. The Abbotts and their network had toiled for decades to create an option for women to be mothers and still retain economic independence and the dignity it afforded in the twentieth-century United States. Because they were committed to, and showed that they were capable of, undermining inequality through the policy they created, the greatest long-term loss has been experienced by the millions of African American children raised by single mothers since 1935. These children would have had a different universe of support had they grown up under the plan of the Abbott sisters and Katherine Lenroot.

Those Old Discriminatory Practices

The Depression, like death, has been a leveler. . . . In this New Deal the Negro has an unusual opportunity of getting in on the ground floor. . . . [T]he whole country is on the threshold of a new era the likes of which the world has not seen in modern times. . . . [However,] unless the Negro can prevent the old discriminatory practices, he is doomed to permanent unemployment, for it is to be remembered that the government and not the individual business man is to be the employer of the future.[1]

How did African Americans become discriminated against through the Social Security Act? The most basic answer is that the Act was structured on a bifurcated, hierarchical model, within the context of an economy that relied on racial inequality. The Act's framers, the Wisconsin group, did not design policy to deliberately discriminate against African Americans, but they structured the Social Security Act in such a way that it would inevitably discriminate against *some* Americans. They rejected a unified approach and instead drew a line in the sand, ensuring that Americans on one side of the line would be able to retain their dignity and independence by contrasting them with those relegated to the other side, who were made economically insecure and dependent. Once the line was drawn and an atmosphere of scarcity established, a scramble ensued as different groups of policymakers sought to differentiate the group they represented from those even more threatened in order to secure the best deal for their own constituencies. With no protections against discrimination built into the Act, and no group of policymakers willing to lay down and die for them, the existing marginality of the country's 12 million African Americans guaranteed that they would fare worst in the scramble.

African Americans were discriminated against, not because they were targeted by "racist intent," but because Social Security rewarded those who were already privileged. In a variety of ways, the Act favored wealthier northern states over the southern states where most African Americans lived. The Act privileged people whose access to health care enabled them to live into their sixties, a group underrepresented by African Americans, over the disproportionate percentage of black children. It gave priority to the dignity and economic security of the working class's top tier, those who were most secure in jobs from which African Americans were barred. So on one level, the Social Security Act discriminated against African Americans because of their marginality in the larger economy.

But that simple answer does not tell the whole story: the bifurcated model itself was a product, not of *racism* per se, of a conscious intent to discriminate, but of the U.S. race paradigm. Back in the 1910s, when John Commons first glimpsed what would become his vision of a national unemployment compensation system, his sight was colored by his culture's belief that Americans could not be understood outside of their designation as "white" or "Negro," and that those categories could only be understood in relation to each other. He drew on that belief as he constructed a new paradigm of the government's relationship to citizens to explain what was wrong and needed to be fixed and how to fix it. His students, those most responsible for the exclusion of African Americans from the Act, did not exhibit "racist intent"; paradoxically, some of them advocated equality. Yet the intent of these policymakers had much less to do with outcomes than their acceptance of the American racial paradigm, that the value of whiteness (of industrial white manhood, in this case) could only be created and maintained through the devaluation of blackness.

This study suggests that *intent* may not the most important lens through which to explore how policy is made discriminatory. The study of discriminatory treatment of African Americans through public policy in the 1930s has been framed as a fight primarily waged between groups of white people, one group with altruistic motives, defending the rights of African Americans, the other group self-interested, seeking to limit those rights. But this model does not fit the story of the Social Security Act. The Act was designed by reformers whose intent was primarily altruistic; they did not set out to enhance their own power and wealth. Nevertheless, they benefited from the policy that they created as "white" men and women. The salvation of white industrial workers was predicated on constructing them as something other than welfare recipients and other than black workers. By enhancing the value of the whiteness of industrial workers, the Act's framers enhanced the value of their own whiteness. The discriminatory policy created through the Social Security Act resulted more from the *positioning* of the Act's framers within the U.S. racial hierarchy than their intent.

None of what happened was an inevitable product of the times; alternatives were offered, and those alternatives would likely have established a much more equitable welfare system. The more unified system that many promoted would have undoubtedly created fewer barriers to equal treatment. But even through the bifurcated structure insisted on by the Wisconsin group, one that separated insurance from welfare programs, more equal policy could have been developed. From the reports drafted by various staffers, it appears that marginal workers, including the majority of African Americans, might easily have been accommodated in the insurance programs through systems in use in Europe, especially the stamp book method. The Children's Bureau's formulas for equalizing funding between states and counties appears to have provided equally for African Americans in the programs under the Bureau's administration and could have done so in the case of Aid to Dependent Children (ADC). Further, the evidence provided to Congress by George Haynes suggests that a combination of nondiscriminatory language and regionally based funding formulas had, in the past, produced nondiscriminatory policies, even in the case of large national programs like funding for higher education.

Not only did policymakers have options that would have created a more equal welfare state. Ironically, it appears that those options would have been easier to administer. Segregating workers from each other, far from preventing administrative problems, actually created logistical nightmares. The problems that surfaced reveal that human beings are not so easily categorized as the Act's framers assumed.

As soon as the Act was passed, the Social Security Board began to have difficulty determining which groups of workers fell into the categories of "domestic" and "agricultural" labor, as claims were submitted from people in all kinds of borderline jobs seeking inclusion or exclusion. The claims came from people working "in orchards, in livery sales, in dairies, in hothouses or on large grounds used for private parks, hunting lodges, golf courses, and similar places."[2] The administration of Old Age Insurance (OAI) was particularly sticky. Because people moved in and out of covered jobs in greater percentages than was originally estimated, their wages were often docked for contributions they would never receive. As late as 1946, House Ways and Means Committee staffers reported that "[t]he quiet movement into and out of [OAI] coverage is such that some 72,000,000 individuals have wage credits but less than half that number have an insured status." Of the 5.3 million "farm operators" in 1938, possibly over a million were "only part-time farmers who receive a sizable share of their income from industrial or commercial business activities or employment." Of the 2.8 million agricultural wage workers, up to one-half were "employed in non-agricultural employment at least during part of the year."[3] In some cases, the exclusions increased the drain on the OAI fund. Some workers were getting more from the system than they were entitled to because of the exclusions. Uncovered workers frequently earned minimum benefits ($10 per month) through part-time employment in covered jobs, which sometimes equaled more than they and their employers had paid in contributions. The same confusion in defining agricultural workers affected workers providing personal services. The confusion still had not been resolved by 1940, when a "nurse-companion," whose job involved full-time care of an older woman, was considered to be a domestic servant under the law and thus was refused coverage under OAI.[4]

Domestic and agricultural workers were not just excluded temporarily; their marginal place in the economy was inscribed in federal law. Domestic workers in New York, Utah, and Washington State actually lost benefits through the Social Security Act. These workers had been covered by fully half of the six state unemployment insurance laws that had been enacted prior to the Act—a small number but a promising percentage. After the Act's passage, however, all but one state—New York—excluded these workers, in accordance with the new federal law.[5] And their situation did not improve with time. Both insurance programs were expanded in the 1950s to theoretically include agricultural and domestic workers, but most of these workers remained uncovered for various reasons. Many employers did not comply with the law: since collection systems were not designed to protect workers employed by families and individuals, these employers were effectively not held accountable. Barbara Armstrong, the chief designer of federal OAI, admitted in 1969 that the people in her neighborhood did not pay Social Security taxes for their hired help. She argued that domestic workers still did not receive adequate coverage because they were not allowed to tack their earnings from one employer onto the earnings from another—that is, they had to make fifty dollars per quarter from each employer.[6] Of course, lack of compliance continues to be a problem today.

In 1939 the Social Security Board appealed to Congress to remove all of the exclusions because of the difficulties they caused. But the lawmakers responded instead by attempting to simplify the programs by expanding the exclusions to an additional 300,000 to 400,000 workers who had been covered by the 1935 Act. These included laborers who processed and packaged fruits and vegetables, as well as those who worked in trucking, poultry hatching, and cotton ginning; naval stores operators; workers in greenhouses and nurseries (often in suburbs); and fur and wild life farmers, mushroom growers, maple syrup producers, and irrigators.[7] These new exclusions, which were felt most keenly in the South,[8] only exacerbated the administrative problems caused by the original exclusions. Also, stricter eligibility requirements imposed by Congress exempted many low-paid workers who had been taxed on their wages since the Social Security Act had been enacted. The outcome of the 1939 amendments was that roughly 550,000 to 850,000 workers who had already been paying Social Security taxes were excluded from coverage and therefore lost all of the money that they and their employers had paid into the system. Letters received by the Social Security Board attest to the unhappiness of these workers.[9]

But the problem did not stop there. Ironically, many African Americans who worked in industry, those lucky few who were considered to be covered by the Act, fared no better than maids and farmworkers. By 1937, a majority of African American workers in northern states (though many more men than women) were technically eligible for OAI and UI.[10] However, almost half of these workers received no benefits because they did not earn the $50-per-employer-per-quarter minimum wage. Those who did tended to earn at the lower end of the benefit scale, which ranged from $10 to $85 per month, because of their low salaries and few years of coverage. UI also provided little help for African Americans, especially in the rural South. Black southerners who were eligible for UI typically received between $5 and $10 per month.[11]

According to a 1977 study of the economic impact of the Social Security Act on African Americans, conducted by Frank G. Davis, UI and OAI may have actually harmed covered African Americans more than they helped. This may still be true under these programs' current structure. Davis argued that Social Security has not lifted black workers out of poverty as was once hoped; on the contrary, it has actually had the effect of transferring income from black workers to white workers by disproportionately burdening black workers with Social Security taxes. Davis found that, as of the mid-seventies, the gap in Social Security benefits between black and white workers was growing at a faster rate than the gap between their relative incomes.[12]

Davis reached this conclusion by looking at both the direct and indirect costs of Social Security: that is, the taxes paid by employees on the one hand and the indirect tax of raised prices on goods that employers pass on to consumers on the other. He found that African American workers, trapped in the lowest-paying jobs, suffering the highest unemployment rates, and, because they died much younger than white workers (thus having fewer years to collect benefits), only received $0.54 in Social Security benefits for every dollar they paid in *direct* contributions. On average, all American workers collected $1.00 for every $1.00 contributed. But over a fifteen-year period (1957–72), African Americans contributed $21.0 billion (in 1977 dollars) to Social Security but received only $11.5 billion in benefits. This significant loss in income was probably doubled, Davis contended, when taking into account the *indirect* contribution African Americans made to the Social Security system during that period as consumers. This drain was a factor in the continued poverty of the larger black community, ensuring that "[a]fter almost 40 years of social security, most Black workers below the low income level in 1970 must look forward to public assistance income, or, now, supplemental security income, rather than income from primary social security benefits." In 1970, 48 percent of African American families living below the "low income level" were on public assistance, though only 24 percent received Social Security.[13]

So one long-term effect of the discriminatory structure of the Social Security Act has been the economic disempowerment of African Americans. But another long-term impact may be just as damaging: the racialization of America's perception of welfare and welfare recipients. The ground was laid in the Social Security Act by funneling black workers away from the insurance programs and therefore making them dependent, when in need, on public assistance. Contemporaries report that beginning with the depression, dependence on government relief became a job category for African Americans, "one of the major Negro 'occupations'" second only to agricultural labor and possibly domestic service.[14] Relief was, at first, a good and necessary thing that kept families from starvation. It was temporary and available to all unemployed Americans. As Gunnar Myrdal asserted, "the institution of large-scale public relief by the

New Deal is almost the only bright spot in the recent economic history of the Negro people."[15]

But that "bright spot" took on a different look when it ceased to be temporary. After passage of the Social Security Act, as African American workers were driven from agriculture, refused a living wage in other fields, and denied benefits through UI when unemployed and OAI when too old to work, they increasingly turned to various forms of public assistance where it was available in the late 1930s and 1940s. Throughout these years, then, African Americans were overrepresented on OAA and ADC rolls, though discrimination continued to be a problem in the South, especially in the program for mothers and children.[16] Moreover, all of those programs were so poorly funded that they did not provide the means for basic sustenance, much less a dignified living.

One problem was that the grant amount of the welfare programs was universally very low. States could, in theory, raise grant levels to any amount, but the programs structurally discouraged them from doing so. ADC and OAA were federally funded through fixed appropriations—the government would budget an amount for welfare that it would not exceed. States budgeted their portion of the programs' budget and then applied for federal matching funds. This plan worked unless the total requested by all of the states was greater than the amount of federal funds budgeted; in that case, the federal funds would be prorated across states, regardless of the actual amount that the state had committed to pay. A state that tried to raise grant levels took a big risk—it would likely get stuck with a huge share of the cost, much more than it had budgeted for, when the federal appropriation ran out. This was not the case with OAI and UI, where appropriations were made according to the amount needed for all covered workers. In short, in the insurance programs, the grant amount paid to individual workers drove the overall cost of the programs, whereas in public assistance, the amount allotted for the programs drove the amount of the grants. Of course, grant levels were further lowered when poor states were unable to match federal dollars, which was also not a factor in the insurance programs because they were matched by businesses, not state governments.[17]

Another problem was that the Social Security Act did not provide structural protections against discrimination, and so the insufficient federal funds were not made equally available to African Americans in poorer states. This was especially the case in the South, where program administration was left in the hands of southern bureaucrats. By 1939, all southern states had at least one public assistance program in place, but these programs were typically run by people appointed through patronage rather than hired through a civil service system. Administration of ADC and OAA was generally left to counties; the federal government could enforce compliance with the law only by completely withdrawing a state's matching funds, an option that was rarely used. States varied widely in their definitions of "need" for public assistance, and standards differed from county to county.[18]

Under the system established by the Social Security Act, African Americans were ghettoized into public assistance programs that stigmatized them as society's dependents. Their unemployment was perceived as a different condition, with a different prescribed treatment, from that of the majority of unemployed white men. The Act treated unemployed white industrial workers as if their unemployment was the fault of an imperfect economy. Unemployed or dislocated African Americans, on the other hand, received assistance only on the basis of their poverty, not their status as workers, the implication being that they, not the system, had failed. The age-old association of African Americans with servitude rather than employment was thus inscribed in federal law.

Before the Act was passed, African Americans expressed great concern about their inability to secure paid work and growing dependence on relief. Forrester Washington feared "Negro chronic dependency" on relief due to the lack of opportunities for employment. He argued that the Federal Emergency Relief Administration (FERA) only helped the masses of blacks at the "lowest" level; the New Deal ignored professional and business-trained African Americans, and New Deal programs discriminated against "Negro" workers. He feared that if such discrimination continued, blacks would never gain a foothold in unskilled and semiskilled work, creating a class of permanent welfare recipients. He viewed this chronic dependence as a new form of slavery.[19]

The same fear was expressed in a study of attitudes of African American families on relief described in the December 1935 issue of *Opportunity* magazine, the official publication of the National Urban League. The author of the study, Newell D. Eason, interviewed members of sixty-five families to catalog what he interpreted as a change in the attitude of black families on relief toward work, home, and life. According to Eason, the advent of federal relief signaled an important development for African

Americans, because it was introduced at a time when "[e]mployers in case after case have undermined the Negroes' ambition as a worker by replacing them in their jobs with white workers." For many African Americans newly arrived in the North and in cities, economic dependence was thrust upon them at a critical moment of disorganization and change, when their identity was already in flux.[20]

Asserting that "[e]mployment is itself a human need, apart from the relation to subsistence," Eason reported that "[r]elief alone is pauperizing Negro families, and is therefore doing more harm than good. It is turning approximately one-fifth of the Negro population into willing professional recipients of charity." His study showed that African American families initially struggled against accepting relief, but in doing so they faced an impossible choice between retaining even marginal independence and going hungry. If unemployed fathers refused relief, their authority over their hungry children could be undermined by government relief workers who stood waiting with bread. One desperate mother enlisted her children's help convincing their father to accept relief by telling them that "the visitor has allowed the money but your father refuses to buy the milk." The relief office inserted itself into the home, in many cases replacing communities and churches as arbiters of family problems. Eason found that children "proudly boasted 'that's my visitor,' where once they boasted 'that's my daddy.'"[21]

Initially, all sixty-five families that Eason studied energetically sought work, "vehemently" declaring that "it is work they want, not relief." But after a while, with no work in sight, their attitude changed. "They soon discover that they have always worked too hard for such a small income so that the idea of receiving an equal sum with no labor attached has a catastrophic effect." With economic dependence came lethargy and dissolution. Eason found that because black men "fall in such large numbers on the relief rolls the general public views him as a chronic dependent. There are few attitudes which have done more to disorganize the Negroes' personality and family life than this attitude. His attitudes are conditioned by the reflection of himself as a chronic dependent that he thinks he sees in the white public." Eason concluded that, having been so distanced in the public mind from white society—from those who were not "dependent"—African Americans turned "wholeheartedly" to the relief agency and developed a new cultural loathing for work. The "general attitude of the families studied was so much an attitude of disgust for work until it leads to the belief that the Negro on relief is becoming pauperized faster than we ordinarily think." Rejected by employment, "Negroes" in turn rejected work.[22]

Eason's study shows the disruption and anguish experienced by African Americans on relief in the 1930s, as well as their disillusionment with work, but it shows something else just as significant. Eason's interpretation of his findings reflects an emerging dominant cultural understanding of the relationship between race and welfare, one that had begun to dissociate African American poverty from its basis in the larger political economy. His conclusion that the damage of relief was perpetuated in "Negro communities" through the dissemination of new and pathological attitudes toward work, ultimately located the cause of this damage within the borders of these communities. "Chronic dependence" did not just describe a material condition for African Americans; for many it was coming to also describe a cultural assignment.

In the context of this developing interest in African American attitudes toward work, Eason's study generally interpreted demands for adequate welfare as evidence, not of material need or resistance to the stigma of dependence, but of hostility toward work. He related the story of a family of eight that had lost its income when the father's employer went out of business and was receiving $12 per week in relief. The family's decision to move to a larger house in a better neighborhood, increasing its rent from $5 to $15 weekly, Eason maintained, was evidence of a diminishing work ethic. The father rejected some used clothing, insisting that his family needed "furniture, shoes, and new clothing instead of secondhand ones." Eason characterized the man's attempts to wrangle these things from the social welfare agency as "begging" and noted with disapproval that the family sent its laundry out. The only examples given in this anecdote relate to securing provisions; there is no indication that anyone in the family rejected work. Yet Eason interpreted the family's "attitude" as resistant to work and negated its efforts to define for itself the meaning of a decent life in the midst of an economic crisis. Even as it critically observed the ways that African American recipients of welfare were being constructed as a group segregated from "normal" society and defined through fear and repulsion of that society, Eason's study contributed to that construction.[23]

Many studies since Easton's have contributed to that interpretation. In the more than five decades since the passage of the Social Security Act,

African Americans who receive welfare have been singled out for scrutiny, punishment, or behavior modification, or to be made examples of social theories or to take the blame for social problems. Sociologists have examined the behaviors of African Americans on welfare; policymakers have argued endlessly about the causal relationships between grant levels, teen pregnancy, and drug use; and politicians have used welfare policy to prove their own humanity and/or thrift. As a dependent, captive audience, African American recipients of welfare are known in American culture only through stereotypes. The "black welfare queen" serves a social/psychological function in the American imagination, embodying the opposite qualities of the self-made, industrious producer and consumer, perhaps even the frightening specter of the unleashed id that rejects work and responsibility, that needs to be controlled and made to conform.

As the Social Security Act gave birth to a welfare system steeped in race, it also re-created the meaning of race, what it means to be "black" or "white." Throughout its history, America has reinvented that meaning to meet changing economic circumstances. One of the most dramatic examples comes from the late nineteenth century, following the legal abolition of slavery and the death of Reconstruction. At that time, white Americans undertook a major effort to reconstruct the meaning of race, to bring the concept into the service of a new system of oppression, one that had to be maintained outside of the law. This freshly minted system — segregation — was supported by new scientific "discoveries" about the biological differences of races and by new arenas of philosophy. A new meaning of "black" was invented. Where white society in southern states once regarded slaves as unruly children needing to be civilized, they now saw African American men as dangerous predators; the physical closeness demanded by the paternalistic plantation family gave way to revulsion at any physical contact between the "races." This change in society's understanding of the meaning of race ensured that, though no longer prevented by slavery, the races would not intermarry, enabling the economic exploitation of black people to continue.

Another example is found more recently, following the civil rights movement, in the creation of both African American Hollywood celebrities and a perpetual "black underclass." Although discrimination is experienced by African Americans at all levels of society, the gap in interests between upper- and lower-income black people has intensified, and the existence of an African American professional class reinforces the idea that the politics of race no longer determines the range of opportunities available to black children growing up on welfare. Scholars of Critical Race Theory suggest that the roots of this shift can be traced to the goals of civil rights. As segregation law was replaced with "equal opportunity" law, it initially appeared that African Americans had won their centuries-old struggle for political equality, which, many believed, would lead eventually to a general leveling of the playing field. But as it turns out, the political gains won through the civil rights movement were not enough. As long as "whiteness" has an economic value, African Americans and other people of color in the United States are undermined in their attempts to build an economic base. As Kimberle Crenshaw has argued, the removal of legal barriers to equality has actually had the effect of diminishing the promise of equality. The "colorblind" law that emerged after the civil rights movement provided the means for masking the continued legal oppression of Americans who are not designated "white." Because Americans believe that equal opportunity reigns today, evidence to the contrary is easily explained as the result of individual failing. "In this new land of equal opportunity," she says, it is "much more difficult for black people to name their reality. There is no longer a perpetrator, a clearly identifiable discriminator."[24]

Stephen Steinberg has argued that this shift took place within federal policy. Federal policy reconstructed the meaning of racial equality itself, basing the realization of equality on intent rather than results. To achieve a state of equality, the government would not have to ensure that equal education, housing, and access to jobs were actually attained. It would only have to establish programs that expressed its commitment to these goals. At the same time, the more limited civil rights agenda—to erase racial difference in employment, housing, and so forth—was submerged in the murky morass of the larger political economy. The civil rights movement sought to remove the barriers preventing African Americans from moving up and through the U.S. class structure, to achieve more proportional representation in each of its layers—a relatively reasonable goal whose achievement, in the mid-1960s, seemed attainable to many. However, the shift in federal policy, best articulated by the 1965 Moynihan Report, argued that racial equality would not be achieved until the related problems of poverty and the "culture of poverty" were solved. Therefore the fight for racial justice became mired in a hopeless sea of quicksand, in the complex intersection of the competing interests of workers, the competitive drive of business, the fluctuating value of property, and all the other factors that maintained the American class structure and relied on the perpetuation of its lower rungs.[25]

Inequality in the post–civil rights era continues to be structurally produced, just as it was through the eras of slavery and of legal segregation. One key to understanding the production of racial inequality today is the economic and social value of whiteness, and the ways that that value is protected institutionally. Just as the elimination of slavery destroyed the economic value embodied in slaves, the creation of true racial equality would have a similar effect on the economic value of whiteness that guarantee for many Americans secure property values, values that they may save, spend, borrow against, and pass on to their heirs.

The Social Security Act provides another example of the structural production of racial inequality through public policy; it suggests that the shift in the meaning of race identified by Crenshaw and others has its roots in the 1930s. The Act did not merely institutionalize existing inequalities; it created a new frontier in the landscape of racial hierarchy. The Act took a diverse group of American workers—farm laborers, welders, cigar rollers, telephone operators, truck drivers, laundry workers, private domestics, and meat packers—and reconfigured them according to their social assignment as either "white" or "black," as two distinct types of workers, with two radically different ties to the rest of society. It built race into the foundations of the welfare state, but in ways that are not easily identified, through a colorblind lens that masks the operation of privilege.

IN RECENT YEARS the social welfare system created by the Social Security Act has undergone big changes, and this is a good time to review them. We have seen the dismantling of Aid to Families with Dependent Children, and we are now embroiled in debates about whether and how to reconstruct the foundations of Social Security. So, what can history teach us about where to go from here? One clear message from the past is that the visions of reformers must be scrutinized, because the most altruistic of dreams can mask, even to the dreamers, the perpetuation of privilege. Another message is that if public policy is to challenge rather than shore up inequality, it must be designed by policymakers with diverse perspectives, at least some of whom do not benefit from current systems of inequality. Policymakers might do well to research the possibility of embracing a unified approach to social welfare, one that does not divide the population and reward some at the expense of others, since all bifurcated models will tend to reinforce existing inequalities. Likewise, any policy that ties bene-fits to an unequal wage structure will reproduce, and possibly enhance, inequality. Those who advocate further privatizing Social Security should take note, especially those who argue that the federal program should be eliminated because it discriminates. The history strongly suggests that fur-ther privatization would only increase discrimination. It may be virtually impossible to ensure mere equal opportunity through colorblind policies in a society that has such a grossly unequal playing field. Those who design policy might want to look at the equalization formulas developed by the Children's Bureau and all of the structural protections against discrimina-tion offered by Walter White and George Haynes.

Ultimately, the Social Security Act can teach us that profound social change can be brought about through public policy, and that is a powerful message. Equally powerful is the knowledge that the segregated structure of the U.S. welfare state was not inevitable: it was neither an inescapable product of a racist era nor the result of the bigoted interests of an omnipo-tent ruling elite. Answers were available within the broad community of those involved with the Act's creation that could have led to a radically dif-ferent social welfare safety net, one that fostered equality rather than pro-moting separation. History can teach us that racial inequality is a relatively recent invention based on the false belief that race is a biological, rather than a socially constructed, reality. It only continues to survive when we continue to breathe life into it. Despite its failings, the Social Security Act teaches us that a reconstructed social welfare policy just might be one of our best future options for eradicating racial inequality from our midst.

Notes

Abbreviations

Abbott
Papers
Edith and Grace Abbott Papers, University of Chicago Library,
Special Collections, Chicago

Altmeyer
Papers
Arthur Joseph Altmeyer Papers, State Historical Society of
Wisconsin, Madison

Bean
Papers
Louis H. Bean Papers, Franklin D. Roosevelt Presidential Library,
Hyde Park, N.Y.

Cohen
Papers
Wilbur J. Cohen Papers, State Historical Society of Wisconsin,
Madison

Commons
Papers
John R. Commons Papers, State Historical Society of Wisconsin,
Madison

Dewson
Papers
Mary Williams Dewson Papers, Franklin D. Roosevelt Presidential
Library, Hyde Park, N.Y.

DOL   U.S. Department of Labor

Du Bois
Papers
William Edward Burghardt Du Bois Papers, University of
Massachusetts Library, Amherst

Ely Papers   Richard Theodore Ely Papers, State Historical Society of
Wisconsin, Madison

ER   Eleanor Roosevelt

FCB   Federal Children's Bureau

FDR Papers   Franklin Delano Roosevelt Papers, Franklin D. Roosevelt
Presidential Library, Hyde Park, N.Y.

FWB   Federal Women's Bureau

Hopkins
Papers
Harry Hopkins Papers, Franklin D. Roosevelt Presidential Library,
Hyde Park, N.Y.

House Files	U.S. House of Representative Records, National Archives, Washington, D.C.
Howe Papers	Louis McHenry Howe Papers, Franklin D. Roosevelt Presidential Library, Hyde Park, N.Y.
Leiserson Papers	William M. Leiserson Papers, State Historical Society of Wisconsin, Madison
Lenroot Papers	Katherine Lenroot Papers, Columbia University, Rare Books and Manuscripts Library, Butler Library, New York, N.Y.
NAACP Papers	National Association for the Advancement of Colored People Papers, Group I, Library of Congress, Manuscripts Division, Department of Research, Washington, D.C.
NUL Papers	National Urban League Papers, Library of Congress, Manuscripts Division, Department of Research, Washington, D.C.
OF	Official Files
PPF	President's Personal Files
Raushenbush Papers	Paul and Elizabeth Brandeis Raushenbush Papers, State Historical Society of Wisconsin, Madison
RG 9	National Recovery Administration Records, Record Group 9, National Archives, College Park, Md.
RG 16	Secretary of Agriculture Records, Record Group 16, National Archives, College Park, Md.
RG 29	Bureau of the Census Records, Record Group 29, National Archives, College Park, Md.
RG 46	U.S. Senate Records, Record Group 46, National Archives, College Park, Md.
RG 47	Social Security Administration Records, Record Group 47, National Archives, College Park, Md.
RG 86	Women's Bureau Records, Record Group 86, National Archives, College Park, Md.
RG 102	Federal Children's Bureau Records, Record Group 102, National Archives, College Park, Md.
SSB	Social Security Board
USDA	U.S. Department of Agriculture

Wagner   Robert F. Wagner Papers, City University of New York, City
Papers   College Archives, New York, N.Y.

Weaver   Robert Clifton Weaver Papers, Schomburg Center for Research in
Papers   Black Culture, The New York Public Library, Manuscripts,
            Archives, and Rare Books Division, New York, N.Y.

Witte Papers   Edwin Emil Witte Papers, State Historical Society of Wisconsin,
               Madison

Introduction

1. Leuchtenburg, *Roosevelt*; Friedel, *F. D. R. and the South*; Schlesinger, *Politics of Upheaval*; Barton Bernstein, *Towards a New Past*.

2. These developments are described by both Berkowitz, in *America's Welfare State*, and Quadagno, in *Transformation of Old Age Security*. The "development" school includes works by Clark Kerr, John T. Dunlop, Frederick Harbison, and Charles Meyers in *Industrialism and Industrial Man*. The "Social democratic" model has been promoted by Frances Fox Piven and Richard Cloward, *Regulating the Poor*.

3. Weir, Orloff, and Skocpol, *Politics of Social Policy*; Quadagno, *Transformation of Old Age Security*.

4. See Sonya Michel and Seth Koven, *Mothers of a New World*, and Robin Muncy, *Creating a Female Dominion*.

5. Barbara Nelson, "Two-Channeled Welfare State"; Linda Gordon, *Pitied but Not Entitled*; Mink, *Wages of Motherhood* and *Whose Welfare?*

6. Berkowitz, *America's Welfare State*, chap. 2.

7. Kessler-Harris, *In Pursuit of Equity*, chaps. 2 and 3.

8. Lieberman, *Shifting the Color Line*. Lieberman's own approach is more nuanced than this phrase implies and more similar to the approach taken in this study.

9. Hale, *Making Whiteness*.

Chapter One

1. Mr. McCauley to the U.S. Senate, April 8, 1935, Records of the U.S. Senate, RG 46, *Social Security Act*, box 14110. I have edited this quotation to help the reader see past the misspelled words and grammatical errors and focus on the arguments it makes. The full transcription is "To the Senat: Govern By a Bodys of Well Educated mens that ar Elected to mak law for Bouth races to live under Now I see a Bill p[os]ed now in Congress about old age pension and it all for one Race Now you ar a body of mens to look for the Ethiopion as well as the caucasion races now What will down one it will down the uther so the Ethiopion race is the foot stol and When he get the age of 65 years he ar she need help to live on in this country [T]her ar a lot of Ethiopian that Was Born and live under president Jefferson

davis and now some of them ar not able to Work so I plee to legislature to look at this mader as you all ar a Body Well Educated men to mak resolution and laws for Bouth Nations . . . the Ethiopian is tilt the Earth and When he ar she riach the age of 65 ar over there ar not much that they can do to mak a living then What must Be don as the Ethiopion Race is submissed to the caucasion Race[?]."

2. W. A. Allen, President, and G. D. Hammonds, Secretary, Plainfield Colored Democratic Club, to FDR, FDR Papers, OF 93, box 2.

3. Those calling for interracial collaboration included the Townsendites; Huey Long's Share the Wealth; followers of Father Charles E. Coughlin; the Technocrats, communists, and socialists; and unemployment councils. See Holtzman, *Townsend Movement*, and Brinkley, *Voices of Protest*.

4. Bunche, *Political Status of the Negro*, quoted in Kirby, *Black Americans*, 149.

5. John J. Cuba to U.S. Government, February 18, 1938, U.S. Unemployment Census, RG 29, PI 183, entry 258, box 17.

6. Of all the "Negro" men who were employed in nonagricultural jobs in 1930, 69 percent were designated "unskilled," in contrast to only 25 percent of white workers. Only 7.5 percent of "Negro" workers were classified as "professionals," "managers," or "clerks," in contrast to 74.9 percent of white workers. Sterner, *The Negro's Share*, 22–28.

7. Foner and Lewis, *Black Workers*, 34.

8. Of 11 million working women in December 1934, 3.2 million were domestic or personal servants, 2 million were clerical workers, 1.9 million had manufacturing or mechanical jobs, 1.5 million were professionals, 963,000 were involved in trade, 909,000 were paid farm laborers, and 281,000 were in transportation or communication. Mary Anderson, "Women Workers Are the Concern of the Women's Bureau" and "Occupations for Women—1930," *Labor Information Bulletin* 1, no. 4 (December 1934), in FWB Papers, RG 47, PI 183, entry 7, box 48. In 1935 there were 1.6 million African American domestic workers, a group that comprised 20.4 percent of all black workers. Reginald A. Johnson, "The Negro and Social Insurance," Atlanta Urban League, February 1935, NUL Papers, ser. 4, box 21, "Regional Conferences"; Ilse M. Smith, "Old-Age Insurance for Domestic Workers," February 24, 1939, RG 47, PI 183, entry 13, box 101, 4; T. Arnold Hill to Mary Anderson, March 15, 1933, FWB, RG 86, entry 8, box 36.

9. "House Maids in Cleveland Ask for Square Deal," unidentified clipping enclosed in Mrs. Joseph F. Novak to Frances Perkins, February 2, 1934, RG 102, Central File 1933–36, entry 3, box 529, 6-1-2-7; Rae Needleman, "Summary of Findings on the Problem of Including Domestic Workers under the Old-Age Benefit Provisions of the Social Security Act," March 26, 1937, CES, RG 47, PI 183, entry 13, box 101; Mary Anderson, "Women Workers Are the Concern of the Women's Bureau."

10. Myrdal, *American Dilemma*, xlix, published in 1944.

11. Ibid., 605–39. Gunnar Myrdal was a Swiss social economist of "international reputation" who was brought to the United States in 1937 by the Carnegie

Corporation to research and draft a report on the current status of the American "Negro."

12. Ibid.

13. Saloutos, *American Farmer*, 179; Wolters, *Negroes in the Great Depression*, 8, 23.

14. Josiah C. Folsom, USDA, "Economic Security of Farmers and Agricultural Workers," November 1934, Witte Papers, box 70, p. 8. In 1920, 997 farm bankruptcies were reported. This number skyrocketed to 7,872 by 1925 (ibid., p. 4). Between 1930 and 1935 the number of farm laborers decreased from 2.7 million to 1.6 million, and unpaid family laborers grew from 1.7 million to 4.3 million. Agricultural Census, 1930 and 1935, graphed in "Rural Poverty," February 1938, Witte Papers, box 202.

15. By the mid-1930s, as the "factory farms" began to move closer to home, sharecroppers and tenant farmers were powerless to protect themselves, and by 1937 waged work was taking over the cotton-growing industry. Thomas Blaisdell Jr., "Some Propositions Regarding Agricultural Labor and Social Security," 1937, Bean Papers, Subject Files, 1923–53, Charts-Conference; "Summary of Agricultural Strikes in California, 1933," in Director of Research of the California Emergency Relief Administration to Dr. Leiserson, January 4, 1935, Leiserson Papers, box 14.

16. Memo on Farmers Home Bill by George Edmund Haynes, April 10, 1935, NAACP Papers, ser. C, box 233.

17. In 1934 African American farmworkers, tenants, and sharecroppers in the South earned only 73 percent of the average income of white farm laborers in the same categories. Wolters, *Blacks in the Depression*, 8.

18. "Estimate of Employment and Unemployment by Months — 1929–1934," RG 47, PI 183, entry 3, box 20; "The American People — How They Are Affected by the Federal-State Program for Social Security," SSB, RG 47, PI 183, entry 13, box 95; 1930 Census.

19. C. W. Rice, quoted in "Negro Labor Leader Here," *A Negro Newspaper*, March 1935, in FDR Papers, OF 93, box 2.

20. T. Arnold Hill to Mary Anderson, March 15, 1933, FWB, RG 86, entry 8, box 36.

21. The few African Americans employed in manufacturing lost their foothold in that industry. In 1931, 31.7 percent of native-born white Americans and 29.9 percent of foreign-born white Americans normally employed in manufacturing and the mechanical trades lost their jobs, whereas 52 percent of African American workers in industry lost theirs. This suggests that many more African Americans were being let go than white workers. Hunter, "Don't Bury Where You Can't Work," 154, 191; Hamilton, "National Urban League," 228.

22. "House Maids in Cleveland Ask for Square Deal," unidentified clipping enclosed in Mrs. Joseph F. Novak to Frances Perkins, February 2, 1934, RG 102, Central File 1933–36, entry 3, box 529, 6-1-2-7.

23. Ilse M. Smith, "Old-Age Insurance for Domestic Workers," February 24, 1939, RG 47, PI 183, entry 13, box 101, 7.

24. Of the country's 11.9 million African Americans in 1930, 4.6 million were under eighteen. "Number of Negroes of All Ages and Number of Negro Children in the United States," Abbott Papers, box 68, folder 3.

25. Willie Edwards, Pelham, Ga., [to the Census of Unemployment and Partial Employment], January 26, 1938, RG 29, PI 183, entry 258, box 17.

26. Albert J. Flowers to "Gentlemen," December 21, 1937, RG 29, PI 161, entry 259, box 17.

27. Mrs. Julia Fisher, Evansville, Ind., to FDR, March 5, 1938, RG 29, PI 161, entry 259, box 17.

28. Mrs. Charlotte Edmonds, Halifax, Va., [to the Census of Unemployment and Partial Unemployment], July 6, 1938, RG 29, PI 161, entry 258, box 17.

29. In 1933 commercial farm income was $40 million above 1932, and in 1934 it was $35 million above 1933. As one relief administrator admitted, "The commercial farmer has thus benefitted considerably from the recovery efforts of the AAA." "Summary of Agricultural Strikes in California, 1933," in Director of Research of the California Emergency Relief Administration to Dr. Leiserson, January 4, 1935, Leiserson Papers, box 14.

30. Rev. E. A. Abbott, Mobile, Ala., to Hugh Johnson, October 10, 1933, RG 9, entry 23, box 359, "581 Negroes."

31. Adrienne Baxter to FDR, August 3, 1933, RG 9, ibid.

32. Robert C. Weaver, "The New Deal and the Negro," 200; "Cotton Production: Another Example of Capitalist Decline," *Social Questions Bulletin*, Methodist Federation for Social Services, May 1935, in NAACP Papers, ser. C, box 233. One document prepared during the establishment of the Social Security Administration claimed that farmers were disproportionately represented on relief rolls: "[I]t will be seen that there were larger proportions of relief people from among farming people than from other classes in the total population." Josiah C. Folsom, USDA, "Economic Security of Farmers and Agricultural Workers," November 1934, in Witte Papers, box 70, p. 4.

33. In October 1933 almost 18 percent of African Americans were on relief, compared with 9.5 percent of whites. In Chicago, where African Americans made up only 7 percent of the population in 1930, 31 percent received relief.

34. Edwin Witte, "The Lundeen (Worker's Unemployment and Social Insurance) Bill: An Analysis of Its Provisions and of the Arguments Advanced by Its Supporters," April 1935, RG 47, PI 183, entry 1, box 9.

35. Ibid.; Brennen Taylor, "UNIA and American Communism in Conflict," 114; John Andrews to Arthur Altmeyer, March 27, 28, 1935, RG 47, PI 183, entry 8, box 54.

36. Alex G. Nordholm, "Some Pertinent Questions Regarding the Lundeen Bill (H.R. 2827)," RG 47, PI 183, entry 3, box 20.

37. Witte to Prof. Mary B. Gilson, April 11, 1935, RG 47, PI 183, entry 4, box 15.

38. Witte, *Development of the Social Security Act*, 36.

39. Brinkley, *Voices of Protest*, 223–24.

40. S. Howard Leech, "Something for Miss Perkins to Read in Her Pastel Bath," *Townsend Weekly*, 1935, in RG 47, PI 183, entry 9, box 43.

41. Resolutions adopted by the Haverhill, Massachusetts, Labor Conference on January 27, 1935, and Rep. A. Piatt Andrew to [Robert] Doughton, February 2, 1935, House Ways and Means Committee Bill Files, HR 74A-F39.1 (Social Security Act).

42. Holtzman, *Townsend Movement*, 55.

43. Percy Green, Secretary-Treasurer, Old Age Pension Society of Mississippi, to Robert Doughton, April 3, 1935, House Ways and Means Committee Bill Files, HR 74A-F39.1.

44. "The Case of the Negro," *The National Forum and Federal Old Age Pension Advocate: Official Publication for the National Old Age Pension Association*, Washington, D.C., December 10, 1934, in RG 47, PI 183, entry 9, box 44. The Pope Plan (HR 2856) sought to redistribute wealth through a tax on income rather than on financial transactions. Under this plan, people earning over $1 million per year would pay 95 percent of it in taxes. Benefits under this plan, which ranged between $30 and $50 per month, were much more modest than those promised under Townsend. J. E. Pope to "Mr. Congressman," January 29, 1935, House Ways and Means Committee Bill Files, HR 74A-F39.1 (Social Security Act).

45. "Resolution" of the Aberdeen Town Meeting, Aberdeen Washington, January 29, 1935, House Ways and Means Bill Files, ibid.

46. Witte, "The Lundeen (Worker's Unemployment and Social Insurance) Bill: An Analysis of Its Provisions and of the Arguments Advanced by Its Supporters," April 1935, RG 47, PI 183, entry 1, box 9.

47. McEvoy, "State-Federal Public Assistance," 134.

Chapter Two

1. *Congressional Record*, vol. 79, pt. 6.

2. Bunche, *Political Status of the Negro*, 29; Key, *Southern Politics*, 130.

3. Bunche, *Political Status of the Negro*, 39–41; Morgan, *Redneck Liberal*.

4. Quoted in Bunche, *Political Status of the Negro*, 207.

5. Swain, *Pat Harrison*, 212–13.

6. Myrdal, *American Dilemma*, 806, 813.

7. Patterson, *Congressional Conservatism*, 26, 28; "Proceedings and Debates of the First Session of the Seventy-fourth Congress of the United States of America," *Congressional Record*, vol. 79, pt. 6, April 25, 1935 (Washington, D.C.: GPO, 1935), 6369.

8. Heinemann, *Harry Byrd*, 62–63.

9. Roger K. Newman, *Hugo Black*, 128; Bunche, *Political Status of the Negro*, 386.

10. See the comments of Senators Ellison Du Rant Smith, George McGill, and others in the *Congressional Record*, April 16, 1935, vol. 79, pt. 6, 5749–50.

11. See, e.g., Witte, *Development of the Social Security Act*, 93; Friedel, *F. D. R. and the South*, 55; and Grace Abbott to Owen E. Pence, April 6, 1935, Abbott Papers, box 54, folder 5.

12. Connally, *My Name Is Tom Connally*, 154.

13. *Congressional Record*, April 13, 1935, vol. 79, pt. 5, 5589.

14. Leuchtenburg, *Roosevelt*, 151.

15. *Congressional Record*, June 14, 1935, vol. 79, pt. 8, 9294.

16. Swain, *Pat Harrison*, 85.

17. Swain, "Pat Harrison and the Social Security Act," 8; *Jackson Daily News*, September 28, 1935, quoted in ibid., 14.

18. Witte, *Development of the Social Security Act*, 96.

19. Key, *Southern Politics*, 217; Bunche, *Political Status of the Negro*, 215; Kennon and Rogers, *Committee on Ways and Means*, 273; *Congressional Record*, April 11, 1935, vol. 79, pt. 5, 5468.

20. Key, *Southern Politics*, 220, 223; Altmeyer, "Reminiscences," 18.

21. Michie and Phylick, *Dixie Demagogues*, 169.

22. Swain, *Pat Harrison*, 92; Michie and Phylick, *Dixie Demagogues*, 73, 77.

23. Patterson, *Congressional Conservatism*, 111–12.

24. Bunche, *Political Status of the Negro*, 386; *Congressional Record*, April 29, 1935, vol. 79, pt. 6, 6533; *Hearings before the Committee on Finance*, Senate, 74th Cong., 1st sess., on S 1130, pt. 2, January 23–25, 1935, p. 135.

25. Patterson, *Congressional Conservatism*, 29; Bunche, *Political Status of the Negro*, 205; Friedel, *F. D. R. and the South*, 77.

26. Patterson, *Congressional Conservatism*, 23–24.

27. Southern Democrats voted three times against antilynching legislation in 1935 and twice in 1937; in 1939 they voted against a prevailing wage rate change in the Works Progress Administration program; in 1943, against a provision opposing discrimination in federal education funding; and in 1945, against a Fair Employment Practices appropriation. Key, *Southern Politics*, 346–52.

28. Witte, *Development of the Social Security Act*, 91–93. The CES staff was heavily involved in advising members of the Senate and participated in executive hearings. Witte to Wilbur J. Cohen, October 2, 1935, Witte Papers, box 53; Cohen, Committee on Public Administration Social Research Council, "Legislative History of the Social Security Act," Witte Papers, box 65; Swain, "Pat Harrison and the Social Security Act," 4–5 (quotation).

29. "Chronological Summary of Activities of the Committee on Economic Security and Developments in Social Security Legislation," *Report of the Committee on Economic Security*, in Witte Papers, box 65.

30. Safier, "Tentative Report," 108; Witte, *Development of the Social Security Act*, 153.

31. *Congressional Record*, April 18, 1935, vol. 79, pt. 6, 5992.

32. *Hearings before the Committee on Ways and Means*, House, 74th Cong., 1st sess., on HR 4120, no. 1, January 21, 1935, pp. 112–13.

33. This statement is based on a 1930 interpretation of the census and does not include "hundreds of thousands" of other families that hired help on a more casual basis. Other estimates were lower. By 1935 the numbers would most likely have increased, as wages for domestic workers were decimated by the depression, in part because many more white women were forced to enter the field, and even working-class urban dwellers could afford domestics for the first time. Safier, "Tentative Report," 129.

34. Safier, "Tentative Report," 114, 119, 128–29.

35. *Hearings before the Committee on Finance*, Senate, 74th Cong., 1st sess., on S 1130, pt. 4, January 30, 31, 1935, p. 239.

36. Hale, *Making Whiteness*, 99.

37. Bunche, *Political Status of the Negro*, 204.

38. "Unemployment, Old Age, and Social Insurance: Hearings before a Subcommittee of the Committee on Labor," February 4–8, 11–15, 1935, House, 74th Cong., 1st sess., on HR 2827, HR 2859, HR 185, and HR 10, RG 47, PI 183, entry 1, box 10.

39. "Distribution of Hired Laborers on Farms in the United States by States and Divisions," January 1935, RG 47, PI 183, entry 13, box 13A.

40. M. M. Libman, "Old-Age Insurance for Agricultural Workers," Bureau of Old-Age Insurance, February 24, 1936, RG 47, PI 183, entry 13, box 101, 2.

41. The eight southern states were South Carolina, Alabama, Texas, Louisiana, Mississippi, and Arkansas, where cotton sharecropping dominated, and Florida and Georgia, with heavy concentrations of agricultural laborers working on larger farms. Ibid.; Safier, "Tentative Report," 50, 95.

42. Safier, "Tentative Report," 50–51, 95, 103; "Distribution of Hired Laborers on Farms in the United States."

43. Hanson, *Gaining Access*, 75.

44. Ibid., *Gaining Access*, 27–29, 75, 87.

45. *Hearings before the Committee on Finance*, Senate, 74th Cong., 1st sess., on S 1130, January 30, 31, 1935, pp. 219–20.

46. This faction was the Farmers Education and Cooperative Union of America, one of the leading organizations. Neil Miller, "The Position of Farm Organizations on the Extension of Old Age and Survivors' Insurance to Farmers and Farm Workers," 1947, Witte Papers, box 202.

47. Witte, *Development of the Social Security Act*, 51, 54; "Advisory Council of the Committee on Economic Security," Minutes of Meetings, December 6–8, 6, and 7, 1934, RG 47, PI 183, entry 7, box 48.

48. Robertson to Doughton, January 18, 1935, House Ways and Means Committee Bill Files, HR 74A-F39.1 (Social Security Act), box 14111.

49. For years Sen. Pat Harrison had received many letters from constituents who sought to gain federal government restitution for cotton seized during the Civil

War and pensions for southern soldiers' families; dozens of these letters arrived in 1935 alone. The government had reimbursed such claims, but only between 1911 and 1917. Those seeking restitution were often very angry: "We know that Nations engage in war for even less things than what the Government did at that time. Even a small insult would sometime [sic] bring about the death of thousands of soldiers to appease such an insult. Yet, Our Government does not think enough of it's [sic] honor to its own citizens to meet its just obligations." Miss Bessie P. Jackson to Harrison, June 20, 1935, RG 46, SEN 74A-F8, box 114. For correspondence between Harrison and Felton Johnson, Mrs. E. B. McRaven, Mrs. C. A. Jackson, and others in 1935, see ibid.

50. *Jackson Daily News*, June 20, 1935, quoted in Swain, *Pat Harrison*.

51. "South Would Get Its Share" (January 10, 1935), "The South's Salvation" (January 15, 1935), and "The War against the States" (November 15, 1934), *Charleston (S.C.) News and Courier*.

52. Editorial (November 16, 1934) and "The Relief Burden" (November 20, 1934), *Atlanta (Ga.) Constitution*.

53. Hale, *Making Whiteness*; Wolters, *Negroes in the Great Depression*.

54. *Hearings before the Committee on Finance*, Senate, 74th Cong., 1st sess., on S 1130, pt. 2, January 23–25, 1935, pp. 165–66.

55. Ibid., January 22, 1935, p. 28.

56. *Hearings before the Committee on Ways and Means*, House, 74th Cong., 1st sess., on HR 4120, no. 1, January 21, 1935, p. 108, and no. 12, February 5, 1935, pp. 853–57.

57. Witte, *Development of the Social Security Act*, 153.

58. *Congressional Record*, April 12, 1935, vol. 79, pt. 5, 5547.

59. *Congressional Record*, April 18, 1935, vol. 79, pt. 6, 6040, 6042.

60. *Congressional Record*, April 17, 1935, 5906–7, ibid.

61. Ibid.; Hari, *The Kingfish*, 210.

62. The phrase "reasonable subsistence compatible with decency and health" first surfaced in a proposal submitted to the CES Technical Board by the board's staff on old-age security. The staff recommended the substance of the Dill-Connery Bill for OAA with the following changes: plans must be statewide; recipients must be citizens, indigent, aged, and residents of the state; financially competent children are liable for their parents; the state may recover funds through liens on estates; and the insertion of some standards for substituting institutional care for the OAA grant. "Report of the Staff on Old-Age Security to the Technical Board Executive Committee," November 16, 1934, in "Technical Board on Economic Security (Minutes of Meetings)," *Report of the Committee on Economic Security*, Witte Papers, box 65.

63. *Hearings before the Committee on Finance*, Senate, 74th Cong., 1st sess., on S 1130, January 22, 1935, p. 20.

64. Altmeyer, *Formative Years*, 39.

65. *Hearings before the Committee on Finance*, Senate, 74th Cong., 1st sess., on S 1130, pt. 2, January 23–25, 1935, pp. 70–72.

66. Altmeyer, *Formative Years*, 39; *Hearings before the Committee on Finance*, Senate, 74th Cong., 1st sess., on S 1130, pt. 2, January 23–25, 1935, pp. 70–72, 75.

67. *Congressional Record*, June 14, 1935, vol. 79, pt. 8, 9268–69; *Hearings before the Committee on Finance*, on S 1130, pt. 2.

68. *Hearings before the Committee on Ways and Means*, House, 74th Cong., 1st sess., January 31, 1935, pp. 598–99.

69. *Congressional Record*, April 11, 1935, vol. 79, pt. 5, 5471–76.

70. Ibid.

71. Witte to Hopkins, February 26, 1935, RG 47, PI 183, entry 8, box 57.

72. Witte to Moley, March 6, 1935, ibid., entry 4, box 15.

73. Witte, *Development of the Social Security Act*, 145.

74. Biles, *The South and the New Deal*, 16, 20, 31.

75. *Congressional Record*, April 16–17, 1935, vol. 79, pt. 6.

76. In 1935 African Americans comprised 11.9 percent of the U.S. population, but because of the earlier death rates of African Americans, they constituted a much smaller percentage of people over age sixty-five.

77. "Summary of Old Age Security Laws," May 1, 1934, in American Association for Social Security, Inc., "Social Security in the United States, 1934," Witte Papers, box 214; Chart [untitled] listing total population over age sixty-five and costs under the proposed Social Security Act by state, RG 46, SEN 74A-E1, S 1118-30, box 18.

78. *Congressional Record*, June 13, 1935, vol. 79, pt. 8, 9246–67.

79. Lenroot to Edwin Witte, February 18, 1835, RG 47, PI 183, entry 8, box 57.

80. Rep. John Clarence Taylor, *Congressional Record*, April 17, 1935, vol. 79, pt. 6, 5877.

81. *Congressional Record*, April 5, 1935, vol. 79, pt. 5, 5800.

82. Draft letter from Perkins to Patman, and memo from Perkins to Witte, December 31, 1935, RG 47, PI 183, entry 8, box 59; Witte to Perkins, January 3, 1935, and draft letter from Witte to Patman, n.d., Cohen Papers, box 25.

83. *Hearings before the Committee on Ways and Means*, House, 74th Cong., 1st sess., on HR 4120, January 21–26, 28–31, February 1–8, 12, 1935, pp. 939–40.

84. "Excerpts from Confidential Hearings before the Committee on Finance, United States Senate, May 1935, p. 17," and "Memo to Hon. Pat Harrison from Edwin Witte, May 14, 1935," RG 47, PI 183, entry 13, box 92, File: "Veterans"; Witte to Sen. Black, May 14, 1935, ibid., entry 8, box 54.

85. Witte to Harrison, May 14, 1935, ibid., entry 8, box 57.

86. "States Rated on Basis of Average per Capita Income and Average Old-Age Assistance Grants," RG 47, PI 183, entry 13, box 96; Myrdal, *American Dilemma*, 359–60; Memo to Executive Director, SSB, from Jane Hoey, Director, Federal Bureau of Public Assistance, Subject: Old-Age Assistance and Confederate

Veterans' Pensions, August 9, 1935, and "Confederate Pensions," both in RG 47, PI 183, entry 13, box 92, File: "Veterans."

87. Memo to Executive Director, SSB, from Jane Hoey, Director, Federal Bureau of Public Assistance, Subject: Old-Age Assistance and Confederate Veterans' Pensions, August 9, 1935, RG 47, PI 183, entry 13, box 92, File: "Veterans."

88. Memo to Members, SSB, from Jack B. Tate, Office of the General Council, regarding "Classifications in Public Assistance Plans — Beneficiaries of Confederate Allowances," January 27, 1938, ibid.

89. Quoted in Skocpol, *Protecting Soldiers and Mothers*.

90. Chalmers, *Hooded Americanism*, 307. Morton Sosna (*Silent South*, 27) argues that southern liberals generally believed that the Civil War was not about slavery and that without it, slavery would gradually have ended and race relations would have been much better, though by 1935 all liberal assumptions about race were beginning to undergo change.

91. Warren, "The Briar Patch," in Twelve Southerners, *I'll Take My Stand*, 249.

92. Dunning, *Reconstruction*; Du Bois, *Black Reconstruction*; Foner, *Reconstruction*.

93. Hale, *Making Whiteness*, 80–81; Bunche, *Political Status of the Negro*.

94. Myrdal, *American Dilemma*, 683–84.

95. Ibid., 593, 595, 725.

96. Warren, "The Briar Patch," in Twelve Southerners, *I'll Take My Stand*, 258.

97. W. J. Cash, *American Mercury* (May 1935), quoted in Walter White, "The South Is a Long Way Off," draft, [May 1935], NAACP Papers, ser. C, box 421, pp. 11–12.

98. Quoted in Morgan, *Redneck Liberal*, 149.

99. Myrdal, *American Dilemma*, 70.

100. Quoted in Sosna, *Silent South*, 47.

101. Quoted in Ashmore, *Hearts and Minds*, 1.

102. Bunche, *Political Status of the Negro*, 33–34.

103. Daniels, *A Southerner Discovers the South*, 344–45.

104. Quoted in Tom Connally, "Under Our Own Power," address by Sen. Connally, San Antonio Rotary Club, November 16, 1934, Connally Papers, box 553.

105. Articles in the southern press regularly suggested that FDR was allowing the federal government to be overrun with "negroes." White Democrats wrote to him demanding to know his true position. See FDR Papers, OF 93, box 2.

106. *Congressional Record*, April 18, 1935, vol. 79, pt. 6, 5981. See also Katherine Lenroot to Grace Abbott, February 26, 1935, Abbott Papers, box 54, folder 2, which discusses attitudes of the Ways and Means Committee toward social workers.

107. *Congressional Record*, April 15, 1935, vol. 79, pt. 5, 5688.

108. Sosna, *Silent South*, 30–34, 38; Hall, *Revolt against Chivalry*.

109. Roger K. Newman, *Hugo Black*, 203; *Congressional Record*, April 29, 1935, vol. 79, pt. 6, 6534. Thaddeus Stevens was an abolitionist and leader of the "Black Republicans," who passed federal civil rights legislation during Reconstruction.

Chapter Three

1. "John R. Commons as a Teacher, Economist, and Public Servant: Remarks by Edwin E. Witte at the John R. Commons Birthday Dinner, October 10, 1950," Witte Papers, box 257, p. 1.

2. Commons, *Myself*, 5.

3. Martin, *Madam Secretary*, 342.

4. According to Cohen, Witte was a "strong friend" of Altmeyer in Wisconsin. See Cohen, "Interview," folder 1, MSS 789, box 23. Barbara Armstrong said that Tom Eliot, legal counsel for the CES, was personally close to Perkins, like a "son," following their work together on the Wisconsin unemployment compensation bill. Perkins lobbied the other CES members to get Eliot hired. Mr. Wyzanski (for Secretary Perkins) to Altmeyer, June 30, 1934, RG 47, PI 183, entry 8, box 55.

5. Thomas H. Eliot, "Reminiscences," 19; Armstrong, "Reminiscences," 190.

6. Burns, "Reminiscences," 34.

7. "Members of the Technical Board of the CES," RG 47, PI 183, entry 1, box 1; Memo from John P. Davis to Walter White with addendum by White, Subject: Suggested Witnesses for Proposed House of Representatives Resolution for Investigation of Status of Negro Labor under the New Deal, [March 1935], NAACP Papers, ser. C, box 278 ("labor on cotton farms"); Witte, *Development of the Social Security Act*, vi ("unbroken horses"). Tugwell was generally known as one of FDR's most radical advisers. See Leuchtenburg, *Roosevelt*, 164, and Biles, *The South and the New Deal*, 44.

8. The "opposition camp" also apparently included Otto Richter, actuary for the Old Age Security Titles; Murray Latimer, chair, Technical Board's section on old-age security; and Burns. Armstrong, "Reminiscences," 104–8.

9. Burns, "Reminiscences," 54, 82.

10. Armstrong, "Possibilities of a Unified System of Insurance against Loss of Earnings," [1934], RG 47, PI 183, entry 3, box 17.

11. See Natalie F. Jaros, "Agricultural Workers in Foreign Unemployment Insurance Schemes," and Constance A. Kiehel, "Agricultural Workers and Farmers in Foreign Social Insurance Systems," both in "Social Insurance," vol. 2, Edwin Witte, CES, Witte Papers, box 70; and Olga Halsey to Witte, memo on "Arguments Advanced in Support of the Proposed Break-down by Industry Groups for Old Age Insurance," and memo from Halsey to Witte, October 27, 1934, "Draft Conventions and Recommendations of the International Organization: Summary and Explanatory Statement," both in RG 47, PI 183, entry 3, box 22.

12. See Ware, *Beyond Suffrage*.

13. Halsey to Edwin Witte, memo on "Arguments Advanced in Support of the Proposed Break-down By Industry Groups for Old Age Insurance," RG 47, PI 183, entry 3, box 22.

14. Witte, *Development of the Social Security Act*, 11. The involvement of FERA is explored further in Chapter 5.

15. CES, Minutes of Meetings, September 26, October 1, 1934, in *Report of the Committee on Economic Security*, Witte Papers, box 65; Witte, *Development of the Social Security Act*, 72.

16. In response to concern expressed by Theo Lunde (of the American Industrial Co.) that the Social Security Act would undermine U.S. capitalism, Arthur Altmeyer wrote: "I am enclosing at this time a copy of the bill which will convince any one who even casually examines it that there is no intention of changing the fundamentals of our present economic order. As a matter of fact, any one who is at all familiar with the history of social insurance knows that Bismarck introduced it in Germany in the 80's as an antidote to Socialism." Altmeyer to Lunde, May 6, 1935, RG 47, PI 183, entry 8, box 54.

17. Correspondence between Commons, Witte, and John Andrews, November 19, 1934–January 31, 1935, ibid., box 55.

18. In November 1934 Commons clarified his plan, and the role of federal UI legislation in it, in a six-page letter to John Andrews with copies to Witte and Perkins. Witte replied to Commons: "The views you express in your letter of November 19 to Andrews are practically all shared by me. I do not know whether they will be recommended by our Committee or not, but I hope that they will be adopted practically in toto." Ibid.

19. Many European and Latin American countries had unemployment compensation systems that covered agricultural and domestic workers through a variety of combinations of stamp tax plans and flat wage taxes. Chile, Czechoslovakia, and Great Britain all had such systems in place by 1925. Many other countries, including France, Germany, Hungary, Italy, the Netherlands, and the USSR provided extended coverage to agricultural and domestic workers before the U.S. Social Security Act was developed. This information had been gathered by the CES and so was available at the time the Act was researched and drafted. Wilbur Cohen, "Foreign Experience in Social Insurance Contributions for Agricultural and Domestic Workers," *Social Security Bulletin*, February 1945, 5–10, in Witte Papers, box 202. See also the volumes of reports on foreign systems in the CES files, RG 47, PI 183.

20. Brown to Wagner, February 22, 1935, Wagner Papers, 566-GF-328, folder 20.

21. Barbara Armstrong, "Advantages of Federal Subsidy Plan," November 9, 1934, RG 47, PI 183, entry 3, box 17; Armstrong, "Reminiscences," 37, 213.

22. Memo from Evelyn Burns to Meredith B. Givens, December 1, 1934, Subject: The Integrated Treatment of Unemployment Insurance, Cash Relief, and Emergency Work, RG 47, PI 183, entry 3, box 17, p. 19.

23. Matthew Rose, "Proportion of Gainful Workers Covered by the Unemployment Compensation Plan by Industries," ibid., box 20.

24. Armstrong claimed that Senator Wagner agreed with her assessment and told her that the Wisconsin group did not want OAA and "wouldn't have it under any circumstances." Douglas Brown later reported that Witte wrote, and Perkins approved, a statement made by FDR in November 1934 that the OAI program

might best be delayed and not included in the Social Security Act. Armstrong said that she broke "the panes in my own bedroom door when I read Miss Perkins' autobiographical book. It wasn't so much what she didn't do for the achievement of Social Security, as the way she took credit for what she had tried her utmost to prevent." Armstrong, "Reminiscences," 12.

25. Burns, "Reminiscences," 54; Thomas H. Eliot, "Reminiscences," 56; Armstrong, "Reminiscences," 12, 111, 165; J. Douglas Brown, "Reminiscences," 14.

26. Armstrong, "Reminiscences," 38, 158.

27. Ibid., 191.

28. Ibid., 157.

29. An employee who had worked 200 weeks in 5 years would, upon retirement, receive 15 percent of his or her average monthly wage, whereas an employee who had worked 800 weeks in that time would receive only 18 percent. Economic Security Act, 74th Cong., sess. 1, chap. 531, August 14, 1935, *The Statutes at Large of the United States of America from January 1935 to June 1936*, vol. XLIX, pt. I, Title II, p. 622.

30. Myrdal, *American Dilemma*, 358, n. 65, 1280.

31. Leuchtenburg, *Roosevelt*, 132–33; Swain, "Pat Harrison and the Social Security Act," 12–13.

32. *Hearings before the Committee on Ways and Means*, House, 74th Cong., 1st sess., HR 4120, January 21, 1935, p. 109.

33. In 1935 ten northern states received more than 30 percent of their total production income from manufacturing. Most southern states (eleven) received only 10–20 percent of their production income from manufacturing, though the percentages were higher in Georgia, South Carolina, and North Carolina (20–30 percent). "Employed Compensable Labor Force by Industry and by Type of Exclusion, United States, April 1930," table 14, RG 47, PI 183, entry 3, box 20.

34. Assuming that agricultural and domestic workers would receive little benefit from these programs, one member of the CES Technical Board felt that "the payment of such unearned pensions to industrial workers would probably be deemed unfair by agricultural workers and domestic servants, as well as by self-employed persons, who under the proposal made will not receive pensions in any form unless they are in need." "The Executive and Old-Age Security Committees" November 22, 1934, "Technical Board on Economic Security (Minutes of Meetings)," *Report of the Committee on Economic Security*, in Witte Papers, box 65, p. 49.

35. American Public Welfare Association, "Social Security for Hired Farm Workers: Questions and Answers," February 1950, Witte Papers, box 202.

36. Ely, "A Job for Everyone," draft of *Work for All*, introduction to chapter, n.d. [after 1934], Ely Papers, box 5, p. 1.

37. Moley, "Reminiscences," 5.

38. Ely, "A Job for Everyone," p. 3.

39. "Preliminary Report of the Staff of the CES," September 1934, Hopkins Papers, FERA, group 24, container 48.

40. Memo from Evelyn Burns to Meredith B. Givens, December 1, 1934, Subject: The Integrated Treatment of Unemployment Insurance, Cash Relief, and Emergency Work (box 17, p. 24), Violet Libby, "Unemployment Compensation or Relief Dole?" [March 15, 1935] (box 19, p. 6), and Ernest K. Lindley, "Morale of Idle New Factor in Shaping of Relief Plans: Survey of Jobless Shows Tendency to Rely on Government and Trend to Radical Thinking: Social Risk Seen in Cutting Aid" (box 32), all in RG 47, PI 183, entry 3; "Report of the CES: Old Age Security Volume," Witte Papers, box 58, pp. 46–48.

41. Correspondence between Edwin Witte, Alfred Briggs, and E. B. Skinner, October 13–30, 1934, RG 47, PI 183, entry 4, box 15.

42. Edwin Witte, "Major Issues in Unemployment Compensation," vol. 2, Witte Papers, box 71, p. 336; Howard Boldt, "Wisconsin Bill Bars Jobless — Is Anti-Strike," *Daily Worker*, New York, August 25, 1934, in ibid., entry 1, box 9.

43. William Leiserson to Abram Epstein, September 16, 1933, Leiserson Papers, box 2.

44. Witte, "Memorandum on the Views Relating to the Work of the Committee on Economic Security Expressed by Various Individuals Consulted," August 19–21, 1934, RG 47, PI 183, entry 9, box 21.

45. Memo from Evelyn Burns to Meredith B. Givens, December 1, 1934, Subject: The Integrated Treatment of Unemployment Insurance, Cash Relief, and Emergency Work, ibid., entry 3, box 17, p. 40.

46. Ibid., p. 36.

47. A CES handout argued that under UI, unemployed workers were "paid as a matter of contractual right, definite compensation for the loss of earnings due to conditions over which he has no control. Such a system upholds rather than lowers the morale of the self-respecting worker." Violet Libby, "Unemployment Compensation or Relief Dole?," March 15, 1935, ibid., box 19, p. 6.

48. "Memorandum on Definitions," SSB, n.d., ibid., entry 13, box 4, Chairman's File, 1935–42.

49. Commons, *Races and Immigrants*, xxv, 113.

50. In 1935 Du Bois asked Commons to participate in the development of the *Negro Encyclopedia*. Commons to Du Bois, October 8, 1935, Du Bois Papers, reel 43, frame 995.

51. Commons, *Races and Immigrants*, chap. 1.

52. Ibid., 2, 7.

53. Ibid., 3, 6–7, 52.

54. Badger, "Fatalism, Not Gradualism."

55. Aubrey Williams, "The Failure of Gradualism," a talk before Alpha Phi Alpha Fraternity, Atlanta, December 28, 1949, pamphlet, 73–1275, 10.

56. Cohen, "Interview," MSS 789, box 23, pp. 10–11.

57. "Preliminary Report of the Staff of the Committee on Economic Security Presented to the CES and the Technical Board on Economic Security," September 1934, RG 47, PI 183, entry 1, box 6.

58. Josiah C. Folsom, USDA, "Economic Security of Farmers and Agricultural Workers," November 1934, Witte Papers, box 70, p. 5. Witte's summary of staff work prepared in September noted that twice as many blacks (18 percent) were on relief as whites, suggesting that the CES was well aware of "Negro" poverty. "Preliminary Report of the Staff of the Committee on Economic Security," September 1934.

59. Frank Fischer (*Technocracy*, 20) argues that the central influence of "experts" in political and economic systems has limited policy options, as these options are constructed to meet the needs of existing institutions. Therefore, the real impact of "objective" administrators comes from the options they present to policy-makers. "Politicians still choose one policy option over another, but it is increasingly the experts who shape the deliberative framework within which they must choose." The New Deal, according to Fischer, was a turning point in this shift.

60. Cohen, "Interview," folder 1, MSS 789, box 23, p. 5. See also Cohen, "The (Lundeen) Worker's Unemployment and Social Insurance Bill," October 1, 1934, RG 47, PI 13, entry 1, box 9, and Ely, "Abstract of an Address on Good Government and Good Business," delivered at Eau Claire Community Institute, January 16, 1917, Ely Papers, box 5, p. 7.

61. Commons, "The 50th Class Leaves," commencement address, Kansas Agricultural College, *The Kansas Industrialist*, June 21, 1913, in Commons Papers, reel 17, frame 291.

62. Witte to Hon. J. W. Garow, August 31, 1934, RG 47, PI 183, entry 4, box 15. Witte acknowledged privately that his sympathies were "naturally" with the British Labour Party and that he feared conservatism in American politics. Witte to Mary Gilson, London, November 18, 1935, Witte Papers, box 33.

63. "The Research Work of Legislative Reference Bureaus: Remarks of Edwin E. Witte, former chief of the Wisconsin Legislative Reference Library, at a Joint Meeting of the Legislation Section of the American Political Science Association and the American Association for Labor Legislation, at Philadelphia, December 27, 1933," Witte Papers, box 257, pp. 5–6.

64. Armstrong, "Reminiscences," 129, 176, 179.

65. Eliot to Mary Dewson, November 27, 1934, Dewson Papers, Subject Files, container 6.

66. CES, "Possible Constructive Amendments to the Social Security Act," marked "Suggested to Wisconsin Congressmen, April 1935, E. E. Witte," RG 47, PI 183, entry 3, box 9.

67. Witte, "Memorandum on the Views Relating to the Work of the Committee on Economic Security Expressed by Various Individuals Consulted," August 19–21, 1934, RG 47, PI 183, entry 9, box 21.

68. For example, Paul Raushenbush and Thomas Eliot strategized about how to get congressmen in line behind the president's bill, referring to Rep. Lewis, one of the sponsors of the Act in the House, as "our weak link . . . he is . . . rather hipped on the ideas of having a blanket security bill." Eliot to Raushenbush, January 25, 1935, Raushenbush Papers, box 24.

69. Witte to Mary Dewson, February 7, 1935, Dewson Papers, Subject Files, container 6; Witte to William Green, June 8, 1934, Witte Papers, box 2; Witte, "Memorandum on the Views Relating to the Work of the Committee on Economic Security Expressed by Various Individuals Consulted," August 19–21, 1934, p. 7; A January 7, 1935, telegram from a Sen. Philip and Sen. Robert La Follette to FDR began: "We are reliably informed that" the draft bill [which had not been released] required industry pooling of UI funds. Cohen Papers, MSS 789, box 25; Witte to Rep. Robert Doughton and Sen. La Follette, July 5, 1935, Witte Papers, box 2; Memo from Frances Perkins to Witte, September 25, 1934 (box 59), and memo from Witte to Harry Hopkins, October 10, 1934 (box 57), RG 47, PI 183, entry 8.

70. For example, Witte was involved in Conference Committee sessions, participated in closed-door meetings of the Senate Finance Committee, and drafted sections of Congressional Committee reports. See Witte, *Development of the Social Security Act*, and "Excerpts from Confidential Hearings before the Committee on Finance, United States Senate, May 1935, p. 17," RG 47, PI 183, entry 13, box 92, File: Veterans.

71. For example, Witte wrote an argument for Sen. William King of Utah against the OAI title of the bill in exchange for his vote in the Senate Finance Committee for the UI title. Witte stated: "I took him up and prepared the best argument I knew how against old age insurance." King read Witte's prepared remarks during the next day's executive session; ironically, another member of the committee asked Witte to rebut King's argument. Witte, *Development of the Social Security Act*, 103.

72. Memo from Frank to Mr. Appleby, January 10, 1935, RG 16, PI 191, entry 17, box 2140.

73. Lenroot, "Reminiscences," 68–69.

74. See July 1935 statement, Witte Papers, box 2. See also, e.g., Witte to Altmeyer, October 3, 1935, Witte Papers, box 33. The individuals who had been most loyal to Witte were the ones who benefited from his recommendations, such as Cohen, Altmeyer, and Ellen Greenblatt. Dozens of letters between Witte and Joseph Harris of the Social Science Research Council attest to the importance Witte attributed to documenting the development of the Act. Witte Papers, box 2; Witte to Martin Foss, November 24, 1934, and to James S. Thompson, February 18, 1935, ibid. The Senate unanimously confirmed Altmeyer's appointment to the SSB. Witte to Altmeyer, August 5, 1939, Altmeyer Papers, MSS 400, box 2.

75. Witte, *Development of the Social Security Act*, vii, 18; Thomas H. Eliot, "Reminiscences," 12; Armstrong, "Reminiscences," 223; Moley, "Reminiscences"; Witte to Moley, July 5, 1935, Witte Papers, box 33. See also Witte to Moley, May 10, 1935, RG 47, PI 183, entry 4, box 15.

76. Kellogg, *Northern Liberals in Black America*, 427, quoted in Kirby, *Black Americans*, 95.

77. Kirby, *Black Americans*, 30, 32. Kelly Miller, who represented more conservative African American positions, argued that FDR's refusal to single out

"Negroes" was a positive sign. He noted with approval that, although the president had been "repeatedly besieged for expressions of his attitudes [on racial equality] he stoutly refused to isolate the Negro as an object of special treatment but insisted that the black man would be integrated in the 'New Deal' without discrimination on account of race and color." Miller, "President Roosevelt and the Negro," *Louisville Courier-Journal*, August 22, 1935, in FDR Papers, OF 93, box 2.

78. See correspondence between Robert Vann, Louis Howe, and Julian Rainey (quotations in text), December 17, 1934–February 15, 1935, Howe Papers: Secretary to the President, 1932–36, container 86.

79. Weiss, *Farewell*, 15; Kirby, *Black Americans*, 133.

80. Correspondence between Joseph Johnson, Missy Durand, and Louis Howe, November and December 1934, Howe Papers: Secretary to the President, 1932–36, container 36.

81. "Recent Negro Appointment by President Roosevelt and His Aides," and Hon. Braswell Deen to Marvin McIntyre, September 25, 1935, FDR Papers, OF 93, box 2; Kirby, *Black Americans*, 109, 154–55.

82. Kirby, *Black Americans*, 56, 58–59, 122.

83. Ibid., 20, 127; John Davis to Weaver, Weaver Papers, Correspondence, 1933–60, "D," reel 1, ScMicro R3701.

84. Berkowitz, *Mr. Social Security*, 32.

85. Schwarz, *The New Dealers*, 181–82.

86. Altmeyer, *Formative Years*, 50.

87. Still, *Milwaukee*, 471–72. There was no NAACP branch in Madison in 1935 (that was still the case in 1938), though early attempts had been made to establish one. The Milwaukee branch was barely active, in conflict within itself and with the national office in 1935. See C. A. Fisher and Chesteua Josey to Walter White, February 13, 1934, and Pickens to Vera S. Lecomte, February 9, 1938, "The Madison Branch of the N.A.A.C.P., Preliminary Organization Meeting Held November 23, 1928," Pickens to the National NAACP, February 24, 1934, and White to Cecil Fisher, March 2, 1934, all in NAACP Papers.

88. Witte Papers, esp. box 203. See the draft MS of Witte, "The Development of the Social Security Act: Confidential Memorandum by Edwin E. Witte, Executive Director of the Committee on Economic Security, 1934–1935 . . .," ibid., box 294. In 1930 Leo Wolfsohn, editor of the *Milwaukee Leader*, claimed that his paper had capitalized the word "Negro" for the prior fifteen years, and Paul Kellogg, editor of the *Survey*, maintained that his newspaper had "always" used the capital *N*. Wolfsohn to Walter White, March 17, 1930, NAACP Papers, ser. C, box 222.

89. "Percent Population of the United States for Specific Ages and Over by White and Negro," and Alex G. Nordholm, "Age Trends in the United States Population: Their Causes and Consequences," [1934], RG 47, PI 183, entry 3, box 20.

90. Edwin Witte, "Major Issues in Unemployment Insurance," February 1935, ibid., p. 18.

91. Ibid.

92. Witte, "Preliminary Report of the Staff of the Committee on Economic Security."

93. Natalie F. Jaros, "Agricultural Workers in Foreign Unemployment Insurance Schemes," in Witte, CES, "Social Insurance," vol. 2, Witte Papers, box 70.

94. "The Collection of Federal Old-Age Benefit Taxes and the Recording of Wages by Means of the Stamp Pass Book System, Prepared Especially for the Treasury Department and the SSB, March 27, 1936," and "Administrative Aspects in the Application of a Stamp System to Agricultural and Domestic Workers under the Old-Age Insurance Program," Analysis Division, Bureau of Old-Age Insurance, March 22, 1939, RG 47, PI 183, entry 13, box 97; Josiah C. Folsom, USDA, "Economic Security of Farmers and Agricultural Workers," November 1934, and Dr. Louis Bean, "The Economic Security Program in Relation to Farm Operators and Employees," December 1934, in Witte, CES, "Social Insurance," vol. 2, Witte Papers, box 70; Thomas Eliot to Paul Raushenbush, December 5, 1934, Raushenbush Papers, box 21; Witte to Frances Perkins, November 10, 1934, RG 47, PI 183, entry 8, box 59; CES, Minutes of Meeting, February 15, 1935, RG 16, PI 191, entry 17, box 2140; "The Executive Committee" October 12, 1934, "The Technical Board on Economic Security (Minutes of Meetings)," *Report of the Committee on Economic Security*, in Witte Papers, box 65.

95. Armstrong, "Provision for Old Age Security," in "Preliminary Report of the CES," September 1934, Hopkins Papers, FRA, group 24, container 48.

96. Ware, *Beyond Suffrage*, 2.

97. Witte to Geline MacDonald Bowman, President, National Federation of Business and Professional Women's Clubs, Inc., November 3, 1934, RG 47, PI 183, entry 8, box 54; Mary Anderson to Frances Perkins RE: Desired Legislation, December 21, 1934, RG 86, entry 12, box 25; Witte, "Major Issues in Unemployment Insurance," February 1935, RG 47, PI 183, entry 3, box 23.

98. "Extent of Gainful Employment of Married Women and Chief Occupation Groups, 1930," RG 47, PI 183, entry 7, box 50.

99. Rae Needleman, "Summary of Findings on the Problem of Including Domestic Workers under the Old-Age Benefit Provisions of the Social Security Act," March 26, 1937, ibid., entry 13, box 101, p. 22.

100. Thomas C. Billig, "Memorandum of Cases Which Illustrate the Position Taken in Its Report to the President and to the Congress by the Social Security Board with Respect to the 'Domestic Service' Exception Contained in the Social Security Act," March 2, 1939, ibid., box 101.

101. Memo from Cohen to Arthur Altmeyer, Subject: Coverage of Domestic Servants, November 1, 1938 (entry 13, box 101), and Marianne Sakmann, CES, to Florence Conley, Editorial Department, *Fortune*, April 19, 1935 (entry 8, box 55), RG 47, PI 183.

102. Witte, *Development of the Social Security Act*; Josiah C. Folsom, USDA, "Economic Security of Farmers and Agricultural Workers," November 1934, and

"Memorandum to Mr. Bean" from William T. Ham, November 20, 1934, in Witte, CES, "Social Insurance," vol. 2, both in Witte Papers, box 70.

103. M. M. Libman, "Old-Age Insurance for Agricultural Workers," Bureau of Old-Age Assistance, February 24, 1939, 2, 12, 18, RG 47, PI 183, entry 13, box 101.

104. CES, Minutes of Meeting, August 13, 1934, *Report of the Committee on Economic Security*, in Witte Papers, box 65, p. 2; Witte, *Development of the Social Security Act*, 14.

105. CES, Minutes of Meeting, December 7, 1934, in Witte Papers, box 65, p. 2; Witte, *Development of the Social Security Act*, 14; Burns, "Reminiscences," 43–48.

106. Josiah C. Folsom to Louis Bean, November 3, 1934, in Witte, CES, "Social Insurance," vol. 2, Witte Papers, box 70; Bryce Stewart, "Unemployment Insurance," app. B, "Preliminary Report of the Staff of the CES," September 1934, 3, and Barbara Armstrong, "Provisions for Old Age Security," Hopkins Papers, FRA, group 24, container 48. See also Armstrong, "Reminiscences," 130, and J. Douglas Brown, "Reminiscences," 30; and "Summary of Discussion of the *Old-Age* Security Committee of the Technical Board, September 26, 1934," in "Technical Board on Economic Security (Minutes of Meetings)," in *Report of the Committee on Economic Security*, Witte Papers, box 65. Witte wrote that the first draft of the report presented to the CES represented his "views of what should be recommended." Witte to Harry Hopkins, December 21, 1934, RG 47, PI 183, entry 8, box 57. See also Witte, *Development of the Social Security Act*, 41.

107. Burns, "Reminiscences," 28.

108. See CES, Minutes of Meeting, November 27, 1934, in *Report of the Committee on Economic Security*, Witte Papers, box 65, p. 7; Witte, *Development of the Social Security Act*, 153; and Altmeyer, *Formative Years*.

109. CES, Minutes of Meeting, December 4, 1934, in *Report of the Committee on Economic Security*; Wallace to Witte, December 1, 1934, RG 16, PI 191, entry 17, box 1959.

110. Armstrong, "Reminiscences," 130; "Miss Perkins Asks Aid for Farm Hand," *New York Times*, October 7, 1934; Perkins, "Reminiscences," 401.

111. "We all went down to see the Southern cotton crop. . . . That was all a farming problem. It never occurred to me that because they were poor people and lived by farming they were the natural charge of the Department of Labor, and I'm sure it didn't occur to the farmers or the people who lived by farming, perhaps not owning any land at all. They were farmers, not laborers. Even the sharecroppers were never laborers." Perkins, "Reminiscences," 425.

112. Perkins suggested that under the right conditions sharecropping was a good system. "There is no master and servant relationship under old common law. That's one of the things that makes it so tragic, as we see it. A man who is working as a sharecropper gets hurt in the course of his employment and there is no recourse. He can't sue. He is not a servant, has no master, but is only an independent contractor. Directly after the Civil War there were some very intelligent Negroes who were delighted with the idea of not being slaves any more. I knew about a

particular Mississippi case and saw some of the people involved. They had always like the family to whom they had belonged, who had apparently been good, honest, kindly people. They then became tenants, or sharecroppers. After five or six years they agreed that life was better when they were slaves. They had done more for them and were better taken care of. Of course, it wasn't good politically, but one can see that economically it has very great advantages, as well as disadvantages. Well, I don't think anyone in the Department of Labor thought this was a labor problem. At that time it struck me as being strictly a Southern problem and a farming problem." Ibid., 428.

113. Perkins to FDR, February 25, 1935, Wagner Papers, 566-GF-328, folder 5.

114. Weiss, *Farewell*, 49.

115. Guzda, "Frances Perkins' Interest in a New Deal for Blacks"; Kirby, *Black Americans*, 16.

116. Witte to Hopkins, February 26, 1935, RG 47, PI 183, entry 8, box 57.

117. Witte, "Major Issues in Unemployment Insurance," February 1935, ibid., entry 3, box 23.

118. *Economic Security Act Hearings before the Committee on Ways and Means*, House, 74th Cong., 1st sess., on HR 4120, no. 12, February 5, 1935.

119. Untitled memo beginning "The Economic Security Bill . . . ," March 2, 1935, Wagner Papers, 566-GF-328, folder 5.

120. Ibid. My assumption that the memo was written by Frances Perkins is based on its similarity to another memo from her, dated February 25, 1935, located in the same folder.

121. Schlabach, *Witte*, 150.

122. Ely, "The Place of Research in Graduate Training: Remarks Made at the Dedicatory Exercises of Wieboldt Hall Northwestern University, June 16, 1927," Ely Papers, box 8.

Chapter Four

1. "Address by Josephine Roche," NAACP Annual Conference, June 30, 1935, NAACP Papers, ser. B, box 11.

2. White to Lee Johnson, Secretary to Sen. Edward P. Costigan, July 5, 1935, ibid., ser. C, box 238.

3. The other large national black organization, the National Association of Colored Women, did not engage in lobbying for national legislation at this time, and the more politically attuned National Council of Negro Women was not established until December 1935.

4. FDR's black appointees included Robert Lee Vann, special assistant to the attorney general; William Hastie, assistant solicitor for the Department of the Interior; Louis Mehlinger, special assistant to the attorney general; James Pyron, confidential secretary to FDR; Robert Weaver, special assistant to Secretary Ickes; Lawrence Oxley, special assistant to DOL; Eugene Kinckle Jones, special assistant

to the Secretary of Commerce; and a Dr. Carver of USDA. "Recent Negro Appointments by President Roosevelt and His Aides" and Hon. Braswell Dean to Marvin McIntyre, September 25, 1935, FDR Papers, OF 93, box 2.

5. Over the protests of George Haynes and John P. Davis, Robert Weaver was hired away from the JCNR in 1933 by the Department of the Interior to act as a special assistant to Secretary Ickes. "Recent Negro Appointments by President Roosevelt and His Aides" and Hon. Braswell Dean to Marvin McIntyre, September 25, 1935, ibid. Davis told Weaver: "We urge that you carry in mind, as we believe that you will, the conviction that you are still the representative of the masses of Negro workers, and that you will view matters more largely from this point of view than from a governmental one. . . . The exploitation of subject peoples and minority groups has been based upon the selection of individual leaders upon whom special favors may be heaped in order that the masses may be kept in their submerged condition. We would not say that your appointment has been based upon this, but we would suggest that the situation does have the possibility of being turned into one of similar dangers . . . we are convinced that no man may serve two masters. We could not adequately compensate you for your services. The advisor to the Secretary of Interior has funds at his disposal to do so, and he has taken one of our key men." Davis to Weaver, November 7, 1933, Weaver Papers, Correspondence, 1933–60, "D," reel 1, ScMicro R3701. Davis and Haynes were also offered jobs, but they turned them down. Perlman, "Stirring the White Conscience," 265. Roy Wilkins said that the NAACP spent "all our waking hours working . . . to get Negroes into government." Quoted in Kirby, *Black Americans*, 154.

6. Memo from Weaver to Lt. Lawrence Oxley, January 21, 1935, NAACP Papers, ser. C, box 406.

7. Weaver wrote an article showing the positive side of the New Deal treatment of blacks, highlighting a couple of small programs while glossing over discrimination in the larger ones. Weaver, "The New Deal and the Negro: A Look at the Facts," *Opportunity*, July 1935, 200.

8. See correspondence between White and Oscar Chapman and Nathan Margold of DOI, NAACP Papers, ser. C, box 44. Frank, Jackson, and others were fired and demoted from AAA, in part because of their defense of "Negro" sharecroppers. Memo from John P. Davis to White with addendum by White, Subject: Suggested Witnesses for Proposed House of Representatives Resolution for Investigation of Status of Negro Labor under the New Deal [March 1935] (box 278), Frankfurter to White, November 27, 1934, White to Frankfurter, November 30, 1934, and White to Arthur Spingarn, November 30, 1934 (box 236), and White to Lee Johnson, Secretary to Sen. Edward P. Costigan, May 9, 1935 (box 238), all in NAACP Papers, ser. C; Kirby, *Black Americans*, x.

9. An incomplete list of administration "friends" of the NAACP can be found in "Memorandum on Proposed Congressional Investigation of Economic Status of the Negro under the New Deal," March 1, 1935, NAACP Papers, ser. C, box 278.

10. Hamilton, "National Urban League," 228; Parris, *Blacks in the City*, 228, 236, 238.

11. Hughes, "Toward a Black United Front," 61–66, 71; Weiss, *Farewell*; Davis Papers, Digital Library Collection, Schomburg Center, New York, ScMicro R-5858; JCNR, Minutes of Meeting, October 19, 1934, NAACP Papers, ser. C, box 42.

12. Holden, *Politics of the Black Nation*, quoted in Bracey, "Impact of Hidden Transcripts."

13. NAACP, Minutes, Meeting of Board of Directors, May 13, 1935, NAACP Papers, ser. A, box 10; Sitkoff, *A New Deal for Blacks*, 244–46.

14. John Kirby (*Black Americans*, 182) called White the most influential "outside" African American in Washington in the 1930s. See also the correspondence between the NAACP and FDR's staff in FDR Papers, PPF 1336, "National Association for the Advancement of Colored People, 1932–1936"; Bigalow, *Contemporary Black Biography*, 257; and White, *A Man Called White*.

15. M. H. McIntyre to White, April 24, 1934, Memo from FDR to Steven Early, April 25, 1935, and Julian Rainey to Louis Howe, April 17, 1933, all in FDR Papers, OF 93, box 7; White to Gardner Jackson, March 22, 1935, NAACP Papers, ser. C, box 278; White to ER, April 20, 1934, FDR Papers, PPF 1336, "National Association for the Advancement of Colored People, 1932–1936"; Lee Johnson to White, November 8, 1934, and White to "Dear Office," May 1, 1935 (box 236), White to Oscar Chapman, May 22, 1935, and Nathan Margold to White, June 5, 15, 1935 (box 44), White to Drew Pearson, March 15, 1935, and Gardner Jackson to White, March 28, 1935 (box 278), all in NAACP Papers, ser. C.

16. Zangrando, *Crusade against Lynching*, 105–6, 279, 284–85; Du Bois, "The Defeat of Judge Parker," *The Crisis*, July 1930, 225; *Christian Science Monitor*, quoted in Du Bois's article above. In his brief tenure as executive director of the NAACP, White had enjoyed two surprising victories: the defeat of Judge Parker's nomination and an investigation into discriminatory treatment of black families in Mississippi by a federal project to control floods, resulting in government aid to the families affected by them.

17. In 1935 African Americans were still barred from the Senate and House cafeterias, and the NAACP expended a great deal of time and energy on that issue. See HR 236, 73rd Cong., 2nd sess., Charles Edward Russell to Walter White, March 16, 1934, White to Hon. Oscar DePriest, January 25, 1934, etc., NAACP Papers, ser. C, box 280; Charles Houston to Stephen Early, August 23, 1933, FDR Papers, OF 93, box 7; and Weiss, *Farewell*, 34.

18. See HR 236, 73rd Cong., 2nd sess.; Charles Edward Russell to White, March 16, 1934, White to DePriest, January 25, 1934, and Morris Lewis to Roy Wilkins, January 25, 1934, and others, all in NAACP Papers, ser. C, box 280.

19. Early to Scheider, August 5, 1935, FDR Papers, PPF Subject File: Walter White, box 173.

20. ER to Steven Early, August 8, 1935, FDR Papers, PPF 1336, "National Association for the Advancement of Colored People, 1932–1936."

21. Quoted in Perlman, "Stirring the White Conscience," 180.

22. Streater, "National Negro Congress," 56.

23. Quoted in ibid.," 61.

24. "Pickens Speaks Briefly at Spingarn Award, Oklahoma City, Oklahoma, June 29, 1934," NAACP Papers, ser. B, box 10.

25. Walter White, "On Segregation," February 5, 1934, ibid., ser. C, box 421.

26. Lewis, "Parallels and Divergences," 543.

27. Talk by Ovington at Annual Conference, NAACP, June 1935, NAACP Papers, ser. B, box 10.

28. J. E. Spingarn, "The Second Quarter-Century of the NAACP," June 25, 1935, ibid., box 11.

29. Diner, *In the Almost Promised Land*, introduction, 3, 13, 96, 98, 112, 128.

30. Lewis, "Parallels and Divergences," 543. Lewis argues that some Jewish elites shared this ideology, including Louis D. Brandeis and Franz Boas.

31. Myrdal, *American Dilemma*, 698.

32. "Memorandum to the Secretary from the Chairman of the Board: *Confidential*," January 10, 1934, NAACP Papers, ser. C, box 287.

33. Du Bois, "Segregation in the North," in "Postscript," *The Crisis*, April 1934, 115.

34. White to Spingarn, January 15, 1934, NAACP Papers, ser. C, box 287.

35. Assistant Secretary of the NAACP to Joel Spingarn, May 23, 1935, ibid., ser. B, box 11.

36. Seligman, "Is the NAACP Highbrow?," draft article, memo from Bagnall to White, November 11, 1931, and memo from Wilkins to White, October 29, 1931, NAACP Papers, ser. C, box 420. Both Bagnall and Wilkins approved the final draft of the proposed article. There is no evidence that it was published.

37. Negro churches were more likely to represent the interests of working-class African Americans than the NAACP, and at least one church conference lobbied FDR for better protection of agricultural and domestic workers through the New Deal. George Bagnall, Secretary, The Conference of Church Workers among Colored People (Episcopal), to FDR, October 15, 1934, FDR Papers, OF 93, box 2.

38. Henderson, "Interpreting the National Association for the Advancement of Colored People as a Religious Ideal," NAACP Papers, ser. B, box 10.

39. White, address at 1935 Annual NAACP Conference, ibid.

40. White to Gertrude B. Stone, April 20, 1935, "Senate Poll (April 19, 1935) on Costigan-Wagner Bill," telegrams from White to fifteen senators on filibuster vote, April 26, 1935, and untitled, "Following Are Expressions from Members of the House of Representatives in Communications re the Costigan-Wagner Anti-Lynching Bill," April 17, 1935, all in NAACP Papers, ser. C, box 238; White to Mr. Barnett, December 13, 1934, ibid., box 236; Zangrando, *Crusade against Lynching*, 125–26; "Are You against Lynching?," enclosed in J. A. MacCallum and D. W. Henry, Committee on Race Relations, Society of Friends, to "Fellow Ministers," January 22, 1935, NAACP Papers, ser. C, box 43.

41. White to Simon Guggenheim and to Robert Kohn, June 3, 1935, and White to Rabbi Sidney E. Goldstein, November 15, 1934, NAACP Papers, ser. C, box 44. See also White to Dr. Louis I. Newman, Temple Rodeph Sholom, October 15, 1935, ibid., box 236.

42. Walter White to Roger A. Baldwin, April 20, 1935, ibid., box 238. See also White to L. C. Dyer, February 2, 1935, and Dyer to White, February 18, 1935, ibid., box 237.

43. Memo from White to Messrs. Wilkins and Schuyler, May 10, 1935, ibid., box 238.

44. Ibid.; Zangrando, *Crusade against Lynching*, 99.

45. Roy Wilkins, "1st draft lynching pamphlet," [1933], NAACP Papers, ser. C, box 205.

46. White to Rockefeller, October 23, 1934, ibid., box 236.

47. Memo from Roy Wilkins to Walter White, May 8, 1935, ibid., box 238.

48. See correspondence between Katherine Gardner, National Federation of Churches, Walter White, William Hastie, and Will Alexander, November 1934, ibid., box 236. See also Roy Wilkins to Rep. Sterling Strong of Texas, January 31, 1934, ibid.

49. Quoted in Sosna, *Silent South*, 53.

50. The NAACP leadership was particularly sensitive to the labeling of "Negroes" as "uncivilized." In response to a *New York Times* editorial that made such a reference, Charles Houston called the statement "malicious libel on all the Negro citizens of this country." Houston to the Editor, *New York Times*, April 19, 1935, in NAACP Papers, ser. C, box 238.

51. Walter White, [draft] "The South Is a Long Way Off," [May 1935], ibid., box 421, p. 11.

52. White, address at 1935 Annual NAACP Conference, ibid., ser. B, box 10.

53. Dr. A. A. Brill and Dr. Fritz Wittels, "Psychologists Analyze Neal Lynching, *The Crisis*, January 1935, in NAACP Papers, ser. C, box 428, p. 18. "[D]e Sade in all his glory could not have invented a more diabolical situation." Ibid.

54. John Kirby (*Black Americans*, 8) argues that in the 1920s, the only organized white liberals who gave any attention to race were those affiliated with Communist organizations or the NAACP and NUL.

55. Hughes, "Toward a Black United Front," 10.

56. James S. Allen, "Lenin and the American Negro," *The Communist*, January 1934, 54–56.

57. A. W. Berry, "Communists Must Build Unity for the Defense of Ethiopian Nation," *Daily Worker*, March 23, 1935, 3.

58. "Negro Editors on Communism: A Symposium of the American Negro Press," *The Crisis*, May 1932, 154.

59. Ibid., April 1932, 117.

60. White to Joel Spingarn, January 15, 1934, NAACP Papers, ser. C, box 287.

61. NAACP Papers, ser. C, box 287.

62. Joel Spingarn informed Walter White: "The Armenia Conference voted in favor of cultural nationalism for the American Negro as the most important thing for the Negro to aim at. This represents the attitude of most of the Negro intelligentsia, or at least of the most advanced groups, and is akin to what certain advanced groups of Jews are aiming at, such as Ludwig Lewison's opposition to all forms of 'assimilation' and the Zionists' desire for political separation. Whether one likes it or not, it is a strong contemporary trend, and is in the direction of self-imposed 'segregation.'" "Memorandum to the Secretary from the Chairman of the Board: *Confidential*," January 10, 1934, NAACP Papers, ser. C, box 287.

63. Hastie, "Du Bois: Ex-Leader of Negroes," *New Negro Opinion*, Washington, D.C., January 25, 1934, in NAACP Papers, ser. C, box 287.

64. Du Bois, "Classes among Negroes," *The Crisis*, June 1930, 210.

65. Myrdal, *American Dilemma*, 796; Du Bois to the Editor, *American Mercury*, New York, November 19, 1934, in Du Bois Papers, reel 41, frame 843.

66. Du Bois, "History of Segregation Philosophy," in "Postscript," *The Crisis*, March 1934, 85–86.

67. Du Bois, "No Segregation," in "Postscript," *The Crisis*, April 1934, 116.

68. Du Bois, "Integration," in "Postscript," *The Crisis*, April 1934, 117.

69. Du Bois to Abram Harris, January 3, [1934], Du Bois Papers, reel 42, frame 426.

70. Du Bois to Mrs. Addie Dickerson, March 21, 1934, ibid., frame 49.

71. Du Bois, "No Segregation."

72. Du Bois to Mrs. Alexina C. Barrell, March 1, 1935, ibid., reel 43, frame 848.

73. Robert Weaver sent suggested language to Lawrence Oxley to prevent discrimination in the distribution of federal funds through the Social Security Act. It read, in part: "[F]or those states where separate public institutions for white and Negro citizens are required by law, shall also show that an equitable distribution of funds in providing facilities and benefits for white and Negro citizens has been made." Memo from Weaver to Oxley, January 21, 1935, NAACP Papers, ser. C, box 406.

74. Du Bois to Harry L. Davis, July 18, 1934, Du Bois Papers, reel 42, frame 27.

75. Pickens to J. E. Spingarn, June 10, 1934, ibid., frame 919.

76. Du Bois, "Segregation in the North," in "Postscript," *The Crisis*, April 1934, 115.

77. Telegram from Walter White to Du Bois, January 11, 1934, Du Bois Papers, reel 43, frame 386.

78. NAACP, "Report of the Secretary for the February Meeting of the Board," February 9, 1934, NAACP Papers, frame I-A-17.

79. Perlman, *Stirring the White Conscience*, 180.

80. Memo, "Evidence Supporting Request for Clause or Clauses against Discrimination on Account of Race or Color in the Economic Security Bill," by George Edmund Haynes, Ph.D., Executive Secretary, Department of Race Relations, Federal Council of Churches, [January or February 1935], RG 46, SEN 74A-E1, S 1130,

box 18; Haynes to Rep. Robert Doughton, January 19, 1935, House Files, HR 74A-F39.3, box 14118; "Urge against Discrimination in Security Laws: Federal Council's Department of Race Relations Wires President and Senator Wagner," January 18, 1935, and Haynes to "Dear Friend," January 22, 1935, NAACP Papers, ser. C, box 43.

81. Haynes, "Lily-White Social Security," *The Crisis*, March 1935, 85.

82. Memo, "Evidence Supporting Request for Clause or Clauses against Discrimination," pp. 14–15.

83. Ibid., p. 18.

84. House Ways and Means Committee, Economic Security Act, 74th Cong., 1st sess., January 31, 1935, 597–600.

85. Hughes, "Toward a Black United Front," 67–68.

86. Streater, "National Negro Congress," 74.

87. Hughes, "Toward a Black United Front," 73; Frances Williams to John Davis, October 8, 1934 (ser. C, box 42), NAACP, Minutes, Meeting of Board of Directors, October 8, 1934 (ser. A, box 10), and JCNR, Minutes of Meeting, September 21, 1934 (ser. C, box 42), all in NAACP Papers.

88. Parris, *Blacks in the City*, 260.

89. In discussions surrounding the 1935 Urban League Regional Conference, the sentiment was expressed that focusing the conference on "The Negro and the Recovery Program" would generate more widespread interest and the participation of "some persons who would not come if they believed it was to be limited to an Urban League subject." Pittsburgh Urban League to T. Arnold Hill, December 21, 1934, February 7, 1935, and note to Maurice Moss from Hill, attached to "Urban League Regional Conference 1935," in NUL Papers, ser. 4, box 21.

90. Hamilton, "National Urban League"; "A Brief Statement Concerning the Activities of the National Urban League during 1935," NUL Papers, ser. 1, box 1.

91. Hill to "City Chairmen," EAC for Negroes, April 25, 1934, ibid., ser. 4, box 4; Abrams, "History of the National Urban League," 54–55.

92. Quoted in Parris, *Blacks in the City*, 249.

93. Hill, "The Negro's Need for Unemployment Insurance," *Unemployment Insurance Review: National Congress Issue* 1, no. 1 [1935], RG 47, PI 183, entry 1, box 9, p. 9.

94. Edwin Witte to Hill, November 9, 1934, ibid., entry 4, box 16.

95. Handwritten minutes of "Morning Session," February 16, 1935, Board Room, Pittsburgh Urban League, and Hill to Executive Secretaries of the Affiliated Branches of NUL, March 18, 1935, NUL Papers, ser. 4, box 21.

96. See, e.g., Jesse O. Thomas to Hill, February 11, 1935, Reginald A. Johnson, "The Negro and Social Insurance," Atlanta Urban League, February 1935, and Handwritten minutes titled "Boycott Discussion," [February 16, 1935], all in NUL Papers, ser. 4, box 21.

97. C. C. Spaulding to State Chairmen of the EACs for Negroes, July 25, 1935,

and EAC for Negroes News Letter, April 25, 1934 (ser. 4, box 4), and A Brief Statement Concerning the Activities of the National Urban League during 1935" (ser. 1, box 1), all in NUL Papers.

98. Hamilton, "National Urban League," 240; Parris, *Blacks in the City*, 247.

99. NAACP Papers, ser. C, boxes 42–44.

100. Assistant Secretary to Spingarn, May 23, 1935, ibid., box 11.

101. Nancy Weiss (*Farewell*, 35) states that "[a]t the outset of the New Deal, in letters, newspaper editorials, and organizational pronouncements, black spokesmen articulated a common racial agenda," of which inclusion in New Deal programs topped the list.

102. These included a Rosenwald-sponsored conference on "Economic Status of the Negro" in May 1933, the Second Amenia Conference in July 1933 on black economic conditions and the Roosevelt administration, and the 1935 Howard University conference of the JCNR. Kirby, *Black Americans* 15.

103. Immediately following the 1932 election, FDR began to receive scores of letters from African American citizens requesting help and recognition, and from black organizations seeking appointments and jobs. See FDR Papers, OF 93, box 2.

104. John Davis stated: "The New Deal is planning, so it says, a new American society. . . . Yet its plans are so shortsighted that it can only see for the next fifty years Negro ghettos, separate and apart from white communities. Although the NAACP fought and won the battle against residential segregation years ago, we find the New Deal extending this principle." "Charges New Deal Re-enslaves Negro; 4 Million on Relief," NAACP Newsletter, [June 1935], NAACP Papers, ser. B, box 11. According to W. E. B. Du Bois: "The government, national and state . . . has entered and entered for good into the social and economic organization of life. We could wish, we could pray, that this entrance could absolutely ignore lines of race and color, but we know perfectly well it does not and will not." Du Bois, "Segregation in the North," in "Postscript," *The Crisis*, April 1934, 115.

105. Abram Harris, "Future Plans and Programs of the NAACP," 3, "Preliminary Report of the Committee on Future Plan and Program of the NAACP," [September 25, 1934], and NAACP, Minutes, Meeting of Board of Directors, June 7, 1935, NAACP Papers, ser. A, box 22.

106. Harris to Du Bois, January 6, 1934, Du Bois Papers, reel 42, frame 427.

107. Granger, Workers Bureau, NUL, to Abram Harris, January 19, 1935, and Harris to T. Arnold Hill, January 2, 1935, NUL Papers, ser. 4, box 4.

108. "Preliminary Report of the Committee on Future Plan and Program of the NAACP," [September 25, 1934] (ser. A, box 22), NAACP, Minutes, Meeting of Board of Directors, June 7, 1935, and "NAACP Annual Conference," June 30, 1935 (ser. B, box 11), NAACP Papers.

109. White to Spingarn, February 7, 1935, ibid., ser. C, box 257.

110. HR 4120, 74th Cong., 1st sess., January 17, 1935, in ibid., box 406.

111. Telegrams from White to Wagner and to William Taylor, Howard University Law School, January 22, 1935, NAACP Papers, ser. C, box 257.

112. Telegram from White to Wagner, February 4, 1935, and memo from Roy Wilkins to White, February 2, 1935, ibid.

113. Telegram from Houston to White, February 5, 1935, ibid.

114. Ibid., Williams to White, [February 1935], ibid.

115. White to Ickes, February 6, 1935, and memo from Wilkins to White, February 2, 1935, ibid.; White to Perkins, February 6, 1035, RG 47, PI 183, entry 8, box 54.

116. See telegrams from White to Henry Morganthau, February 6, 1935, RG 47, PI 183, entry 8, box 54; NAACP, Minutes, Meeting of Board of Directors," February 11, 1935 (ser. A, box 10), and memo from White to Members of the Committee on Old-Age Pensions and Unemployment Insurance, February 14, 1935 (ser. C, box 257), NAACP Papers.

117. Morganthau to White, February 13, 1935, NAACP Papers, ser. C, box 406.

118. Altmeyer to White, February 11, 1935, Witte to White, February 18, 1935, and White to Davis, February 20, 1935, all in ibid., box 257.

119. Williams to William Lloyd Imes, February 15, 1935, ibid.

120. Mrs. Kendall Emerson, Chairman, Public Affairs Committee, YWCA, to Rep. Robert Doughton, February 11, 1935, ibid.; *Hearings before the Committee on Finance*, Senate, 74th Cong., 1st sess., on S 1130, pt. 7, February 6, 7, 1935; Mrs. Emerson to FDR, February 15, 1935, NAACP Papers, ser. C, box 257.

121. Cuthbert, "Variety, Spice and Life II," *The Womans Press*, November 1934, 502.

122. "Testimony of Charles H. Houston Representing the National Association for the Advancement of Colored People," *Hearings before the Committee on Finance*, Senate, 74th Cong., 1st sess., on S 1130, February 9, 1935; Houston testimony, *Economic Security Act Hearings before the Committee on Ways and Means*, House, 74th Cong., 1st sess., January 1935, pp. 641–43.

123. Henriette C. Epstein, Interview, box 1, pp. 9, 24, 92.

124. Abraham Epstein, "The Social Security Act," *The Crisis*, November 1935, 337–38.

125. Memo from Wilkins to Rev. Imes, Mr. Delany, Mr. Studin, Miss Williams, February 26, 1935, In Re: Wagner-Lewis Economic Security Bill, NAACP Papers, ser. C, box 257.

126. NAACP, Minutes, Meeting of Board of Directors, March 11, 1935, ibid., ser. A, box 10.

127. Memo from Wilkins to Rev. Imes, Mr. Delany, Mr. Studin, Miss Williams, February 26, 1935.

128. White to Ben Stern, Secretary to Hon. Frederick Van Nuys, May 15, 1935, and Lee Johnson to White, August 17, 1935 (ser. C, box 238), and NAACP, "Report of the Secretary for the September Meeting of the Board," [September 1935] (ser. A, box 18, p. 2), NAACP Papers.

129. NAACP, Minutes, Meeting of Board of Directors, March 11, 1935, NAACP Papers, ser. A, box 10.

130. White to P. L. Prattis, Associated Negro Press, April 10, 1935, ibid., ser. C, box 238.

131. Memo from John P. Davis to White with addendum by White, Subject: Suggested Witnesses from Proposed House of Representatives Resolution for Investigation of Status of Negro Labor under the New Deal, [March 1935] (ser. C, box), NAACP, "Report of the Secretary," August 1935 (ser. A, box 18), White to Mother Katherine, April 11, 1935 (ser. C, box 278), and John C. Dancy, Director of the Detroit Urban League, to White, March 15, 1935, and White to Dancy, March 18, 1935 (ser. C, box 278), all in NAACP Papers. White refused to work with the NUL, concerned that "T. Arnold Hill would try to grab off the whole thing for the Urban League and hog the show." White to Forrester B. Washington, March 11, 1935, White to Houston, March 16, 1935, and telegram from White to Houston, March 30, 1935, all in ibid., ser. C, box 278.

132. P. L. Prattis, Associated Negro Press, to White, March 13, 1935, "Memorandum on Proposed Congressional Investigation of Economic Status of Negro under the New Deal," March 1, 1935, and White to Forrester B. Washington, March 11, 1935 (ser. C, box 278), NAACP, Minutes, Meeting of Board of Directors, March 11, 1935 (ser. A, box 10), and White to Prattis, April 10, 1935, and White to Mother Katherine, April 11, 1935 (ser. C, box 278), all in NAACP Papers.

133. Telegram from Edward P. Costigan to White, March 29, 1935, and White to "Chief" Costigan, April 1, 1935, ibid., ser. C, box 278.

134. Memo from Walter White to Charles Houston, July 12, 1935, ibid., ser. C, box 278.

Chapter Five

1. Cushman, "Report of Field Trip, Public Health Nursing, Alabama, September 26, October 1, 2, 3, 4, 5, 6, 7, 1936," RG 102, Central File 1933–36, entry 3, box 615, 13-2-1(2).

2. Abramovitz, *Regulating the Lives of Women*, 318.

3. Quoted in Costin, *Two Sisters*, 127.

4. According to her biographer, Grace Abbott's inner circle also included Josephine Roche, Florence Kelley, Julia Lathrop, Josephine Goldmark, Alice Hamilton, M.D., Carrie Chapman Catt, Rose Schneiderman, Harriet Tayler Upton, Emily Balch, Margaret Drier Robins, and Cornelia Pinchot. Ibid.

5. Ibid., 162–63, 204; Abbott Papers, box 25, folder 10.

6. Lenroot, "Transcript of Oral History," 6, 10–11; Draft titled "Early Childhood and Youth," Lenroot Papers, box 1, File: Letters re. Articles etc. Lenroot was never officially a graduate student of Common's, though when she was an undergraduate he gave her research projects, even, apparently, getting her excused from exams in other classes so that she could devote herself to his work.

7. Lundberg and Lenroot lived together in a six-room apartment at the Woodward in Washington, directly above Lenroot's mother and father; they apparently also shared an apartment in New York City, where Lundberg was director of research for the New York City Temporary Emergency Relief Administration. Article, ". . . in the Federal Government," entry 2, [1936–39], Lenroot Papers, box 3, p. 2; Lenroot to Lundberg, November 8, 1934, January 27, 1931, Lenroot to C. W. Areson, October 25, 1934, and Lenroot to Areson, November 8, 1934, RG 102, Central File 1933–36, entry 3, box 463, 0-1-0-4(3); Lenroot, "Transcript of Oral History," 7, 14–15; Costin, *Two Sisters*, 128.

8. Costin, *Two Sisters*, 141–42.

9. See Linda Gordon, *Pitied but Not Entitled*; Muncy, *Creating a Female Dominion*; Molly Ladd Taylor, *Mother-Work*; Michel, "Limits of Maternalism"; and Mink, *Wages of Motherhood*, 46.

10. Goodwin, *Gender and the Politics of Welfare Reform*, 46, 99.

11. Quoted in ibid.

12. Lenroot, "What America Expects of Her Daughters," *Philadelphia Public Ledger*, October 25, 1931, in Lenroot Papers, box 2, p. 3.

13. Costin, *Two Sisters*, 181.

14. Herschel Alt to Florence W. Hutsinpillar, January 24, 1929, and Hutsinpillar to Alt, January 29, 1929, RG 102, Central File 1929–32, entry 3, box 404, 7-3-3-1.

15. Memo from Lenroot to Edwin Witte, December 1, 1934, RG 47, PI 183, entry 8, box 57; Grace Abbott, "Recent Trends in Mothers' Aid" [1934], Abbott Papers, box 24, folder 13; Lenroot, "Recent Developments in Provision for Children Born out of Wedlock," National Florence Crittenton Conference, Washington, D.C., May 29, 1929, Lenroot Papers, box 3, box 2, pp. 1, 5, 8. The Federal Children's Bureau was fully aware that a disproportionate percentage of unmarried mothers were African American. Agnes K. Hannah to Grace Abbott, November 22, 1935, RG 102, Central File 1933–36, entry 3, box 550, 7-4-0-3; Lenroot, "Recent Developments in Provision for Children Born out of Wedlock." Shortly after the passage of the Social Security Act, Grace Abbott, through the FCB staff, began to gather data on illegitimacy and state legislation regarding illegitimate births and children; she obtained a commitment from the Bureau to study the matter more closely in the spring. Hannah to Abbott, November 22, 1935.

16. Agnes K. Hannah to F. F. Pettiford, May 10, 1933; D. E. Webster to DOL, May 6, 1933, RG 102, Central File 1933–36, entry 3, box 477, 0-2-9-1-3.

17. Lenroot to Paul Kellogg, October 28, 1935, ibid., box 476, 0-2-9-1-0; Lenroot, "Transcript of Oral History," 129.

18. Miss F. B. King to Lenroot, May 16, 1933, and Lenroot to King, June 1, 1933, RG 102, Central File 1933–36, entry 3, box 476, 0-2-9-1-0.

19. Dr. Ro[berts], "Maternal Mortality Study," draft, [1928?], Abbott Papers, box 63, folder 3.

20. The FCB discouraged states from hiring older women as midwives and nurses. Albert McCown to George M. Cooper, February 13, 1936, RG 102 (box 622,

13-2-1[35]; Memo from Ruth Heintselman to Miss Deutsch, August 19, 1936 (box 615, 13-2-3[0]), RG 102, Central File 1933–36, entry 3,

21. *Hearings before the Committee on Finance*, Senate, 74th Cong., 1st sess., on S 1130, pt. 6, February 4, 5, 1935, p. 411.

22. Lenroot (to be "Furnished" to Lt. Exley), "Sections of the Secretary's Speech at the National Conference on Problems of the Negro," December 24, 1936, RG 102, Central File 1933–36, entry 3, box 476, 0-2-9-1-0.

23. Albert McCown, FCB, to G. Lombard Kelly, University of Georgia, March 28, 1936, ibid., box 617, 13-2-2-12.

24. Frances Kelley to Grace Abbott, RG 102, Central File 1929–32, entry 3, box 367, 0-2-9-1-1.

25. There is no correspondence with the NAACP on record for the years between 1933 and 1936; there are a handful of letters between the Bureau and the NUL and only one exchange with the National Association of Colored Women for the same period. See RG 102, Index to the Central File 1933–36, entry 1, box 85, p. 71, and White to "Director," FCB, September 21, 1929 (box 367, 0-2-9-1-3), George Arthur to Katherine Lenroot, December 27, 1933 (box 47, 0-2-9-1-2), Letitia R. Myles to Clara Beyer, October 15, 1933 (box 477, 0-2-9-1-4), Grace Abbott to Robert R. Moton, October 14, 1929, and Moton to Abbott, October 9, 1929 (box 367, 0-2-9-1-1), and Lenroot to White, September 24, 1929 (box 367, 0-2-9-1-3), Agnes K. Hannah to T. Arnold Hill, December 30, 1932, and Ann Tannyhill, Secretary to Hill, to Hannah, December 31, 1932 (box 404, 7-3-3-1), all in RG 102, Central File 1929–32, entry 3.

26. Edith Abbott, "Grace Abbott: Her Sister's Story of Her Life and Work," Abbott Papers, addendum, box 7, folder 7.

27. "The United States Supreme Court and the Scottsboro Case," "Notes and Comments," *Social Service Review* 8, no. 3 (September 1934): 337. In April 1931 an all-white grand jury in Scottsboro, Ala., convicted nine African American teenagers of raping two white women, all of whom were riding in a freight train southbound from Chattanooga, Tenn. The jury convicted the young men only two weeks after the alleged incident. The evidence against the "Scottsboro boys" was extremely shaky, resting entirely on the contradictory and possibly coerced testimony of the two women who had been their traveling companions. All but the youngest of the nine boys were sentenced to death. The Communist Party's International Labor Defense headed legal appeals on the boys' behalf. The case came to stand as an indictment of Jim Crow segregation. See correspondence with members of the NIC in box 367, 0-2-9-1-0, and Grace Abbott to Edwin Embree, June 6, 1933, Embree to Abbott, June 1, 1933; Abbott to George Arthur, Rosenwald Fund, January 6, 1933, RG 102, Central File 1933–36, entry 3, box 477, 0-2-9-1-3; Abbott Papers, box 25, folder 10.

28. Irene Graham, University of Chicago, *Social Service Review* 3, no. 4 (December 1929): 541–62.

29. See correspondence between Abbott and the NIC, RG 102, Central File

1929–32, entry 3, box 367, 0-2-9-1-0, and Edwin Embree to Abbott, June 1, 1933, Abbott to Embree, June 6, 1933, and Abbott to George Arthur, Rosenwald Fund, January 6, 1933, RG 102, Central File 1933–36, entry 3, box 477, 0-2-8-1-3.

30. [Grace Abbott], Untitled draft, n.d., edited in Abbott's handwriting, Abbott Papers, box 68, folder 3.

31. Katherine Lenroot, "The Health-Education Program of the Children's Bureau, with Particular Reference to Negroes," *Journal of Negro Education* (July 1937): 506.

32. RG 102, Central File 1929–32, entry 3, box 404, 7-3-3-1; Agnes K. Hannah to Miss Isabel V. D. Traver, November 12, 1935, RG 102, Central File 1933–36, entry 3, box 477, 0-2-9-1-3.

33. Untitled reported, edited by Grace Abbott, [after 1931], Abbott Papers, box 63, folder 3.

34. Lenroot to Sarreals, June 28, 1934, and February 13, 1934, RG 102, Central File 1933–36, entry 3, box 476, 0-2-9-1-0. The FCB's interest in black mothers and children contrasts with its almost total lack of concern about other minority groups during this period. In response to requests, the Bureau reported that it had no statistical information on American children of Chinese and Japanese descent; it forwarded inquiries about Indian and Mexican American children to the Bureau of Indian Affairs. Antoinette Lagana, FCB, to Miss Ella Arvilla Merritt, Council of Women for Home Missions, August 6, 1934, ibid., box 477, folder 0-2-9-2; see also folders 0-2-9-4 and 0-2-9-5-0. The exception to this rule was the Bureau's interest in Puerto Rican immigrants. The FCB argued that Puerto Rican nationals should not be sent home, as was the policy of the Relief Administration in New York City, because conditions in Puerto Rico were even more desperate than those in the United States, nor should they be given relief through a separate program. Sarreals to Lenroot, June 19, 1934, ibid., box 476, 0-2-9-1-0. The Bureau tried, unsuccessfully, to get Puerto Rican citizens included in the provisions of the Social Security Act. Memo from Arthur Altmeyer to Lenroot, June 12, 1935, ibid., box 467, 0-1-0-7-3(1), and Lenroot, "The Children's Bureau," in *Twenty-fourth Annual Report of the Secretary of labor for the Fiscal Year Ended June 30, 1936* (Washington, D.C.: GPO), 1936, 135. See also Florence Hutsinpillar to Frances Griggs, August 30, 1932, and Griggs to Hutsinpillar, August 11, 1932, RG 102, Central File 1929–32, entry 3, box 404, 7-3-3-1; Harold Goldstein, Women's Trade Union League, to Director, FCB, January 14, 1935, Ella Arvilla Merritt to Goldstein, January 22, 1935, Annette Davis, YWCA, to FCB, February 1, 1935, Merritt to Davis, February 20, 1935, and Merritt to NAACP, February 20, 1935 (box 477, 0-2-9-1-4), "References on Child Welfare Work among Negroes" (box 476, 0-2-9-1-3), and Ruth Bloodgood, FCB, to Wilda Mullins, December 19, 1935 (box 476, 0-2-9-1-2), all in RG 102, Central File 1933–36, entry 3.

35. Dr. Haven Emerson, responding to a subreport comparing maternal mortality rates, insisted that the national statistics did not fully describe how race factored into these death rates: "International uniformity if ever attained will be of

little or no value in helping to reduce our maternal mortality. The use of rates of different countries may be an excusable device to arouse women's clubs to indignation and even to action, but this does not help the Negro in Alabama, the Indian in Arizona or the Jew in New York City. Only by local studies which analyze the deaths with some such minuteness as is given to each death in our maternity hospitals . . . will the multifarious causes of unnecessary maternal deaths be brought to light." Emerson to Dr. Elizabeth Tandy, May 22, 1934. Tandy, of the FCB, was delighted with Emerson's response. RG 103, Central File, 1933–36, entry 3, box 463, 0-1-0-4(3).

36. This study had originally been undertaken to save the Sheppard-Towner Act from sunsetting in 1929 and to shame organized medicine into supporting it. Through the study, the Bureau investigated the deaths of 7,537 women, a figure that included all the maternal deaths in certain states between 1927 and 1928. FCB, "Trend of Maternal Mortality by Color in the U.S. Birth Registration Area and in States Having 1,500 or More Negro Births in 1932, 1915–1932," February 9, and "Trend of Infant Mortality in the U.S. Birth Registration Area and in States Having 1,500 or More Negro Births in 1932, 1915–1932," November 11, 1934, RG 47, PI 183, entry 3, box 23. See also Abbott Papers, box 68, folder 3; Fred Adair to Elizabeth C. Tandy, February 15, 1934 (box 463, 0-1-0-4[3]), and memo from Tandy, FCB, to Katherine Lenroot, November 12, 1934, RE: Economic Security (box 466, 0-1-0-7-3[1]), RG 102, Central File 1933–36, entry 3.

37. Costin, *Two Sisters*, 139.

38. Mrs. Ben Roach to Grace Abbott, August 25, 1933, and Lenroot to Roach, August 31, 1933, RG 102, Central File 1933–36, entry 3, box 476, 0-2-9-1-0.

39. Miss Mary Elizabeth Moore to Frances Perkins, December 12, 1933, and Abbott to Moore, December 19, 1933, ibid. See also Beatrice McConnell, FCB, to O. Singleton, Irvington, Ky., April 1, 1936, "The Cause and Cure of Crime and the Rational Solution of the Vexatious Negro Problem," and L. B. Austin to Dr. M. O. Bousfield, July 20, 1936, ibid., box 477, 0-2-9-1-6.

40. The FCB referred the letter to the Eugenics Laboratory. Georgia Tann, Tennessee Children's Home Society, to FCB, April 13, 1936, Ella Oppenheimer to Dr. Charles S. Davenport, April 24, 1936, and Davenport to Tann, May 4, 1936, ibid., box 493, 4-4-0-1.

41. Pickens, *Eugenics*, 87, 90. The American Eugenics Society held a roundtable discussion in May 1936; the speakers included a professor of philosophy from the New School of Social Work in New York City, and Arthur E. Morgan, director of the federal Tennessee Valley Authority. "The American Eugenics Society Round Table Conference and Annual Meeting," May 7, 1936, New York, RG 102, Central File 1933–36, entry 3, box 493, 4-4-0-4; Grace Abbott, "The United States Children's Bureau," draft, for publication in magazine of the St. Paul's Roman Catholic Orphan Asylum, Pittsburgh, May 4, 1934, Abbott Papers, box 24, folder 14; Grace Abbott, excerpts of address at National Women's Trade Union League, [1934], Abbott Papers, box 24, folder 13. In response to requests for information about

heredity, the FCB sent out a form letter stating: "Your best sources of information on the subject of heredity are the publications of the following organizations: The Human Betterment Foundation[,] . . . Pasadena, California[;] . . . The Race Betterment Foundation[,] . . . Battle Creek, Michigan[;] . . . [and the] American Eugenics Society[,] . . . New Haven, Connecticut." Agnes K. Hannah, FCB, to Virginia Wyatt, East Gadson, Ala., February 17, 1934, RG 102, Central File 1933–36, entry 3, box 493, 4-4-8-1.

42. Lenroot, "Address of the Chairman of the United States Delegation, Sixth Pan American Child Congress, Lima, Peru, July 4–11, 1930," Lenroot Papers, box 2, pp. 2–4. See also RG 102, Central File 1933–36, entry 3, box 463, 0-1-0-4(3), and Lenroot, "Setting Goals for Child Welfare in America," *Pan American Magazine*, October 1930, in Lenroot Papers, box 2. Lenroot chaired the U.S. delegation to the Sixth Pan American Child Congress, and Grace Abbott chaired the sixteen-person delegation to the Seventh, held in Mexico City in October 1935.

43. The FCB took great pride in the appointment of Frances Perkins to the president's cabinet; she was identified with social work circles and, along with the Abbott sisters and Lenroot, with the network of women employed by New Deal agencies. Perkins trusted Grace Abbott especially and often turned to her for advice about DOL. Abbott only stepped down from the FCB when Perkins was appointed secretary of labor, because she felt secure that Perkins would protect the FCB's interests. In some cases, Perkins authorized Abbott to speak on her behalf without her prior approval. On becoming reacquainted with Edwin Witte just after his appointment to the CES staff in August 1934, Katherine Lenroot told Abbott enthusiastically: "I think Mr. Witte will be a real friend for the Children's Bureau." Ware, *Beyond Suffrage*; Lenroot, "Women in Government Service," Radio Broadcast, National Federation of Business and Professional Women's Clubs, March 27, 1935, in Lenroot Papers, box 2; Costin, *Two Sisters*, 213–15; Lenroot to Abbott, August 1, 1934, Lenroot Papers, box 1.

44. Lenroot to Witte, November 21, 1934, RG 47, entry 8, box 57, "Lenroot." The second proposal could not be located in the FCB's files or in the personal papers of either Lenroot or Abbott.

45. "Memorandum on Legislative Program for Coming Year," enclosed in Lenroot to Abbott, August 3, 1934, RG 102, Central File 1933–36, entry 3, box 485, 1-10-4. Lenroot later claimed that Abbott's main interest in the Act was the expansion of mothers' pensions and that she did not initially consider reviving the Sheppard-Towner maternity and infant program through the Act. Lenroot, "Transcript of Oral History," 52. Lenroot wrote to Abbott requesting that she meet with Witte in Chicago soon, as he was "eager" for her views. During a "long talk" with Lenroot and Martha Eliot on August 16, Witte said that the bill would cover three areas: unemployment insurance, old-age pensions, and a program for low-income children. "He is thinking in terms of a maternity and child health program which would provide for much of the work carried on under Sheppard-Towner without designating the program as such, provisions for a mothers' aid program involving

federal subsidies, and such other measures for child health and child welfare as appear to be necessary." Lenroot to Abbott, August 17, 1934, Abbott Papers, box 54, folder 1. The idea to include the Sheppard-Towner program may have originated in a meeting between Witte, Lenroot, and Martha Eliot in August 1934. Eliot to Abbott, September 13, 1934, Abbott Papers, box 37, folder 3. Lenroot claimed that she originally had proposed federal aid for child welfare services. Lenroot, "Transcript of Oral History," 52. Martha Eliot also may have been the catalyst for inclusion of child welfare funds in the bill. She noted that the first report submitted to Witte in September made no reference to child welfare services beyond mothers' pensions and asked "whether something could not be included." Martha Eliot, "Reminiscences," 46. That preliminary proposal, a mere four pages long, had been "boiled down . . . at Mr. Witte's suggestion." Ibid. In very brief, straightforward language, it called for a revival of the Sheppard-Towner Act, now expanded to include women and children beyond infancy, at Eliot's suggestion, and a mothers' pension program. Lenroot, "Special Measures for Children's Security," from app. E, CES Preliminary Report, RG 47, PI 183, entry 3, box 23.

46. Lenroot and Abbott, "Security for Children: Relationship of Special Measures for Children to a General Security Program," 1. Memo from Lenroot to Witte, November 21, 1934, RG 47, PI 183, entry 8, box 57.

47. Ibid., 4.

48. Ibid., 12–13.

49. That exception was a draft outline for the mothers' pension title of the Act, which defined eligible children as those of "widowed or divorced mothers or mothers deserted by their husbands for one year or more, or whose husbands are physically or mentally incapacitated or under sentence of at least one year to a correctional institution." However, this language differed strikingly from that used in the rest of the proposal and may not have survived; the outline was attached to the back of the report and marked "Tentative" because, as Lenroot explained, Grace Abbott had not yet reviewed it. Lenroot and Abbott, "Security for Children," and Lenroot to Edwin Witte, November 21, 1934, RG 47, PI 183, entry 8, box 57, "Lenroot."

50. Eighty-two percent of families that benefited from mothers' pension programs were headed by widows. Lenroot and Abbott, "Security for Children," 4–5, 17.

51. In a letter dated October 16, Lenroot noted that Abbott "thought we might allow special funds for States in special need, owing to drought or other emergencies." Lenroot to Abbott, October 16, 1934, RG 102, Central File 1933–36, entry 3, box 467, 0-1-0-7-3(1).

52. Lenroot and Abbott, "Security for Children," 30.

53. Albert McCown to B. F. Austin, Director of the Bureau of Hygiene and Nursing, Alabama, February 24, 1936, RG 102, Central File 1933–36, entry 3, box 615, 13-2-5(2).

54. In southern states, much smaller percentages of black women received

mothers' pensions than their numbers required. For example, in Jacksonville, Fla., only 0.8 percent of recipients were African American, though the city was 34.3 percent black. In many northern and border cities, including Baltimore, Philadelphia, and Washington, black women received a disproportionate number of mothers' pensions. Florence Hutsinpillar to Frances Griggs, August 30, 1932, and Griggs to Hutsinpillar, August 11, 1932, RG 102, Central File 1929–32, entry 3, box 404, 7-3-3-1. Of Texas's 23 mothers' pension programs, not one was located in the state's 43 southwestern counties with large Mexican-American populations (30 percent or more). "Mothers' Aid in Texas for Year Ended June 30, 1931," in Agnes K. Hannah to Mrs. Violet S. Greenhill, December 5, 1932, ibid.; Key, *Southern Politics*, 272.

55. McEvoy, "State-Federal Public Assistance.

56. Lenroot and Abbott, "Security for Children," 4, 7; Lundberg, *Child Dependency in the United States: Methods of Statistical Reporting and Census of Dependent Children in 31 States* (New York: Child Welfare League of America, [1934?]), 28, 50.

57. Arthur W. James, Virginia Department of Public Welfare, to Agnes K. Hannah, July 28, 1931, RG 102, Central File 1929–32, entry 3, box 404, 7-3-3-1.

58. Lenroot to Witte, January 26, February 18, 1935, RG 47, PI 183, entry 8, box 57. Lenroot began to lobby Witte on this matter almost immediately after the CES bill was introduced, providing him with statistics on mothers' aid by state. Ibid.; Confidential Committee Printing, March 19, 1935, House Ways and Means Committee Bill Files, HR 74A-F39.1, p. 34. Martha Eliot suggested that distribution be made according to state deficits, which, again, would have ensured greater percentages for southern states. In her Senate testimony, Grace Abbott argued for equalization to poorer states. Eliot to Lenroot, March 1, 1935, RG 102, Central File 1933–36, entry 3, box 467, 0-1-0-7-3(1); *Hearings before the Committee on Finance*, Senate, 74th Cong., 1st sess., on S 1130, pt. 2, February 16, 18–20, 1935.

59. Lenroot, "The Health-Education Program of the Children's Bureau, with Particular Reference to Negroes," *Journal of Negro Education* (July 1937): 510.

60. E. A. Callis, M.D., to Lenroot, December 23, 1935, Lenroot to Callis, October 28, 1935, to Mary Irene Atkinson, Director, Child Welfare Division, FCB, November 9, 1935, Atkinson to Hill, October 24, 1935, and Hill to Lenroot, October 22, 1935, RG 102, Central File 1933–36, entry 3, box 476, 0-2-9-1-0.

61. Memo from Dr. Daily to Dr. McCown, December 11, 1936, ibid., box 615, 13-2-5(2); Naomi Deutsch, Directory of Public Health Nursing, Report of Field Trip, April 1, 2, 1936, ibid., box 622, 13-2-1(35). See also memo from Dr. Daily to Dr. Eliot and Dr. McCown, November 16, 1936, ibid., box 615, 13-2-3(2).

62. Texas's state plan stated that, under "Requirement No. VII," "[w]e have selected a county for this demonstration—Van Zandt, having a population of about 35,000, of which 8 percent covers the negro population." It is interesting that the plan referred to the Negro population, which comprised about one in seven of the state's population, but made no mention of the larger Mexican American population. John W. Brown, State Health Officer, Texas, to Albert McCown, February 15,

1936, RG 102, Central File 1933–36, entry 3, box 624, 13-2-5(47). See also Key, *Southern Politics*, 254, 271.

63. Edith Rockwood, "State Plans for Maternal and Child Health Services Demonstration under Fund A, May 6, 1936, and memo from FCB to S. B. McAllister, July 29, 1936, RG 102, Central File 1933–36, entry 3, box 615, 13-2-5(8); Katherine Lenroot, "The Health-Education Program of the Children's Bureau, with Particular Reference to Negroes," *Journal of Negro Education* (July 1937): 511.

64. Memo from Eliot to Dr. Rothert, July 26, 1935, RG 102, Central File 1933–36, entry 3, box 615, 13-2-3(2).

65. Lenroot, "The Health-Education Program of the Children's Bureau."

66. Lenroot, [to be Furnished to Lt. Oxley], "Sections for the Secretary's Speech at the National Conference on Problems of the Negro," December 24, 1936, RG 102, Central File 1933–36, entry 3, box 476, 0-2-9-1-0.

67. Dr. A. E. Thomas to Edwin F. Daily, July 2, 1936, and Daily, M.D., Acting Director, MCH Division, FCB, to Thomas, July 11, 1936, ibid., box 615, 13-2-5(2).

68. "A Practical Plan of Reducing Maternal and Infant Morbidity and Mortality in the State of North Carolina," by Ivan Proctor, M.D., submitted July 3, 1935, ibid., box 622, 13-2-1(35).

69. M. O. Bousfield, M.D., to Dr. Martha Eliot, July 22, 1935, and Eliot to Bousfield, July 26, 1935, ibid., box 622, 13-2-2(35).

70. Eliot to George M. Cooper, February 26, 1935, ibid., box 622, 13-2-1(35).

71. Lenroot and Abbott, "Security for Children," 18.

72. Ibid., 14, 18, 30.

73. Witte to John Andrews, April 25, 1935, RG 47, PI 183, entry 8, box 54.

74. Lenroot and Abbott, "Security for Children," 4.

75. Ibid., 9.

76. Grace Abbott, "Recent Trends in Mothers' Aid," [1934], Abbott Papers, box 24, folder 13.

77. Memo from Lenroot to Witte, December 1, 1934 (entry 8, box 57), and "Report to the President of the Committee on Economic Security," 1935 (entry 1, box 7, pp. 35–38), RG 47, PI 183.

78. Lenroot to Grace Abbott, January 1, 1935 (box 61, folder 4), and Martha Eliot to Abbott, January 19, 1935 (box 54, folder 2), Abbott Papers.

79. CES, Minutes of Meeting, January 7, 1935, RG 16, PI 191, entry 17, box 2140, 2.

80. Abbott to Lenroot, February 21, 1935, Abbott Papers, box 61, folder 4.

81. FERA, "Security Employment—A Part of a Program of National Economic Security," November 21, 1934, Hopkins Papers, FRA, group 24, container 48.

82. Ibid.

83. Ibid.

84. "American Association of Social Workers Special Bulletin, 1935 Delegate Conference," February 8, 1935, Abbott Papers, box 28, folder 12.

85. Ibid.

86. *Hearings before the Committee on Finance*, Senate, 74th Cong., 1st sess., on S 1130, pt. 2, February 16, 18–20, 1935, pp. 1084–85. Martha Swain (*Ellen S. Woodward*, 98) found that black women were especially discriminated against by local welfare offices that were unwilling to identify them as "employable." Local officials used the categories "employable" and "unemployable" to define "acceptable" work for blacks. Their lack of a recognized occupational status was used to undermine their attempts to secure relief work.

87. Abbott to Frances Perkins, February 3, 1936, Abbott Papers, box 68, folder 7; Abbott to Perkins, October 26, 1934, RG 47, PI 183, entry 8, box 54.

88. Lenroot, "Transcript of Oral History," 55.

89. Eliot to Abbott, "Tues Evening," [February 1935], Abbott Papers, box 37, folder 4.

90. Ruth M. Jones, Director, Mothers' Pension Department, Cincinnati, to Katherine Lenroot, February 8, 1935, RG 102, Central File 1933–36, entry 3, box 467, 0-1-0-7-3(1).

91. Lurie to Abbott, August 24, 1934, "Committee to Outline a National Social Welfare Program," July 20, 1934, and Abbott to Lurie, November 7, 19, 1934, Abbott Papers, box 28, folder 11; "The Montreal Conference," *Conference Bulletin, NCSW* 38, no. 4 (July 1935), in RG 102, Central File 1933–36, entry 3, box 471, 0-2-0-4(9); Lurie to Abbott, June 19, 1934, Abbott Papers, box 28, folder 11.

92. Abbott to Lurie, March 4, 1935, Abbott Papers, box 28, folder 12.

93. Linda Gordon, *Pitied but Not Entitled*, 210; Correspondence between Perkins and Katherine Lenroot, February 1, 1935, to July 29, 1935, RG 102, Central File 1933–36, entry 3, box 471, 0-2-0-4(9).

94. Katherine Lenroot to Rep. Vinson, April 22, 1935, RG 102, Central File 1933–36, entry 3, box 467, 0-1-0-7-3(1); Lenroot to Grace Abbott, January 22, 1935, Abbott Papers, box 54, folder 2; Memo from Lenroot to Arthur Altmeyer, February 18, 1935, RG 47, PI 183, entry 3, box 23.

95. Elizabeth Criswell to Agnes K. Hannah, July 20, 1935, "Field Visit to Mississippi by Mary Ruth Colby, August 12–14, 1935, and Margaret Leach to Hannah, August 1, 1935, RG 102, Central File 1933–36, box 464, 0-1-0-6; Mrs. W. T. Bost to Robert Doughton, February 18, 1935, RG 102, Central File 1933–36, entry 3, box 467, 0-1-0-7-3(1).

96. *Hearings before the Committee on Finance*, Senate, 74th Cong., 1st sess., on S 1130, pt. 6, February 4, 5, 1935, pp. 339, 342.

97. Lenroot to Abbott, March 9, 1935, Abbott Papers, box 54, folder 3.

98. Telegram from Breckinridge to Katherine Lenroot, January 28, 1935, RG 102, Central File 1933–36, entry 3, box 467, 0-1-0-7-3(1); Letters to Robert Doughton, esp. February 18–20, 1935, HRA74-39.1, House Files, box 14110; Lenroot to Grace Abbott, January 10, 1935, Perkins to Abbott, February 1, 1935, Abbott Papers, box 61, folder 4; Correspondence between Abbott and Witte, February 25, 27, March 28, 1935, RG 47, PI 183, entry 4, box 16.

99. Witte to Abbott, January 21, 1935, Abbott Papers, box 54, folder 2.

100. Telegram from Lenroot to Abbott, March 3, 1935, ibid., folder 3.

101. See "Urgent" letter from C. W. Areson, Assistant Executive Director, Child Welfare League of America, to Membership, March 27, 1935, RG 102, Central File 1933–36, entry 3, box 467, 0-1-0-7-3(1).

102. In a letter to Edith Abbott, Witte wrote: "Our committee is not necessarily wedded to the social insurance approach. It certainly is not confined to that approach and intends to give consideration to other measures which might promote economic security no less than to the conventional forms of social insurance." Correspondence between Witte and Edith Abbott, August 3–October 26, 1934, RG 47, PI 183, entry 8, box 54.

103. Witte Papers, box 2; Witte to Arthur Altmeyer, August 25, 1934, RG 47, PI 183, entry 8, box 54.

104. Notes and Comments, "Social Insurance and/or Social Security," *Social Service Review* 8, no. 3 (September 1934): 539.

105. Although, in Abbott's words, the CES Advisory Council was "staged for the public and that little will be decided by it," the Wisconsin group kept a tight rein over who would be invited to participate. The FCB's list of suggested members was severely edited; the names of many social workers were removed and Wisconsin supporters added, including John Commons, Paul Raushenbush, and Elizabeth Raushenbush. Abbott to Lenroot, November 3, 1934, Lenroot Papers, box 1; Lenroot to Abbott, November 6, 7, 1934, Abbott Papers, box 54, folder 1.

106. Edwin Witte to Edith Abbott, October 18, 1939 (box 54, folder 50, Grace Abbott to Mr. Steelman, Assistant to Frances Perkins, January 9, 1935 (box 37, folder 4), and Dr. Luther Gulich to Grace Abbott, March 29, 1935 (box 66, folder 6), all in Abbott Papers; Press release, Washington, D.C., March 16, 1935, prepared by Katherine Lenroot, RG 102, Central File 1933–36, entry 3, box 467, 0-1-0-7-3(1); "To the Congress of the United States," March 20, 1935, HRA74-39.1, House Files, box 14112; *Hearings before the Committee on Finance*, Senate, 74th Cong., 1st sess., S 1130, pt. 2, February 16, 18–20, 1935, pp. 1076–78.

107. Louise Cutter to Sen. Robert F. Wagner, May 27, 1935, Wagner Papers, 566-GF-328, folder 5; Dozens of letters in the files of the House Ways and Means Committee, HRA74-39.1, House Files, box 14110.

108. The vast majority of social workers who protested their exclusion through letter or petition were women. See correspondence between Frances Perkins and Violet Kittner, Executive Director, Jewish Social Service Bureau, March 26, 28, 1935, RG 47, PI 183, entry 8, box 54.

109. HRA74-39.1, House Files, box 14110–12, and HRA74A-D38, box 13956; Jacob Kepecs to Grace Abbott, June 8, 1934, Katherine Lenroot to Kepecs, June 14, 1934, Kepecs to Lenroot, June 25, 1934, and Lenroot to Kepecs, June 28, July 7, 1934, all in RG 102, Central File 1933–36, entry 3, box 540, 7-2-3-0. Kepecs was deeply involved in the issue of the exclusion of charitable workers.

110. See, e.g., Pence to Abbott, March 16, 1935, and Abbott to Pence, April 6, 1935, Abbott Papers, box 54, folder 5.

111. Abbott to West, March 29, 1935, Abbott Papers, box 28, folder 12.

112. Andrews lobbied Sen. Robert Wagner to include AALL in the exemption of charitable workers. He wrote that to exempt charitable organizations, to which contributions were deductible, "would have an unfortunate and unintentionally bad result" on organizations such as AALL that were (unfairly) excluded from tax-exempt status. Therefore, "if it is deemed desirable to exempt non-profit making public welfare organizations from the proposed excise tax, we earnestly urge that it be done by some other device" that would include AALL. Andrews to Wagner, April 2, 1934, Wagner Papers, 566-GF-328, folder 2.

113. See Abbott Papers, box 54, folder 4.

114. Lenroot to Abbott, February 26, 1935, Abbott Papers, ibid., p. 2.

115. Ruth M. Jones, Chair, Mothers' Aid Section, National Conference of Social Work stationery: Hamilton County [Ohio] Court of Common Pleas, to Lenroot, February 8, 1935, and Agnes K. Hannah to Jones, February 15, 1935, RG 102, Central File 1933–36, entry 3, box 467, 0-1-0-7-3(1).

116. Memo from Niels Christensen to Mr. Resnick, July 14, 1936, RG 47, PI 183, entry 20, box 234, file 631.21.

117. Lenroot, "Transcript of Oral History," 109.

118. Memo from Niels Christensen to Mr. Resnick, July 14, 1936.

119. Memo from A. L. Cannon to Miss Atkinson and Miss Lundberg, April 15, 1936, RG 102, Central File 1933–36, entry 3, box 482, 0-6-15.

120. McEvoy, "State-Federal Public Assistance," 24, 34.

121. Myrdal, *American Dilemma*, 360.

122. Ibid.

123. Abramovitz, *Regulating the Lives of Mothers*, 138.

Conclusion

1. Hazel W. Harrison, "The Status of the American Negro in the New Deal," *The Crisis*, November 1933, 256.

2. Lieberman, *Shifting the Color Line*.

3. House Ways and Means Committee, Technical Staff on Social Security, "Issues in Social Security," 79th Congress, 1st sess., 1946, 19, in Witte Papers, box 202; "Some Notes on Old-Age Insurance for Agricultural Workers in Western Europe," Bureau of Research Statistics, SSB, February 11, 1938, RG 47, PI 183, entry 13, box 101.

4. Memo from John J. Corson, Director, Bureau of Old-Age and Survivor Insurance, to Wilbur Cohen, Technical Adviser to SSB, November 28, 1940, RG 47, PI 183, entry 13, box 101.

5. Rae Needleman, "Summary of Findings on the Problem of Including Domestic Workers under the Old-Age Benefit Provisions of the Social Security Act," March 26, 1937, RG 47, PI 183, entry 13, box 101. Before the Act was passed, New York, Utah, and Washington State all covered domestic workers in private homes.

After passage, New York continued to include these workers in theory, but only those working for large employers with steady work.

6. Armstrong, "Reminiscences," 130.

7. "Tentative Statement on Extension of Old-Age and Survivors Insurance Coverage to Agricultural Workers," November 14, 1939, RG 47, PI 183, entry 13, box 101 (quotation); Memo from Corson to Cohen, November 28, 1940; "Message from the President of the United States, Transmitting a Report fo the Social Security Board Recommending Changes in the Social Security Act," January 16, 1939, 76th Cong., House, HD 110; Altmeyer, *Formative Years*, 97.

8. The *New York Times* reported that the 1939 amendments would exclude a much higher percentage of people "in the low-wage areas of the South than in the North and East. In Mississippi . . . the proportion of persons who would be disqualified would be more than twice the national average." Louis Stark, "Proposed Changes in Social Security Contain 'Inequities,'" *New York Times*, June 25, 1939.

9. Arthur J. Altmeyer, "Social Security for Industrialized Agriculture," *Social Security Bulletin*, 1945, 2–5, in Witte Papers, box 202.

10. In 1937 over 32 million workers were covered by OAI, and 6.9 percent were African American. Only one-quarter of nonwhite women were covered nationally. Myrdal, *American Dilemma*, 358.

11. In 1935, 42 percent of covered black workers and 22 percent of covered white workers had annual incomes of less than $200—over 50 percent of covered black women earned this little. Myrdal, *American Dilemma*, 358, n. 65, 1280.

12. Frank G. Davis, *Black Community's Social Security*.

13. Ibid., 111, 62.

14. Myrdal, *American Dilemma*, 206.

15. Ibid.

16. African Americans were better represented on OAA rolls (12 percent) than their percentage of the population over age 65 (7 percent), according to national averages. In the South, the average African American got a $7 grant, compared to a white recipient's grant of $11. Myrdal, *American Dilemma*, 359.

17. Edwin Witte, "To the Senate and Assembly of the Legislature of Wisconsin," July 5, 1935, Witte Papers, box 2.

18. Altmeyer, *Formative Years*, 80.

19. "Report of Forrester Washington," July 1, 1934, CWA "Interracial Correspondence," in Kirby, *Black Americans*, 140, 145.

20. Eason, "Attitudes of Negro Families on Relief toward Work, toward Home, toward Life," *Opportunity*, December 1935, 367.

21. Ibid., 379, 369.

22. Ibid., 368.

23. Ibid., 367.

24. Crenshaw, "Race, Reform, and Retrenchment."

25. Steinberg, "Liberal Retreat from Race."

Bibliography

Archival Collections

Amherst, Massachusetts
  University of Massachusetts Library
    William Edward Burghardt Du Bois Papers, 1803–1968 (inclusive), 1877–
      1963 (bulk)
Baltimore, Maryland
  Johns Hopkins University Library
    Douglas Southall Freeman Papers, 1902–22
Berkeley, California
  University of California, Bancroft Library
    Southern Tenant Farmers' Union Papers, 1934–70
Bethesda, Maryland
  National Association of Colored Women's Clubs Records, 1895–1992
Chicago, Illinois
  University of Chicago Library, Special Collections
    Edith and Grace Abbott Papers, 1893–1967
    Julius Rosenwald Papers
College Park, Maryland
  National Archives
    Federal Children's Bureau Records, Record Group 102
    Social Security Administration Records, Record Group 47
Hyde Park, New York
  Franklin D. Roosevelt Presidential Library
    Louis H. Bean Papers, 1894–1994
    Mary Williams Dewson Papers, 1898–1961
    Harry Hopkins Papers, 1928–46
    Louis McHenry Howe Papers, 1912–36
    Henry Morganthau Papers, 1866–1953
    Franklin Delano Roosevelt Papers
      Official Files, 1933–45
      President's Personal Files, 1933–45
    Henry Wallace Papers

Ithaca, New York
>Cornell University, Labor-Management Documents Center, M.P., Catherwood Library
>>John Rogers Commons Papers, 1859–1967 (bulk), 1887–1945

Madison, Wisconsin
>State Historical Society of Wisconsin
>>Arthur Joseph Altmeyer Papers, 1904–73
>>John B. Andrews Papers, 1910–22
>>Wilbur J. Cohen Papers, 1941–80
>>John R. Commons Papers, 1862–1945
>>Richard Theodore Ely Papers, 1912–63
>>Abraham Epstein Papers, 1918–30, 1973
>>William M. Leiserson Papers, 1901–59
>>Milwaukee Urban League Records, 1919–79
>>Paul and Elizabeth Brandeis Raushenbush Papers, 1918–80
>>Edwin Emil Witte Papers, ca. 1905–67

New York, New York
>City University of New York, City College Archives
>>Robert F. Wagner Papers, 1926–64
>Columbia University, Rare Books and Manuscripts Library, Butler Library
>>Katherine Lenroot Papers
>>Frances Perkins Papers, ca. 1895–1965
>Schomburg Center for Research in Black Culture, The New York Public Library, Manuscripts, Archives, and Rare Books Division
>>John Preston Davis Papers, 1891–1972 (bulk)
>>National Negro Congress Records, 1933–47
>>William Pickens Papers, 1906–54
>>Robert Clifton Weaver Papers, 1869–1970, 1923 (bulk)

Washington, D.C.
>Library of Congress, Manuscripts Division, Department of Research
>>Hugo Lafayette Black Papers, 1883–1976 (bulk), 1926–71
>>National Association for the Advancement of Colored People Papers, 1909–60
>>National Urban League Papers
>>Roy Wilkins Papers, 1915–80

Oral Histories

Altmeyer, Arthur J. "Reminiscences of Arthur Joseph Altmeyer," by Peter Corning. Social Security Project, 1967. Oral History Research Office, Columbia University, New York.

Armstrong, Barbara Nachtrieb. "Reminiscences of Barbara Nachtrieb Armstrong," by Peter Corning. Social Security Project, 1965. Oral History Research Office, Columbia University, New York.

Brown, J. Douglas. "Reminiscences of James Douglas Brown: Oral History," by Peter Corning. Social Security Project, 1965. Oral History Research Office, Columbia University, New York.

Burns, Evelyn Mabel. "Reminiscences of Evelyn Mabel Richardson Burns," by Evangeline C. Cooper. Unemployment Insurance Project, 1981. Oral History Research Office, Columbia University, New York.

Cohen, Wilbur J. "LBJ Oral History Transcript Interview with Wilbur J. Cohen," by David G. McComb, December 8, 1968. Wilbur J. Cohen Papers, State Historical Society of Wisconsin, Madison.

Eliot, Martha. "Reminiscences of Martha May Eliot," by Peter Corning. Social Security Project, 1966. Oral History Research Office, Columbia University, New York.

Eliot, Thomas H. "Reminiscences of Thomas Hopkinson Eliot," by Peter Corning. Social Security Project, 1966. Oral History Research Office, Columbia University, New York.

Epstein, Henriette Costex. Interview with Mrs. Abraham Epstein, by Janice O'Connell, May 21, 1973, New York. Abraham Epstein Papers, State Historical Society of Wisconsin, Madison.

Lenroot, Katherine. "Transcript of Oral History," by Peter Corning. Social Security Project, 1965. Oral History Research Office, Columbia University, New York.

Moley, Raymond. "Reminiscences of Raymond Charles Moley," by Peter Corning. Social Security Project, 1965. Oral History Research Office, Columbia University, New York.

Perkins, Frances. "Reminiscences of Frances Perkins: Book IV, US Department of Labor and the First Year of the New Deal," by Dean Albertson, December 3, 1955. Oral History Research Office, Columbia University, New York.

Raushenbush, Paul A., and Elizabeth Brandeis. "Reminiscences of Paul A. and Elizabeth Brandeis Raushenbush," by Peter Corning. Social Security Project, 1966. Oral History Research Office, Columbia University, New York.

Secondary Sources

Aaron, Daniel, and Robert Bendiner, ed. *The Strenuous Decade: A Social and Intellectual Record of the 1930's*. Garden City: Anchor-Doubleday, 1970.

Abbott, Grace. *From Relief to Social Security*. Chicago: University of Chicago Press, 1941.

———. *The Immigrant and the Community*. New York: Century, 1917.

Abramovitz, Mimi. *Regulating the Lives of Women: Social Welfare from Colonial Times to the Present*. Boston: South End Press, 1988.

Abrams, Robert S. "History of the National Urban League, 1910–1935." Ph.D. diss., University of Minnesota, 1961.

Achenbaum, W. Andrew. *Social Security: Visions and Revisions*. Cambridge University Press, 1986.

Akin, William E. *Technocracy and the American Dream: The Technocrat Movement, 1900–1941*. Berkeley: University of California Press, 1977.

Altmeyer, Arthur J. *The Formative Years of Social Security*. Madison: University of Wisconsin Press, 1968.

Anderson, Kristi. *The Creation of a Democratic Majority, 1928–1936*. Chicago: University of Chicago Press, 1979.

Anderson, Nels. *The Right to Work*. 1938. Reprint, New York: Greenwood Press, 1973.

Armstrong, Barbara. *Ensuring the Essentials: Minimum Wage, Plus Social Insurance—A Living Wage Program*. New York: Macmillan, 1932.

Ashmore, Harry S. *Hearts and Minds:The Anatomy of Racism from Roosevelt to Reagan*. New York: McGraw-Hill, 1982.

Auerbach, Jerold S. "Southern Tenant Farmers: Socialist Critics of the New Deal." *Labor History* 7 (Winter 1966).

Avery, Sheldon. *Up from Washington: William Pickens and the Negro Struggle for Equality, 1900–1954*. London: Associated University Presses, 1989.

Badger, Tony. "Fatalism, Not Gradualism: The Crisis of Southern Liberalism, 1945–1965." In Brian Ward and Tony Badger, eds., *The Making of Martin Luther King and the Civil Rights Movement*. New York: New York University Press, 1996.

Bain, George W. "How Negro Editors Viewed the New Deal." *Journalism Quarterly* 44 (Autumn 1967): 552–54

Balough, Brian. "Securing Support: The Emergence of the Social Security Board as a Political Actor, 1935–1939." In Critchlow and Hawley, eds. *Federal Social Policy: The Historical Dimensions*. Pennsylvania State University Press, 1988.

Bandler, Jean T. D. "Family Protection and Women's Issues of Social Security." *Social Work* 34 (July 1939).

Beland, Daniel. *Social Security: History and Politics from the New Deal to the Privatization Debate*. Lawrence: University of Kansas Press, 2005.

Berger, Samuel R. *Dollar Harvest: The Story of the Farm Bureau*. Lexington: D. C. Heath, 1971.

Berkowitz, Edward D. *America's Welfare State from Roosevelt to Reagan*. Baltimore: Johns Hopkins University Press, 1991.

———. *Creating the Welfare State: The Political Economy of Twentieth-Century Reform*. Lawrence: University Press of Kansas, 1992.

———. "The First Social Security Crisis." *Prologue* 15 (Fall 1983).

———. "History, Public Policy and Reality." *Journal of Social History* 18, no. 1 (1984).

———. *Mr. Social Security: The Life of Wilbur J. Cohen*. Lawrence: University Press of Kansas, 1995.

———. *Social Security after Fifty: Success and Failures*. New York: Greenwood Press, 1987.

Bernstein, Barton. *Towards a New Past*. New York: Pantheon, 1968.

Bernstein, Irving. *A Caring Society: The New Deal, the Worker, and the Great Depression*. Boston: Houghton Mifflin, 1985.

———. *Turbulent Years: A History of the American Worker, 1933–1941*. Boston: Houghton Mifflin, 1970.

Bigelow, Barbara Carlisle, ed. *Contemporary Black Biography*. Vol. 4. Detroit: Gale Research Inc., 1993.

Biles, Roger. *The South and the New Deal*. University Press of Kentucky, 1994.

Blackwelder, Julia Kirk. *Women of the Depression: Caste and Culture in San Antonio, 1929–1939*. College Station: Texas A&M University Press, 1984.

Bracey, Earnest Norton. "The Impact of Hidden Transcripts on Decision Making and Organizational Effectiveness: A Study of the Washington Bureau of the National Association for the Advancement of Colored People." Ph.D. diss., George Mason University, 1993.

Braeman, John. "The New Deal: The Collapse of the Liberal Consensus." *Canadian Review of American Studies* 20, no. 1 (1989).

Bremner, Robert. *From the Depths: The Discovery of Poverty in the United States*. New York: New York University Press, 1966.

Brinkley, Alan. *Voices of Protest: Huey Long, Father Coughlin and the Great Depression*. New York: Vintage Books, 1982.

Brock, William. *Welfare, Democracy, and the New Deal*. New York: Cambridge University Press, 1988.

Brown, Douglas. *An American Philosophy of Social Security: Evolution and Issues*. Princeton, N.J.: Princeton University Press, 1972.

———. *The Genesis of Social Security in America*. Princeton, N.J.: Industrial Relations Section, Princeton University Press, 1969.

Brown, Michael. *Race, Money, and the American Welfare State*. Ithaca, N.Y.: Cornell University Press, 1999.

Bunche, Ralph J. "A Critique of New Deal Social Planning as It Affects Negroes," 1936, in *Selected Speeches and Writings*, ed. Charles P. Henry. Ann Arbor: University of Michigan Press, 1995.

———. *The Political Status of the Negro in the Age of FDR*. Chicago: University of Chicago Press, 1973.

Burns, James MacGregor. *Roosevelt: The Lion and the Fox*. New York: Harcourt, Brace, 1956.

Campbell, Christiana McFadyen. *The Farm Bureau and the New Deal: A Study of the Making of National Farm Policy, 1933–40*. Urbana: University of Illinois Press, 1962.

Campbell, Rita Ricardo. *Social Security: Promise and Reality*. Stanford, Calif.: Hoover Institution Press, 1977.

Cates, Jerry. *Insuring Inequality: Administrative Leadership in Social Security, 1935–54*. Ann Arbor: University of Michigan Press, 1983.

Chalmers, David. *Hooded Americanism: The History of the Ku Klux Klan*. Durham: Duke University Press, 1987.

Chambers, Clarke A. "Toward a Redefinition of Welfare History." *Journal of American History* 73, no. 2 (1986).

Charles, Clephus. "Roy Wilkins, The NAACP and the Early Struggle for Civil Rights: Towards the Biography of a Man and a Movement in Microcosm, 1901–1939." Ph.D. diss., Cornell University, 1981.

Clegg, Brenda Faye. "Black Female Domestics during the Great Depression in NYC, 1936–40." Ph.D. diss., University of Michigan, 1983.

Cobb, James C., and Michael V. Namorato, eds. *The New Deal and the South*. Jackson: University Press of Mississippi, 1984.

Coburn, Mark D. "America's Great Black Hope." *American Heritage* 29 (October–November 1978): 82–91.

Cohen, Wilbur. "The Social Security Act of 1935: Reflections Fifty Years Later." *Fiftieth Anniversary Edition: The Report of the Committee on Economic Security of 1935*. Washington, D.C.: National Conference on Social Welfare, 1985.

Coll, Blanche D. *Safety Net: Welfare and Social Security, 1929–1979*. New Brunswick, N.J.: Rutgers University Press, 1995.

Commons, John. *Myself: The Autobiography of John Commons*. Madison: University of Wisconsin Press, 1964.

———. *Races and Immigrants in America*. 1907, 1920. Reprint, New York: Macmillan, 1967.

Connally, Tom. *My Name Is Tom Connally, by Tom Connally, as Told to Alfred Steinberg*. New York: Crowell, 1954.

Cook, Blanche Wiesen. *Eleanor Roosevelt: Volume 1, 1884–1933*. New York: Viking-Penguin Press, 1992.

Costin, Lela B. *Two Sisters for Social Justice: A Biography of Grace and Edith Abbott*. Chicago: University of Illinois Press, 1983.

Crenshaw, Kimberle Williams. "Race, Reform, and Retrenchment: Transformation and Legitimation in Antidiscrimination Law." In E. Nathaniel Gates, ed., *Critical Race Theory: The Judicial Isolation of the 'Racially' Oppressed*. New York: Garland, 1997.

Daniels, Jonathan. *A Southerner Discovers the South*. New York: Macmillan, 1938.

Davies, Garreth, and Martha Derthick. "Race and Social Welfare Policy: The Social Security Act of 1935." *Political Science Quarterly* 11 (November 2, 1997): 217–35.

Davis, Frank G. *The Black Community's Social Security*. Washington, D.C.: University Press of America, 1977.

Davis, Kenneth S. *FDR: The New Deal Years: 1933–1937: A History*. 1979. Reprint, New York: Random House, 1986.

Derthick, Martha. *Agency under Stress: The Social Security Administration in American History*. Washington, D.C.: Brookings, 1990.

———. *Policymaking for Social Security*. Washington, D.C.: Brookings, 1979.

Deutrich, Mabel E., and Virginia C. Purdy, eds. *Clio Was a Woman: Studies in the History of American Women*. Vol. 16 of *National Archives Conferences*. Washington, D.C.: Howard University Press, 1980.

Diner, Hasia R. *In the Almost Promised Land: American Jews and Blacks, 1915–1935*. 1977. Reprint, Baltimore: Johns Hopkins University Press, 1995.

Du Bois, W. E. B. *Black Reconstruction in America*. 1935. Reprint, New York: Simon and Schuster, 1998.

Dunning, William A. *Reconstruction: Political and Economic, 1865–1877*. 1907. Reprint, New York: Harper, 1962.

Dykeman, Wilma, and James Stokely. *Seeds of Southern Change: The Life of Will Alexander*. 1962. Reprint, New York: Norton, 1976.

Egerton, John. *Speak Now against the Day: The Generation before the Civil Rights Movement in the South*. New York: Knopf, 1994.

Ekirch, Arthur A., Jr. *Ideologies and Utopias: The Impact of the New Deal on American Thought*. Chicago: Quadrangle Books, 1969.

Eldersfeld, Samuel J. "The Influence of Metropolitan Party Pluralities in Presidential Elections since 1920." *American Political Science Review* 43 (December 1949): 1189–1206.

Eliot, Thomas. *Recollections of the New Deal: When the People Mattered*. Boston: Northeastern University Press, 1992.

Elsner, Henry, Jr. *The Technocrats: Prophets of Automation*. Syracuse, N.Y.: Syracuse University Press, 1967.

Epstein, Abraham. *Insecurity: A Challenge to America: A Study of Social Insurance in the United States and Abroad*. 1933. Reprint, New York: Random House: 1938.

Ermer, Virginia B., and John H. Strange. *Blacks and Bureaucracy: Readings in the Problems and Politics of Change*. New York: Crowell, 1972.

Fischer, Frank. *Technocracy and the Politics of Expertise*. Newbury Park, N.Y.: Sage, 1990.

Fitzgerald, Tracey A. *The National Council of Negro Women and the Feminist Movement, 1935–1975*. Georgetown Monograph in America Studies, no. 2. Washington, D.C.: Georgetown University Press, 1985.

Fitzpatrick, Ellen. *Endless Crusade: Women Social Scientists and Progressive Reform*. New York: Oxford University Press, 1990.

Fletcher, John Gould. *Selected Letters of John Gould Fletcher*. Edited by Leighton Rudolph et al. Fayetteville: University of Arkansas Press, 1990.

Foner, Eric. *Reconstruction: America's Unfinished Revolution, 1863–1877*. New York: Harper and Row, 1988.

Foner, Eric, and Ronald Lewis, eds. *Black Workers: A Documentary History from Colonial Times to the Present*. Philadelphia: Temple University Press, 1989.

Fraser, Steve, and Gary Gerstle, eds. *The Rise and Fall of the New Deal Order, 1930–1980*. Princeton, N.J.: Princeton University Press, 1989.

Friedel, Frank. *F. D. R. and the South*. Baton Rouge: Louisiana State University Press, 1965.

Gates, E. Nathaniel. *Critical Race Theory: The Judicial Isolation of the "Racially" Oppressed.* New York: Garland, 1997.

Gieske, Millard L. *Minnesota Farmer-Laborism: The Third Party Alternative.* Minneapolis: University of Minnesota Press, 1979.

Glazer, Nathan. "Is Assimilation Dead?" *Annals of the American Academy of Social Science* 530 (November 1993).

Goodson, Martia Graham, ed. *Chronicles of Faith: The Autobiography of Frederick D. Patterson.* Tuscaloosa: University of Alabama Press, 1991.

Goodwin, Joanne. *Gender and the Politics of Welfare Reform: Mothers' Pensions in Chicago, 1911–1929.* Chicago: Chicago University Press, 1997.

Gordon, Lawrence. "A Brief Look at Blacks in Depression Mississippi, 1929–1934: Eyewitness Accounts." *Journal of Negro History* 64 (Fall 1979): 377–90.

Gordon, Linda. *Pitied but Not Entitled: Single Mothers and the History of Welfare.* New York: Free Press, 1994.

———. "Social Insurance and Public Assistance: The Influence of Gender in Welfare Thought in the United States, 1890–1935." *American Historical Review* 97 (February 1992): 19–54.

——— ed. *Women, the State, and Welfare.* Madison: University of Wisconsin Press, 1990.

Gosnell, Harold F. *Negro Politicians: The Rise of Negro Politics in Chicago.* Chicago: University of Chicago Press, 1935.

Graebner, William. *A History of Retirement: The Meaning and Function of an American Institution, 1885–1978.* 1980. New Haven: Yale University Press, 1984.

Graham, Otis L., Jr. *An Encore for Reform: The Old Progressives and the New Deal.* New York: Oxford University Press, 1967.

Grant, Philip A., Jr. "Southern Congressmen and Agriculture, 1921–1932." *Agricultural History* 53 (January 1979).

Grossman, James R. *Land of Hope: Chicago, Black Southerners, and the Great Migration.* Chicago: University of Chicago Press, 1989.

Grubbs, Donald H. *Cry from the Cotton: The Southern Tenant Farmers' Union and the New Deal.* Chapel Hill: University of North Carolina Press, 1971.

Gunther, Lenworth Alburn, III. "Flamin' Tongue: The Rise of Adam Clayton Powell, Jr., 1908–1941." Ph.D. diss., Columbia University, 1985.

Guzda, Henry P. "Frances Perkins' Interest in the New Deal for Blacks." *Monthly Labor Reviews: U.S. Department of Labor, Bureau of Labor Statistics* (April 1980).

Hale, Grace Elizabeth. *Making Whiteness: The Culture of Segregation in the South, 1890–1940.* New York: Pantheon, 1998.

Hall, Jacquelyn Dowd. *Revolt against Chivalry: Jessie Daniel Ames and the Women's Campaign against Lynching.* New York: Columbia University Press, 1993.

Hamby, Alonzo L., ed. *The New Deal: Analysis and Interpretation.* 1969. Reprint, New York: Longman, 1981.

Hamilton, Dona Cooper. "The National Urban League and New Deal Programs." *Social Service Review* 58 (June 1984): 227–43.

Hamilton, Dona Cooper, and Charles V. Hamilton. *The Dual Agenda: Race and Social Welfare Policies of Civil Rights Organizations*. New York: Columbia University Press, 1997.

Hanson, John Mark. *Gaining Access: Congress and the Farm Lobby, 1919–1981*. Chicago: Chicago University Press, 1991.

Hari, William Ivy. *The Kingfish and His Realm: The Life and Times of Huey P. Long*. Baton Rouge: Louisiana State University Press, 1991.

Harris, Abram. *The Negro as Capitalist: A Study of Banking and Business among American Negroes*. Philadelphia: American Academy of Political and Social Sciences, 1936.

Heinemann, Ronald L. *Harry Byrd of Virginia*. Charlottesville: University Press of Virginia, 1996.

Herrick, John M., and Paul H. Stuart, eds. *Encyclopedia of Welfare History in North America*. Thousand Oaks, Calif.: Sage, 2004.

Hine, Darlene Clark. "Blacks and the Destruction of the Democratic White Primary, 1935–1944." *Journal of Negro History* 62 (January 1977): 43–59.

Holcombe, Arthur N. *The Middle Classes in American Politics*. 1940. Reprint, New York: Russell and Russell, 1965.

Holden, Matthew. *The Politics of the Black Nation*. New York: Chandler Press, 1973.

Holt, Rackham. *Mary McLeod Bethune: A Biography*. Garden City, N.Y.: Doubleday, 1964.

Holt, Thomas. "Making Race, Race-making, and the Writing of History." *American Historical Review* 100, no. 1 (1995).

Holtzman, Abraham. *The Townsend Movement: A Political Study*. New York: Bookman Associates, 1963.

Hughes, Cicero Alvin. "Toward a Black United Front: The National Negro Congress Movement." Ph.D. diss., Ohio University, 1982.

Hunter, Gary. "Don't Bury Where You Can't Work: Black Urban Boycott Movements during the Depression, 1929–1941." Ph.D. diss., Michigan State University, 1977.

Huthmacher, J. Joseph. *Senator Robert F. Wagner and the Rise of Urban Liberalism*. New York: Atheneum, 1968.

Ickes, Harold L. *The Secret Diary of Harold L. Ickes: The First Thousand Days, 1933–1936*. New York: Simon and Schuster, 1953.

Irish, Marian D. "The Southern One-Party System and National Politics." *Journal of Politics* 4 (February 1942): 80–94.

Jones, Jacqueline. *Labor of Love, Labor of Sorrow: Black Women, Work, and the Family from Slavery to the Present*. New York: Vintage Books, 1986.

Kalmar, Karen. "Southern Black Elites and the New Deal: A Case Study of Savannah, Georgia." *Georgia Historical Quarterly* 65 (Winter 1981): 341–55

Katz, Michael. *In the Shadow of the Poorhouse: A Social History of Welfare in America*. New York: Basic Books, 1996.

———. *Poverty and Policy in American History*. New York: Academic Press, 1983.

———— ed., *The "Underclass" Debate: Views from History*. Princeton, N.J.: Princeton University Press, 1993.

Katznelson, Ira. *When Affirmative Action Was White: An Untold History of Racial Inequality in Twentieth-Century America*. New York: Norton, 2005.

Kellor, Frances A. *Out of Work: A Study of Unemployment*. New York: Arno Press and New York Times Co., 1971.

Kennedy, Stetson. *Southern Exposure*. 1946. Reprint, University Press of Florida, 1991.

Kennon, Ronald R., and Rebecca M. Rogers. *The Committee on Ways and Means: A Bicentennial History, 1789–1989*. Washington, D.C.: GPO, 1989.

Kerr, Clark, and Others. *Industrialism and Industrial Man: The Problems of Labor and Management in Economic Growth*. Cambridge: Harvard University Press, 1960.

Kessler-Harris, Alice. "Designing Women and Old Fools: The Construction of the Social Security Amendments of 1939." In Linda Kerber, Alice Kessler-Harris, and Kathryn Kish Sklar, eds. *U.S. History as Women's History: New Feminist Essays*. Chapel Hill: University of North Carolina Press, 1995.

————. *In Pursuit of Equity: Women, Men and the Quest for Economic Citizenship in Twentieth-Century America*. Oxford: Oxford University Press, 2001.

————. *Out to Work: A History of Wage Earning Women in the United States*. Oxford: Oxford University Press, 1982.

Key, V. O. *Southern Politics in State and Nation*. New York: Knopf, 1950.

King, Gail B. "Women and Social Security: An Applied History Overview." *Social Science History* 6 (Spring 1982): 223–27.

Kirby, John B. *Black Americans in the Roosevelt Era: Liberalism and Race*. Knoxville: University of Tennessee Press, 1980.

————. "Ralph J. Bunche and Black Radical Thought in the 1930's." *Pylon* 35 (Summer 1974): 129–41.

Kneebone, John T. *Southern Liberal Journalists and the Issue of Race, 1920–1944*. Chapel Hill: University of North Carolina Press, 1985.

Knupfer, Anne Marie. *Toward a Tenderer Humanity and a Nobler Womanhood: African American Women's Clubs in Turn-of-the-Century Chicago*. New York: New York University Press, 1996.

Koeniger, A. Cash. "The New Deal in the States: Roosevelt versus the Byrd Organization in Virginia." *Journal of American History* 68 (March 1982): 876–96.

Kyvig, David E., and Mary Ann Blasio. *New Day/New Deal: A Bibliography of the Great American Depression, 1929–1941*. New York: Greenwood Press, 1988.

Laird, William E., and James R. Rinehart. "The Post–Civil War South and the Great Depression: A Suggested Parallel." *Mid-America* 48 (July 1966): 206–10.

Leff, Mark. "Taxing the Forgotten Man: The Politics of Social Security Finance in the New Deal." *Journal of American History* 70 (September 1983): 359–81.

Leiby, James. *A History of Social Welfare and Social Work in the United States*. New York: Columbia University Press, 1978.

Leuchtenburg, William E. *Franklin D. Roosevelt and the New Deal, 1932–1940*. New York: Harper Torchbooks–Harper and Row, 1963.

Lewis, David Levering. "The Appeal of the New Deal." *Reviews in American History* (December 1984).

————. "Parallels and Divergences: Assimilationist Strategies of Afro-American and Jewish Elites from 1910 to the Early 1930's." *Journal of American History*.

————. *W. E. B. Du Bois: Biography of a Race, 1868–1919*. New York: Henry Holt and Co., 1993.

————. *W. E. B. Du Bois: The Fight for Equality and the American Century, 1919–1963*. New York: Henry Holt and Co., 2000.

Lieberman, Robert. *Shaping Race Policy: The United States in Perspective*. Princeton, N.J.: Princeton University Press, 2005.

————. *Shifting the Color Line: Race and the American Welfare State*. Cambridge: Harvard University Press, 1998.

Lobove, Roy. *The Struggle for Social Security, 1900–1935*. Cambridge: Harvard University Press, 1968.

Lorence, James J. *Gerald J. Boileau and the Progressive-Farmer-Labor Alliance: Politics of the New Deal*. Columbia: University of Missouri Press, 1994.

Loucheim, Katie, ed. *The Making of the New Deal: The Insiders Speak*. Cambridge: Harvard University Press, 1983.

Marquis, Alice G. *Hopes and Ashes: The Birth of Modern Times, 1929–1939*. New York: Free Press, 1986.

Martin, George. *Madam Secretary: Frances Perkins*. Boston: Houghton Mifflin, 1976.

McBride, David, and Monore H. Little. "The Afro-American Elite, 1930–1940: A Historical and Statistical Profile." *Pylon* 42 (June 1981): 105–19.

McEvoy, Richard E. "State-Federal Public Assistance, 1935–1946." Ph.D. diss., University of Maryland, 1980.

McJimsey, George. *Harry Hopkins: Ally of the Poor and Defender of Democracy*. Cambridge: Harvard University Press, 1987.

McKinley, Charles, and Robert W. Frase. *Launching Social Security: A Capture-and-Record Account, 1935–1937*. Madison: University of Wisconsin Press, 1970.

Meier, August, and Elliot Rudwick. "Communist Unions and the Black Community: The Case of the Transport Workers Union, 1934–1944." *Labor History* 23 (Spring 1982): 165–97.

Mettler, Suzanne. *Divided Citizens: Gender and Federalism in New Deal Public Policy*. Ithaca, N.Y.: Cornell University Press, 1998.

Michel, Sonya, and Seth Koven, eds. *Mothers of a New World: Maternalist Politics and the Origins of Welfare States*. New York: Routledge, 1993.

Michie, Allan A., and Frank Phylick. *Dixie Demagogues*. New York: Vanguard Press, 1939.

Miller, Jan. "Annotated Bibliography of the Washington-DuBois Controversy." *Journal of Black Studies* 25, no. 2 (December 1994).

Mink, Gwendolyn. *The Wages of Motherhood: Inequality in the Welfare Sate, 1917–1942*. Ithaca, N.Y.: Cornell University Press, 1995.

———. *Welfare's End*. Ithaca, N.Y.: Cornell University Press, 1998.

———. *Whose Welfare?* Ithaca, N.Y.: Cornell University Press, 1999.

Mitchell, H. L. *Mean Things Happening in This Land: The Life and Times of H. L. Mitchell, Co-Founder of the Southern Tenant Farmers Union*. Montclair, N.J.: Allanheld, Osmun, 1979.

Moon, Henry Lee. *Balance of Power: The Negro Vote*. Garden City, N.Y., 1948.

Morgan, Chester. *Redneck Liberal: Theodore G. Bilbo and the New Deal*. Baton Rouge: Louisiana State University Press, 1985.

Muncy, Robin. *Creating a Female Dominion in American Reform, 1890–1935*. New York: Oxford University Press, 1991.

Myrdal, Gunnar. *An American Dilemma: The Negro Problem and Modern Democracy*. 1944. Reprint, New York: Harper and Row, 1962.

Naison, Mark. "Communism and Harlem Intellectuals in the Popular Front: Anti-Fascism and the Politics of Black Culture." *Journal of Ethnic Studies* 9 (Spring 1981): 1–25.

———. *Communists in Harlem during the Depression*. Urbana: University of Illinois Press, 1983.

Nash, Gerald, Noel H. Pugach, and Richard F. Thomas. *Social Security: The First Half Century*. Albuquerque: University of New Mexico Press, 1988.

Nelson, Barbara. "The Origins of the Two-Channeled Welfare State." In Linda Gordon, ed., *Women, the State, and Welfare*. Madison: University of Wisconsin Press, 1990.

Nelson, Viscount. "The Philadelphia NAACP: Race versus Class Consciousness during the Thirties." *Journal of Black Studies* 5 (March 1975): 255–76.

Newman, Debra L. *Black History: A Guide to Civilian Records in the National Archives*. Washington, D.C.: National Archives Trust Fund Board, 1984.

Newman, Richard. *Black Index: Afro-Americana in Selected Periodicals, 1907–1949*. Vol. 4 of *Critical Studies on Black Life and Culture*. New York: Garland, 1981.

Newman, Roger K. *Hugo Black: A Biography*. New York: Pantheon, 1994.

Ovington, Mary White. *The Walls Came Tumbling Down*. 1947. Reprint, New York: Schocken Books, 1970.

Parris, Guichard, and Lester Brooks. *Blacks in the City: A History of the National Urban League*. Boston: Little, Brown, 1971.

Patterson, James T. *Congressional Conservatism and the New Deal: The Growth of the Conservative Coalition in Congress, 1933–1939*. Lexington: University of Kentucky Press, 1995.

Paul, Diane B. *Controlling Human Heredity, 1865 to the Present*. New Jersey: Humanities Press, 1995.

Perkins, Frances. *The Roosevelt I Knew*. New York: Viking Press, 1946.

Perlman, Daniel. "Stirring the White Conscience: The Life of George Edmund Haynes." Ph.D. diss., New York University, 1972.

Pickens, Donald K. *Eugenics and the Progressives*. Nashville, Tenn.: Vanderbilt University Press, 1968.

Piven, Frances Fix, and Richard A. Cloward. *Regulating the Poor: The Functions of Public Welfare*. 1971. New York: Vintage Books–Random House, 1993.

Potter, Barrett. "The Civilian Conservation Corps and New York's 'Negro Question': A Case Study in Federal-State Race Relations during the Great Depression." *Afro-Americans in new York Life and History* 1 (1977): 183–200.

Quadagno, Jill. *The Color of Welfare: How Racism Undermined the War on Poverty*. New York: Oxford University Press, 1994.

———. *The Transformation of Old Age Security: Class and Politics in the American Welfare State*. Chicago: University of Chicago Press, 1988.

Raper, Arthur. "The Southern Negro and the NRA." *Georgia Historical Quarterly* 64 (Summer 1980): 128–45.

Raushenbush, Paul, and Elizabeth Brandeis Raushenbush. *Our U.C. Story, 1930–1967*. Raushenbush, 1979.

Record, Wilson. "Negro Intellectual Leadership in the National Association for the Advancement of Colored People, 1910–1940." *Phylon* 27 (3rd Quarter 1956): 375–89.

———. *Race and Radicalism: The NAACP and the Communist Party in Conflict*. Ithaca, N.Y.: Cornell University Press, 1964.

Reed, Christopher Robert. "Black Chicago Political Realignment during the Great Depression and the New Deal." *Illinois History Journal* 78 (Winter 1985): 242–56.

Reisch, Michael. *The Road Not Taken: A History of Radical Social Work in the United States*. Philadelphia: Brunner-Routledge, 2002.

Roediger, David. *The Wages of Whiteness: Race and the Making of the American Working Class*. London: Verso, 1992.

Rosen, Elliot A. "Roosevelt and the Brains Trust: An Historiographical Overview." *Political Science Quarterly* 87, no. 4 (1972).

Ross, Joyce B. "J. E. Spingarn and the Rise of the NAACP." In August Meier, ed., *Studies in American Negro Life*. New York: Atheneum, 1972.

———. "Mary McLeod Bethune and the National Youth Administration: A Case Study of Power Relationships in the Black Cabinet of Franklin D. Roosevelt." *Journal of Negro History* 60 (January 1975): 1–28.

Ryan, Eleanor. "Toward National Negro Congress." *New Masses* 4 (June 1935).

Saloutos, Theodore. *The American Farmer and the New Deal*. Ames: Iowa State University Press, 1982.

Scharf, Lois. *To Work and to Wed: Female Employment, Feminism, and the Great Depression*. Contributions to Women's Studies, no. 15. Westport, Conn:: Greenwood Press, 1980.

Schlabach, Theron F. *Edwin E. Witte: Cautious Reformer*. Madison: State Historical Society of Wisconsin, 1969.

Schlesinger, Arthur M., Jr. *The Politics of Upheaval*. Vol. 3 of *The Age of Roosevelt*. Boston: Houghton Mifflin, 1960.

Schwarz, Jordan A. *The New Dealers: Power Politics in the Age of Roosevelt*. New York: Knopf, 1993.

Scotchie, Joseph. *Barbarians in the Saddle: An Intellectual Biography of Richard Weaver*. New Brunswick, N.J.: Transaction Publishers, 1977.

Scott, Daryl Michael. *Contempt and Pity: Social Policy and the Image of the Damaged Black Psyche, 1880–1996*. Chapel Hill: University of North Carolina Press, 1997.

Scott, William R. "Black Nationalism and the Italio-Ethiopian Conflict, 1934–1936." *Journal of Negro History* 63 (April 1978): 118–34.

Shouse, Sarah Newman. *Hillbilly Realist: Herman Clarence Nixon of Possum Trot*. Tuscaloosa: University of Alabama Press, 1986.

Singleton, Jeff. *The American Dole: Unemployment Relief and the Welfare State in the Great Depression*. Westport, Conn.: Greenwood Press, 2000.

Sitkoff, Harvard, ed. *Fifty Years Later: The New Deal Evaluated*. Philadelphia: Temple University Press, 1985.

———. *A New Deal for Blacks: The Emergence of Civil Rights as a National Issue: The Depression Years*. Oxford: Oxford University Press, 1978.

Skocpol, Theda. *Protecting Soldiers and Mothers: The Political Origins of Social Policy in the United States*. Cambridge: Belknap-Harvard University Press, 1992.

Slamond, John. "'Aubrey Williams Remembers': A Note on Franklin D. Roosevelt's Attitude toward Negro Rights." *Alabama Review* 25 (January 1972): 62–77.

Smith, Elaine M. "Mary McCleod [sic] Bethune and the National Youth Administration." In Mabel E. Deutrich and Virginia C. Purdy, eds. *Clio Was a Woman: Studies in the History of American Women*. Washington, D.C.: Howard University Press, 1980.

Sosna, Morton. *In Search of the Silent South: Southern Liberals and the Race Issue*. New York: Columbia University Press, 1977.

Stedman, Murray S., Jr. and Susan W. Stedman. *Discontent at the Polls: A Study of Farmer and Labor Parties, 1827–1948*. New York: Russell and Russell, 1950.

Steele, Richard W. *Propaganda in an Open Society: The Roosevelt Administration and the Media, 1933–1941*. Westport, Conn.: Greenwood Press, 1980.

Steinberg, Stephen. "The Liberal Retreat from Race during the Post-Civil Rights Era." In Wahneema Lubiano, ed., *The House That Race Built*. New York: Random House, 1997.

Steiner, Gilbert Y. *Social Insecurity: The Politics of Welfare*. Chicago: Rand McNally, 1966.

Sterner, Richard. *The Negro's Share: A Study of Income, Consumption, Housing, and Public Assistance*. New York: Harper and Brothers, 1943.

Stevens, Robert B. *Statutory History of the United States: Income Security*. New York: Chelsea House–McGraw-Hill, 1970.

Stewart, William. *The Era of Franklin D. Roosevelt: A Selected Bibliography of Peri-*

odical, Essay, and Dissertation Literature, 1945–1971. Hyde Park: Franklin D. Roosevelt Presidential Library, 1974.

Still, Bayard. *Milwaukee: The History of a City*. Madison: State Historical Society of Wisconsin, 1981.

Streater, John Baxter, Jr. "The National Negro Congress, 1936–1947." Ph.D. diss., University of Cincinnati, 1981.

Strickland, Arvarh E. *History of the Chicago Urban League*. Urbana: University of Illinois Press, 1966.

Susman, Warren. *Culture and Commitment, 1929–1945*. New York: George Braziller, 1973.

Swain, Martha H. *Ellen S. Woodward: New Deal Advocate for Women*. Jackson: University Press of Mississippi, 1995.

———. *Pat Harrison: The New Deal Years*. Jackson: University Press of Mississippi, 1976.

———. "Pat Harrison and the Social Security Act of 1935." *Southern Quarterly* 15 (October 1976).

Tatum, Elbert Lee. *The Changed Political Thought of the Negro, 1915–1940*. New York: Exposition, 1951.

Taylor, Brennen. "UNIA and American Communism in Conflict, 1917–1928: An Historical Analysis in Negro Social Welfare." Ph.D. diss., University of Pittsburgh, 1964.

Taylor, Carl C. *The Farmer's Movement, 1620–1920*. New York: American Book Co., 1953.

Taylor, Molly Ladd. *Mother-Work: Women, Child Welfare, and the State, 1890–1930*. Urbana: University of Illinois Press, 1994.

Tindall, George B. *The Emergence of the New South, 1913–1945*. Baton Rouge: Louisiana State University Press, 1967.

Trattner, Walter I. *From Poor Law to Welfare State: A History of Social Welfare in America*. 1974. Reprint, New York: Free Press–Macmillan, 1989.

Trotter, Jo William, Jr. *Black Milwaukee: The Making of an Industrial Proletariat, 1915–45*. Urbana: University of Illinois Press, 1985.

Twelve Southerners. *I'll Take My Stand*. 1930. Reprint, New York: Harper and Brothers, 1962.

Valelly, Richard M. *Radicalism in the States: The Minnesota Farmer-Labor Party and the American Political Economy*. Chicago: University of Chicago Press, 1989.

Van Raaphorst, Donna. *Union Maids Not Wanted: Organizing Domestic Workers, 1870–1940*. New York: Praeger, 1988.

Vedder, Richard, and Lowell Gallaway. *Out of Work: Unemployment and Government in Twentieth-Century America*. New York: Holmes and Meier, 1993.

Wandersee, Winifred D. *Women's Work and Family Values, 1920–1940*. Cambridge: Harvard University Press, 1981.

Ware, Susan. *Beyond Suffrage: Women in the New Deal*. Cambridge: Harvard University Press, 1981.

————. *Holding Their Own: American Women in the 1930's*. Boston: Twayne, 1982.

Watson, Denton L. *Lion in the Lobby: Clarence Mitchell Jr.'s Struggle for the Passage of Civil Rights Laws*. New York: William Morrow, 1990.

Weaver, Carolyn L. *The Crisis in Social Security: Economic and Political Origins*. Durham, N.C.: Duke University Press, 1993.

Weaver, Robert C. "The New Deal and the Negro: A Look at the Facts." *Opportunity*, July 1935.1

Weir, Margaret. *Politics and Jobs: The Boundaries of Employment Policy in the U.S.* Princeton, N.J.: Princeton University Press, 1993.

Weir, Margaret, Ann Shola Orloff, and Theda Skocpol, eds. *The Politics of Social Policy in the United States*. Princeton, N.J.: Princeton University Press, 1988.

Weiss, Nancy J. *Farewell to the Party of Lincoln: Black Politics in the Age of FDR*. Princeton, N.J.: Princeton University Press, 1983.

————. *The National Urban League, 1910–1940*. New York: Oxford University Press, 1974.

White, Graham, and John Maze. *Henry A. Wallace: His Search for a New World Order*. Chapel Hill: University of North Carolina Press, 1995.

White, Walter. *A Man Called White*. New York: Arno Press and New York Times Co., 1969.

Wilkins, Roy, with Tom Mathews. *Standing Fast: The Autobiography of Roy Wilkins*. New York: Viking Press, 1982.

Williams, Aubrey. *The Failure of Gradualism*. Pamphlet, self-published, 1949.

Williams, Linda Faye. *Constraints of Race: Legacies of White Skin Privilege in America*. University Park: Pennsylvania State University Press, 2004.

Williams, Vernon J., Jr. *From a Caste to a Minority: Changing Attitudes of American Sociologists toward Afro-Americans, 1896–1945*. New York: Greenwood Press, 1989.

Witte, Edwin E. *The Development of the Social Security Act: A Memorandum on the History of the Committee on Economic Security and Drafting and Legislative History of the Social Security Act*. Madison: University of Wisconsin Press, 1963.

————. *Social Security Perspectives*. Madison: University of Wisconsin Press, 1962.

Wolters, Raymond. *Negroes in the Great Depression: The Problem of Economic Recovery*. Contributions in American History, no. 6. Westport, Conn.: Greenwood Press, 1970.

Woods, Thomas A. *Knights of the Plow: Oliver H. Kelley and the Origins of the Grange in Republican Ideology*. Ames: Iowa State University Press, 1991.

Wye, Christopher. "The New Deal and the Negro Community: Toward a Broader Conceptualization." *Journal of American History* 59 (December 1972): 621–39.

Young, James O. *Black Writers of the Thirties*. Baton Rouge: Louisiana State University Press, 1973.

Zangrando, Robert L. *The NAACP Crusade against Lynching, 1909–1950*. Philadelphia: Temple University Press, 1980.

Zangrando, Robert L., and Joanne Schneider Zangrando. "ER and Civil Rights." In Joan Hoffman Wilson and Marjorie Lightman, eds., *Without Precedent: The Life and Career of Eleanor Roosevelt*. Bloomington: Indiana University Press, 1984.

Zinn, Howard, ed. *New Deal Thought*. Indianapolis: Bobbs-Merrill, 1966.

Index

Printed in the USA
CPSIA information can be obtained
at www.ICGtesting.com
LVHW090138310823
756702LV00005B/138

9 780807 856888